For all those who help to
fill my days ...

First published 2013

The History Press
The Mill, Brimscombe Port
Stroud, Gloucestershire, GL5 2QG
www.thehistorypress.co.uk

British Library Cataloguing in Publication Data.
A catalogue record for this book is available from the British Library.

ISBN 978 0 7524 6866 2

Typesetting and origination by The History Press
Printed in India

THE NEWCASTLE BOOK OF DAYS

JO BATH
WITH RICHARD F. STEVENSON

May your days be eventful!

Rich F. Stevenson

March '18.

JANUARY 1ST

1756: On this day, Ralph Carr opened the Bank of Newcastle – the country's first provincial bank. Other towns and cities had businesses which called themselves 'banks', like Woods at Gloucester and Smiths of Nottingham. Those institutions carried out a range of financial services and business dealings. But Carr's innovation was a new and risky venture – the Bank of Newcastle was the first institution outside of London and Edinburgh to rely solely on the business of banking. With £2,000 in capital – drawn equally from four partners – the company took premises in Pilgrim Street. Bank of Newcastle banknotes depicted the city's coat of arms and a view from the Bigg Market towards St Nicholas's Church. Initially, there were some difficulties in getting all merchants to take the notes seriously – Ralph Jackson records in his diary, in March 1756, that 'Mr Surtees paid me in Bank Notes (viz the Bank of Newcastle) but Mr Featherston would not take them … ' In the first year, the Bank of Newcastle issued notes amounting to over £15,000, received deposits for £10,000 (including gaining the custom of Lord Ravensworth, and the trustees of the Infirmary), and made just over £1,000 in profit. While it had initially been a risky venture, the experiment proved so successful that it was replicated all over the country. Locally, Carr's enterprise became known as 'the Old Bank' to distinguish it from competitors. Carr's bank remained in business until 1839, when it was taken over by the Northumberland and Durham Bank. (Diary of Ralph Jackson; *Monthly Chronicle of North Country Lore and Legend*, 1889

JANUARY 2ND

1548: On this day, an inventory was taken of all the munitions and ordnance of war held within Newcastle. These give us a fascinating insight into the machinery of sixteenth-century warfare, as well as Newcastle's often surprising provisions for conflict. Most of the foot soldiers were equipped with black bills (a hooked blade on a 5-6 feet long stick) or bows – there were 2,000 of each! Others had pikes (400), and demi-lances (250) with smaller numbers of staves. Also held in the city were weapons made by converting farming equipment – hedging bills, scythes, sickles and axes. Cannons were now an important part of the city's armoury, with one 'saker' and forty-four 'bases' – both early forms of cannon – and 1,700 iron shots of various types for them. Two hundred smaller guns, called 'hackbuts', were also available. The inventory also lists chemicals such as serpentine powder (gunpowder), and the ingredients to make it: saltpetre, sulphur and charcoal, plus mortars and pestles. Added to the munitions were tools – an array of spades and pick axes, mining equipment, leather buckets, coils of thick rope, and cressets (metal cages for making lit torches). And to carry it all? Newcastle had fifty new carts and six old ones, twenty privy carts, and gear for 100 horses. (Welford, R., *History of Newcastle and Gateshead*, 1884)

JANUARY 3RD

1430: On this day, Roger Thornton, 'the Dick Whittington of Newcastle', died in his lavish house in Broad Chare. As the legend tells it, 'at the Westgate came Thornton in, With a hap, and a halfpenny, and a lambskin'. We really don't know whether his beginnings were this humble, though his brother was probably John Thornton, a town bailiff. But wherever he started, Roger Thornton's rise was staggering, as he worked his way up to be (according to King's Antiquary, Leland) 'the richest marchant that ever was dwelling in Newcastell' and a substantial landowner, able to marry his children into noble households. He really was connected with 'lambskin' – he made his money trading in wool, as well as coal, wine, and lead. But he is best remembered for his work for the medieval town. He was Mayor nine times, and served as a collector of taxes and customs, a bailiff and commissioner of enquiry, and four times as Member of Parliament for Newcastle. In 1400, he was involved in the deal that made Newcastle a county, and five years later he spent 1,000 marks of his own money defending the town against the Earl of Northumberland's rebel forces. In later life he donated a lot of money to charitable and religious ventures, like the Maison Dieu (hospital) of St Katherine in Sandhill, a chantry at All Saints' Church and the east window of St Nicholas's Church. He is buried under a fine brass in All Saints' Church. (www.historyofparliamentonline.org)

JANUARY 4TH

1770: On this day, a rather unusual advert appeared in the *Newcastle Chronicle*: 'This is to acquaint the public that on Monday the first inst., being the Lodge (or monthly meeting night) of the Free and Accepted Masons of the 22nd Regiment, held at the Crown Inn, Newgate, Mrs. Bell, the landlady of the house, broke open a door (with a poker) that had not been opened for some years past, by which means she got into an adjacent room, made two holes through the wall and by that stratagem discovered the secrets of Masonry, and she, knowing herself to be the first woman in the world that ever found out that secret, is willing to make it known to all her sex. So any lady that is desirous of learning the secrets of Freemasonry by applying to that well learned woman Mrs. Bell (that lived fifteen years in and about Newgate Street) may be instructed in all the Secrets of Masonry.' We don't know whether this is a genuine story, promotion for the pub, or something else. It has been suggested that the story is a hoax, designed to ridicule and silence Mrs Bell. Perhaps she really had learned a bit about the Masons, and even boasted about her knowledge, but this advert would have made her very unpopular with some of the loacals. (www.masonicworld.com)

JANUARY 5TH

1967: At 5.15 a.m. on this snowy morning, the body of Angus Sibbett was found on the backseat of his car, under a bridge in South Hetton, County Durham. He had been shot three times. The two men accused of Sibbett's murder were his work colleagues, Michael Luvaglio and Dennis Stafford, who worked for a company supplying fruit machines to Newcastle businesses (Luvaglio was the boss's son), hence the crime soon became known as the 'One Armed Bandit Murder'. Luvaglio and Stafford were thought to have believed that Sibbett had begun to siphon money off from the business. Although they had been in The Birdcage public house in Newcastle for most of the night in question, and despite the fact that the blood in Sibbett's car did not match theirs, the jury controversially found Luvaglio and Stafford guilty, reasoning they would just have had time to make it to the crime scene. The two men continued to fight to clear their names long after their release from prison in 1979, and the case has been challenged twice, taken to the House of Lords, and reviewed a further time. Sibbett's life and death was (very loosely) the inspiration for the gangland film *Get Carter*. (Wade, S., *The Torso in the Tank and Other Stories*, Black and White Publishing, 2005)

January 6th

1954: On this day, the Lord Mayor received a letter from the French Consul suggesting a formal friendship tie between Newcastle and Nancy, capital of the Lorraine district. After some formal visits, the two cities were formally 'twinned'. The Civic Centre retains links with Nancy's local government, and BBC North has ties with local TV station FR3 Nancy. This was not Newcastle's first twinning – in the late 1940s, ties were made with Groningen (Netherlands), and Gelsenkirchen (Germany). More recently, Newcastle has been twinned with Haifa (Israel), Newcastle (Australia), Bergen (Norway), and Atlanta (USA). In 1961, the Russians judged a link between Newcastle and Rostov-on-Don 'a waste of time and money'.

———◆———

1955: On this day, the comedian and actor Rowan Atkinson was born in a nursing home on Jesmond Road, Newcastle. He didn't stay long – his father was a farmer, and Atkinson spent the first seventeen years of his life in Consett, County Durham. Still, it was at the Theatre Royal on Grey Street, aged eleven, that he first experienced live theatre; a pantomime starring Terry Scott. In 1972 he started at Newcastle University, studying electrical engineering. He recalls: 'I wasn't a terribly exciting student. I lived in a hall of residence – Henderson Hall – for all my time there and I worked very hard for that degree. I did some revues at Newcastle but they weren't very good ones really. They consisted mainly of Monty Python rewrites as I recall'. (Gibson, J., *Spirit of Tyneside*, John Donald Publishers Ltd, 1990)

JANUARY 7TH

1594: On this day, thousands of people gathered to witness the execution of Catholic priest Edward Waterson. A Londoner, as a young adult Waterson travelled to Turkey with some merchants. While there, he was reputedly offered a prestigious bride – if he would convert to Islam. He refused, but started thinking about his faith, and, returning back via Rome, converted to Catholicism. Unfortunately, that set him on a collision course with the policies of Protestant Elizabethan England. Returning in the summer of 1592, he travelled around, preaching and performing Mass for almost a year before being arrested. Found guilty of performing as a Catholic priest, he was sentenced to be hanged, drawn, and quartered. According to a Catholic Archdeacon who witnessed the event, the horses refused to drag the hurdle (to which Waterson was bound) to the scaffold, and when he finally got there, the ladder jumped around of its own accord, and couldn't be used until Waterson himself made the sign of the cross over it.

Waterson was not the first to suffer this fate in Newcastle – only six months earlier, another priest, Joseph Lampton, went the same way. It was recorded that the executioner got halfway through drawing the unfortunate man's intestines out when he staggered away, horrified at his own actions. A local butcher stepped up to complete the sentence.

Edward Waterson was beatified in 1929. (Challoner, R., *Memoirs of Missionary Priests*, Burns Oates and Washbourne, 1924)

JANUARY 8TH

1842: On this day, 200 workmen were given a slap-up meal with extra strong ale at the Unicorn Inn in the Bigg Market, accompanied by a lively band. The occasion was the completion of the Victoria Tunnel, a stone and brick tunnel 7 feet 5 inches high and over two miles long. This connected the Spital Tongues (or Leazes Main) Colliery, which opened in 1835, with the River Tyne, thus avoiding the cumbersome horse-drawn cart transportation of coal through town. The tunnel was officially opened on April 7th. Unfortunately, while the tunnel did its job well – carrying coal wagons moving under gravity, with the aid of a stationary steam engine – the Spital Tongues Colliery only lasted until 1860. The tunnel was left unused, and both ends were soon lost in housing developments. Nothing more happened until 1928-9, when the Victoria Tunnel Mushroom Company took an interest. The company did not last long, but the council continued to rent the tunnel to mushroom growers until 1950. In 1939, almost the whole length was converted for use as an air-raid shelter for the people of Newcastle, with seven entrances positioned along the way. This was a massive undertaking, with the provision of electric lighting, chemical toilets, seating for 9,000 people and bunks for 500. Doubtless it was uncomfortable, but a civil servant's report of the time notes that this being a mining district, those sheltering would be 'fitted constitutionally' to withstand the conditions! (Jones, M., *Victoria Tunnel: Newcastle's Hidden Heritage*, Ouseburn Trust, 2010)

JANUARY 9TH

1537: On this day, Newcastle's Augustinian Friary was surrendered as part of the Dissolution of the Monasteries. This monastery, founded in 1291, had seen some illustrious visitors over the years, partly because it was on one of the main roads to the North. King Edward I stopped there only a few years after it opened, giving each of the brethren 3s 4d. Richard II must have been unimpressed when he came through town as he ordered the bailiffs of Newcastle to take steps to tackle locals' dumping of 'excrements, filth, and garbage, near to the house of the Austin Friars, to their great annoyance and peril.' When the friary was seized in 1537, it was somewhat diminished, with only seven brethren and three novices. Unusually, the importance of the place did not diminish immediately after the Reformation. Thomas Cromwell specifically asked that the site be left intact, so that it could be used for the King's Council of the North, when they needed to be further north than York (Elizabeth I decreed that this should be at least twenty days a year). At about the same time a tower was added to the building, for the storage of the town's weaponry (which still survives), but by the end of the century the buildings were in disrepair and during the Civil War it was handed to the Corporation. Thirty years later they built the Holy Jesus Hospital on the site; only one sacristy wall remains of the Augustinian Friary.

JANUARY 10TH

1932: On this day, Jesmond's real tennis court was opened to the public. This historic sport, the ancestor of lawn tennis, is played on a court around 34 metres by 12. The heavy cork ball can be bounced off the walls within play, so real tennis courts are usually indoors. Jesmond's court, also notable for its row of large circular windows, had been built in 1894 as a private facility for the Noble family, who lived in Jesmond Dene House. They hired a professional tennis player, and built up a list of those allowed to use the court. In the 1900s, the professional was Charles Lambert, one of the best in the world – and on this court, in 1904, he beat the world champion Edgar Lambert. During the First World War, the open space was used to make balloons for airships. Afterwards it reverted to the family, but in 1931, when Lady Noble died aged 103, the house and grounds were given to Newcastle City Council. The court became public, with a club set up to keep things running smoothly. The first match was between Charles Lambert and another (visiting) professional, and caused some consternation because it was refereed by an amateur. However, real tennis remained a niche sport, very much in the shadow of the immensely popular lawn tennis, which was played just outside the real tennis building. But the court was kept going, on a joint use agreement with a badminton club. During the Second World War, it was mothballed and used for storage, and thereafter badminton had the court to itself – until 1981, when real tennis made a comeback. The court is now one of only twenty-six in the country, and forty-five in the world. (www.jdrtc.co.uk)

JANUARY 11TH

1828: On this day, the self-proclaimed medical expert William Henderson died. Henderson was a pitman, and, while in Newcastle Infirmary convalescing from an injury, he met and married a young nurse. When the House of Recovery was opened in 1804, she became its matron, and he (in spite of a complete lack of training) its inspector. Eventually he felt he had learned enough on the job to start calling himself a doctor, and in 1827 J. Marshall of the Old Flesh Market printed his work, *Every man his own doctor ... with rhymes to gratify the mind*. Henderson claimed this book, costing 3s 6d, would 'make the pupil a wiser man, his voice may give the sound and say, 'tis worth a hundred pound!' – although whether anyone but him thought so is open to question. (Sykes, J., *Local Records*, Volume II, 1833)

· ◆ ·

2002: On this day, psychic Uri Geller started his world tour in Newcastle. The previous month, he had worked to break Newcastle United's London losing streak by asking people to channel their positive vibes through looking at his picture in the *Newcastle Evening Chronicle* (which was behind the scheme). He also ran several times around the stadium during the match. United won, making Geller immensely popular with the fans. The *Chronicle* had previously tried calling in the aid of an exorcist and two witchdoctors. (*Newcastle Chronicle* / www.uri-geller.com)

JANUARY 12TH

1654: On this day, Newcastle's streets were granted freedom from a decade of dirt, grime and waste. The city's Corporation passed a law dictating that the city's inhabitants should oversee a thorough cleaning of their buildings and their environs every Saturday night. This had, it seems, been a custom until 'the Reducing of this town' – the Civil War siege of 1644. Apparently, 'time out of mind … it hath been the constant practice of the Burgesses and Inhabitants every Saturday at night … to sweep and make clean their [house] fronts'. However, since the siege, the practice had been neglected. The 1654 order complains that even when the Mayor and Aldermen had continued to send out the Bellman to order individuals to clean their areas, 'little or no obedience [had] been given'. This negligence led to the 'dishonour of the Magistrates, the Disparagement of the Town, Discouragement to traffic and trade, and the begetting of noisesome smells and diseases amongst us'. The Corporation stipulated that all inhabitants now *must* clean in front of their houses every Saturday night, and when otherwise told. If they did not do it, they were liable to a fine – with the sum varying depending on where they lived, from 3 shillings and sixpence, to 12 pence for those outside the city walls – which would go straight into the poor rates. (Tyne and Wear Archive)

JANUARY 13TH

1740: By this day, the continuing bitter winter, finally reached the point where the people might as well use the River Tyne as a road. It had frozen over in December; ships could not move, and indeed many were damaged by the press of ice. On this date, the inhabitants of Tyneside took to the ice until the river resembled a market, with stalls selling meat and drink, footraces, and even a football match. The next day, Sir John Fenwick of Bywell held a birthday party on the river for his son – he erected a tent on the ice, where they roasted a sheep, and also travelled across the ice in a carriage. For the poor, of course, the continued cold was less enjoyable, although the Newcastle MP, Walter Blackett, ordered the distribution of £350 to the needy. The river was still frozen a month later, at which point the coal owners hired 200 men to start cutting a channel through the ice, a mile and a half long, from the staithes to the open water. It took them a week, but by that time a great mass of ice had travelled downstream, which needed clearing out. That done, Sir Henry Liddell tried to extend the channel to other staithes, but stopped when two men drowned. On February 24th the thaw finally came. (Sykes, J., *Local Records*, Volume I, 1833)

JANUARY 14TH

1845: On this day, the River Tyne was the setting for an extraordinary journey. The Theatre Royal had been showing a pantomime, and wanted to advertise the show. So, a clown named Wood hatched a plan – to hook a wash tub up to four geese, and sail in it down the Tyne, encouraging the geese along with a stick. Starting at King's Meadows, an island near Scotswood (dredged away in the 1870s), Wood's geese pulled him all the way to the Tyne Bridge, witnessed by thousands of spectators. So many came, in fact, that the banks, quays and bridge were reported as being extremely crowded, and, unsurprisingly, the Theatre Royal was packed that evening. What most of the awed spectators did not realise was that the geese were being helped – Wood's tub was actually connected by an underwater rope to a small steamboat moving some metres ahead. Just four months later, another clown was pulling the same trick on the people of Yarmouth when the chains of a suspension bridge gave way and tipped most of the crowd into the river, killing eighty people, many of them children. (*Monthly Chronicle of North Country Lore and Legend*, 1887)

JANUARY 15TH

1959: On this day, at 5 p.m., Tyne Tees Television began to broadcast. Initially it was based in a converted warehouse on City Road, where it remained until 2005. Tyne Tees Television aimed to be strongly regional and independent, and they produced their own listing magazine, 'The Viewer'. That night, Tynesiders were also able to watch a television commercial for the first time! After an opening ceremony by the Duke of Northumberland, the channel chose to kick-off with episodes of *Robin Hood* and *Popeye*. The highlight of the evening was a live interview with Prime Minister Harold Macmillan, who had been MP for Stockton-on-Tees for many years. This was followed by a live variety show, and episodes of US imports *Highway Patrol*, *Double your Money*, and *I Love Lucy*. These American shows gave Tyne Tees a fashionable appeal – the BBC, on the same night, offered Vera Lynn in concert, a documentary on Kathmandu and a philosophical discussion. No great surprise then that Tyne Tees soon found an audience. Later productions of Tyne Tees Television included *Supergran*, several Catherine Cookson adaptations, and *The Tube* (produced for Channel 4 from the Tyne Tees studios). (*Evening Gazette*)

JANUARY 16TH

1988: On this day, the BBC started to broadcast from new northern headquarters on Barrack Road. They had been using the former lying-in hospital in town, which housed a single studio for Look North and BBC Radio Newcastle. But with new technology, more space was needed, and the small, listed building was no longer suitable. It was last used on Friday, January 15th 1988. The new building took over smoothly, with its first live radio broadcast the following day, and its first television broadcast (Look North) on the 18th. Back then there were two studios, where they produced regional news, radio, and a few shows mostly for children's television. In 1989, for instance, the Look and Read series *Geordie Racer* introduced a whole generation of children to the Geordie accent, while showing Newcastle as a hotbed of pigeon smuggling and long-distance running. The building's capacity was later reduced to just one studio, but it has so far avoided losing television filming completely (as has happened to some regions). The building itself was officially opened by Prince Charles, and with its slight pink-brown tint to the glazed exterior quickly gained the nickname 'the Pink Palace'!

JANUARY 17TH

1851: On this day, reformer and editor Joseph Clark died. Born in Newcastle in 1770, and orphaned soon after, he was brought up by his eldest sister. Hearing the preaching of John Wesley, he switched from Presbyterianism to Methodism, where he developed his natural talent for public speaking. By the age of seventeen, he was preaching for the chapel, travelling from village to village; he may even have met Wesley himself. But when the Methodist New Connexion split from the mainstream, he went with them. His first appearance in print was a tribute to his dead sweetheart, published in the New Connexion's first magazine. In accordance with her wishes, he then married her sister! In 1806, while undertaking religious rounds, he uncovered a scandal – that the inmates of the Holy Jesus Hospital were so badly paid that one had died of starvation. He campaigned, and eventually succeeded, in getting their pension increased. This got him into the world of campaigning, and he threw himself in with vigour, mostly concerning the rights and responsibilities of the trade companies, burgesses and Corporation, for instance with regard to the Town Moor. He was also responsible for pushing through a proposal for a home for the elderly freemen and their widows in the west of town. This was the 'Peace and Unity' hospital, so-called because the foundation stone was laid on the day that peace with France was declared, in 1814. (*Monthly Chronicle of North Country Lore and Legend*, 1889)

January 18th

1370: On or around this day, Richard Helmslay, a Dominican friar based in Newcastle (in what is now called Blackfriars), began a series of controversial sermons which eventually led him to a courtroom in Rome. The Church at the time was riven with dispute between the parish church system and the monasteries. Helmslay, of course, stood with the monasteries and attacked the standards and privileges of parish priests – and in particular that of Matthew de Bolton, the elderly vicar of Newcastle. Helmslay argued that friary churches deserved the same honour as parish churches, that women did not have to be 'churched' (a ceremony marking her return to church after childbirth), that no one should be forced to offer candles on Candlemas day, or pay mortuary fees. He said that eighty curates within the diocese were illiterate and several had criminal tendencies. He was found guilty in Rome of holding unorthodox opinions and ordered to publicly recant in St Nicholas, Newcastle. But what sealed his notoriety was his interpretation of the 21st decree of the Third Lateran Council. The decree said that everyone 'of both sexes' (*utriusque sexus*) must make confession each year. Helmslay remarked that this only applied to those of both sexes – hermaphrodites. Presumably he was just being witty – but his opponents used it to discredit him, and he became widely known as Richard 'of Both Sexes'! (ed. Newton, D. and Pollard, A., *Newcastle and Gateshead Before 1700*, The History Press, 2009)

JANUARY 19TH

1674: On this day, magistrates heard accusations of witchcraft against Peter Banks of Newcastle. Banks was no stereotypical witch – at least the way the witnesses told it – but a learned sorcerer able to command the spirits of sea and air. Apparently, one of his favourite promises – made for the sum of 20s – was that he could keep sailors safe from the dangers of the sea, for the space of a year, by ordering the spirits of the storms and rocks to assist them. He also claimed that he could undo bewitchment – ordering harmful spirits to leave – and, perhaps most tempting of all, that he 'could make ill husbands be good to their wives'. Love was only half the price, at 10s for a year's domestic bliss. Witness Jane Burrell, a shipwright's wife, said that when she discovered that her husband was using Bank's services, she was angry, and threw into the fire a piece of paper central to the magic. She said Banks 'threatened that he would plague the informant, and she should never be worth a groat', and that the family had suffered many problems since then. The jury was not convinced, though, and on September 1st, Banks – described by the court as a Newcastle labourer – was found not guilty of witchcraft. (Public Record Office)

JANUARY 20TH

1823: On this day, workmen began the demolition of the Maison Dieu. This 'house of God' was a medieval hospital dedicated to St Katherine, founded in 1412 for a priest, nine poor men and four poor women, who would live as lay brothers and sisters and be provided with their meat and drink – so long as they prayed daily. Since the place was founded by Mayor Roger Thornton, this prayer had to be for the health of the Mayor, Sheriff, Aldermen and people of Newcastle, and after their deaths, for the souls of Thornton's family members, and other hospital benefactors. It was situated on Sandhill and was not large, measuring only 100 feet by 24 feet, though in its heyday it owned land across the region. Oddly, from 1456, Thornton's son granted the use of the hospital's hall, 'for a young couple, when they were married, to make their wedding dinner in, and receive the offerings and gifts of their friends'. After the Reformation, the Thorntons continued to run the Maison Dieu as a home for the poor and elderly, until they gave it to the Corporation in 1629. By the time of its demolition, it had long been serving as a warehouse; a fish-market was then built on the site. From 'house of God' to 'house of cod' in just over 400 years … (Sykes, J., *Local Records*, Volume II, 1833)

JANUARY 21ST

1788: On this evening, the Theatre Royal opened its doors for the first time. This was the Mosley Street predecessor to the current Theatre Royal. The theatre company had previously been based in a Bigg Market pub. Technically, they didn't stage dramatic performances – that was illegal. Instead, the entertainment was billed as a concert of music, which you paid for, with 'free' drama presented in the gaps! The opening night comprised several short pieces, including *The Way to Keep Him* (as you might expect, a comedy, with lead characters including Mr and Mrs Lovemoor, and the marvellously named Sir Brilliant Fashion), and *The Sultan: or A Peep into the Seraglio* (a farce involving a sultan, his servant, and three harem women). Before the show, the *Newcastle Chronicle*, looking at the cast list, was unconvinced: stating that the company 'appears to have been strengthened by the addition of several new names, but we are sorry it has not been improved by the absence of several old ones …' The building was knocked down in the Grainger redevelopment, but one legacy remains – the alley which once ran alongside the theatre is still called Drury Lane. (Oswald, H., *The Theatres Royal in Newcastle*, Northumbria Press, 1936)

January 22nd

1822: On this day, James Miller, a Warkworth carrier, came to an unfortunate end on the Newcastle Turnpike. Some distance away, three young men were enjoying a bit of target practice, setting a target up against a high wall of the 'bullpark' on the Town Moor (this was where the city's bull was penned for stud, a triangle of land now occupied by the Great North Museum). But one of them, Thomas Burnet, misjudged his shot, and the bullet went over the wall, right across the park and as far as the road, where it entered Miller's right temple and crossed the brain, being found lodged by the left ear. Following an inquest, and a criminal trial, Burnet was found guilty of manslaughter. Shooting practice so close to a public highway was illegal, and the judge roundly condemned it in his summing up. Nonetheless, Burnet's respectability helped him out. Several other gentlemen had spoken on his behalf and he was allowed to go free until the next meeting of the court – but not before he paid £100, and another four men each put up £50 in sureties. At the next meeting of the court, he received the strikingly lenient punishment of a £10 fine. (Sykes, J., *Local Records*, Volume II, 1833)

JANUARY 23RD

2002: On this day, workers in protective suits began tearing down Burnside Farm, a stone's throw from the border between Newcastle and Northumberland. Outbuildings were flattened and burned, and JCBs dug massive trenches to bury the rubble of the buildings. When the demolition was complete, a month later, the whole site was thoroughly disinfected.

The farm had stood abandoned for almost a year, since it first hit the headlines on February 22nd 2001. On that day, foot and mouth disease had been identified in the pigs, and the government identified the Heddon-on-the-Wall farm as the most likely source of the national outbreak. The farmer had sold pigs to the abattoir in Essex, where the disease was first identified, and, as an intensive farm which was also under investigation for hygiene and welfare concerns, it made a likely candidate. However, the identification of Burnside as the starting point of the epidemic – rather than merely an early stage carrier – remains controversial, the evidence contradictory. Equally there are many theories as to the first cause, from imported swill, to infection from a forty-year-old mass grave from the last major foot and mouth outbreak, one of which is close to Burnside. (*Evening Chronicle*)

JANUARY 24TH

1814: On this day, the River Tyne was frozen solid. It had begun to freeze over on January 15th, and stayed that way until February 6th, with an average depth of 10 inches of ice. That was plenty to allow walking with confidence (it even supported a horse and carriage), and whenever people had the chance they made their way onto the ice. The scene, it is said, resembled a country fair, with races (with and without skates), booths selling drink, or cutting hair, and people walking around selling cakes, playing music, and recruiting for the army. The ballad 'Tyne Fair' describes the scene beautifully:

> Hats, stockings, and handkerchiefs, still hung as prizes,
> Was run for by skaters and lads of all sizes;
> Razor grinders quite tipsy, with Balmbro' Jack,
> And God Save the King, sung by Willy the Black.

Willy the Black is probably William Fifefield, a West Indian who had made his way to Newcastle and was well known both as a drummer in local volunteer regiments and as a the rower of a commercial 'comfortable' – a boat with a covered section to keep out the elements, which did well until the steam boats overtook them in the 1830s. (Livsey, *William Fifefield: A Different Drummer* (e-book) / Mackenzie, E., *A Descriptive and Historical Account of the Town and County of Newcastle upon Tyne: Including the Borough of Gateshead*, 1827)

JANUARY 25TH

1768: On this day, Sandhill saw its last bull baiting. Here, a bull would be loosely tied by around 15 feet of rope to a ring set into the ground, and three or so dogs – often, but not always, bulldogs – set upon it. The dogs would try to avoid the bull's horns and get around to bite the soft under parts; the bull would try to gore the dogs, potentially throwing them many feet into the air with his horns. Large gatherings to watch the 'sport' were commonplace – there had been another in Sandhill only four days before, when the bull was bought by several gentlemen, butchered and the meat given to the poor. However, at this event things went badly wrong. The bull managed to break free, injuring several people. Worse, a young sailor was badly gored, and died the following morning. In response to these events, the magistrates ordered the removal of the bull ring. The last known bull baiting in Newcastle was six years after the Sandhill fatality. On August 10th 1774, a group of the freemen of Newcastle organised a bull baiting on the Town Moor, protesting the fact that the land had been made available to rent by the Common Council. It seems enthusiasm for bull baiting died out gradually from the north downward, with the southern counties continuing to bait bulls until it was made illegal in 1835. (*Monthly Chronicle of North-country Lore and Legend*, 1889)

JANUARY 26TH

1769: On this day John White, newspaper editor and the son of a York printer of the same name, died. As an interesting aside, his father had (after a brief spell in prison) done well out of printing the propaganda of William of Orange in 1688, when no one else would. The nineteen-year-old John White Jnr moved to Newcastle in 1708, and three years later founded the *Newcastle Courant*, initially printed three times a week, later only once a week, from premises initially in the Close, then a larger building in Side. He was now producing the only provincial paper north of the Trent (though for a brief period, in 1710, the *Newcastle Gazette* had been attempted by John Saywell of Gateshead); a month later he started publishing sermons and other tracts too. His father died in 1715, leaving him the majority of his estate. Meanwhile, in 1718, his mother started producing a newspaper in York, only to pass this on to her husband's pupil, Thomas Gent. There was some sort of falling out, and White, while continuing his Newcastle business, ran a rival paper in York, the *York Courant* (1725-35). Active to the last (though he'd taken on a partner a few years before), White was eighty years old when he died, and was thought to have been, at that time, the oldest master printer in England. (Mackenzie, E., *A Descriptive and Historical Account of the Town and County of Newcastle upon Tyne: Including the Borough of Gateshead*, 1827)

JANUARY 27TH

1879: On this day, Byker Bridge, crossing the Ouseburn Valley, was opened to carts and carriages. It had been taking pedestrians across its twenty-two arches since October 19th of the previous year. There was a half-penny toll to cross, which was withdrawn in 1895. Four years later, major work was done to widen it from 30 feet to 50 feet. It is today 1,130 feet long. Byker Bridge was important in that, previously, travellers eastward would have had to climb the sides of the Ouseburn Valley. As the eastern suburbs were developing, there was more need for a quick route. Ouseburn, after all, wasn't really an area to walk through if you didn't have to: the proximity of the River Tyne, and ships bringing in useful ballast like limestone or flint, had encouraged industry to take over. Victorian Ouseburn saw brickworks and lead works, toffee factories, potteries, smelly tanneries, and lots of stables for carting all the products to the Quayside. In fact, the previous year Maling Pottery had opened a new factory, the Ford B, which was the largest pottery in the country. So it made sense to stay above it all, even if it did cost a penny.

JANUARY 28TH

1848: On this day, Newcastle Infirmary was the site of a landmark tragedy – the first death to be caused by anaesthetics. Hannah Greener was a healthy fifteen year old who had already experienced an ether anaesthetic. But within three minutes of being given chloroform, her face went white and her pulse stopped. The coroner blamed congestion of the lungs as a result of the chloroform. However, Dr James Simpson, who had discovered chloroform's use only a year before, contended that the brandy given to try to revive her, combined with inadequate oxygen, was the issue, and that mouth-to-mouth resuscitation would have done the trick. The Queen's anaesthetist John Snow (also a Geordie) argued that the handkerchief method of giving chloroform was imprecise, and recommended an inhaler. Modern examination cannot solve the case, though an additional possibility relating to a heart spasm demonstrated in lightly chloroformed patients, seems plausible. The anaesthetist at the heart of all this, Robert Glover, was an expert anaesthetist, the first to really study the bodily processes involved. He later became a chloroform addict himself, and at one point married an escaped lunatic, Sarah Hickson, with whom he spent one week before she was taken back! He died of chloroform overdose, at just forty-three. (Knight, P. and Bacon, D., 'An Unexplained Death: Hannah Greener and Chloroform', *Anaesthesiology*, 2002 / Defalque, R. and Wright, A., 'The Short, Tragic Life of Robert M. Glover', *Anaesthesiology*, 2004)

JANUARY 29TH

1897: On this day, the Chief Constable of Newcastle wrote his report for the year. The 1890s saw a peak in drinking, and more beer was being produced in the country than any time before or since. Among other things, the report shows 3,905 proceedings for drunkenness, including one man who was arrested twelve times, and another eleven. With an arrest rate over three times the national average, Newcastle had one of the worst drinking problems in the country (or the most zealous police). Around a hundred people escaped prosecution, for instance because they were soldiers handed over to the military, or because they gave false addresses. Of those prosecuted, around three quarters were male; a third were labourers. The second biggest group, at twelve per cent, were prostitutes. Five per cent were miners, with smaller numbers identifying themselves as fitters, hawkers, sailors and cartmen. Over a third of those arrested were not native to the town, probably having come to Newcastle specifically for a night on the town. At the time there was one alehouse for every 300 people – that's one for every forty-three dwellings! (Bennison, B., 'Drunkenness in Turn of the Century Newcastle upon Tyne', *Local Population Studies*, 1994)

JANUARY 30TH

1787: On this day, workmen levelling part of St John's graveyard found a body. You wouldn't think this too exciting an occurrence, but this body – a young woman of around fifteen – was only a few inches below the surface, wrapped in a bloody cloth, and had no head. When examined, the surgeon coroner believed that it had been in the ground about a year, and the coroner's jury recorded a verdict of wilful murder. Of course, this led to a massive amount of gossip and conjecture as to who the girl, and her killer, might be. The magistrates placed an advertisement in the Newcastle papers: 'in a situation that induced a suspicion of some person being murdered, a Reward of Twenty Guineas is offered by the Corporation of Newcastle to any person who shall give such information as shall lead to a discovery, or to a satisfactory explanation of the circumstances occasioning the suspicion.' But although it was examined closely, the body was so putrefied that no distinguishing marks could be found, and no one came forward with a good enough case to warrant an arrest. (Richardson, M., *Local Historian's Table Book*, 1841)

JANUARY 31ST

2011: On this day, footballer Andy Carroll was bought by Liverpool from Newcastle United for £35m, a record sum for a transfer of a British player between British clubs. This wasn't the first time that Newcastle broke this record – in February 1904, Andy McCombie's transfer from Sunderland for £700 was a world record at the time. He was probably worth it – he stuck with the team as player and trainer, not retiring until 1950. Carroll is from Gateshead, and came to the attention of NUFC at an early age. When he first came onto the pitch in a UEFA Cup match in November 2006, as a late substitute, he was just seventeen years and 300 days old, the youngest man to ever play for Newcastle in Europe. In 2007, he debuted in the FA Cup and Premier League, and was awarded the Wor Jackie trophy for promising young north-eastern players. By 2010 he was a regular fixture and scoring a high percentage of the team's goals. Perhaps it was his performance against Liverpool in December of that year that encouraged Liverpool to start negotiating a transfer. Their second offer was accepted. Still, Liverpool didn't end up feeling the pinch too badly – at the same time, they had sold Fernando Torres to Chelsea for £50m. At the time of writing, that sale remains the most expensive one in Britain, and Carroll's the joint second most expensive.

FEBRUARY 1ST

1937: On this day, the Newcastle News Theatre opened on Pilgrim Street. It was the brainchild of Dixon Scott, a local entrepreneur (and also the great-uncle of directors Ridley Scott and Tony Scott). Scott saw an opportunity to get in on the craze for local news theatres which was sweeping the country. At the time, Newcastle had around forty-seven cinemas with over 40,000 seats – but no news theatres. The building Scott designed was full of rich colours, inspired by his travels in the Middle and Far East. For sixpence, you could go in any time between 10.30 a.m. and 9.30 p.m. and watch seventy-five minutes of newsreels, which were played on a loop. Customers could arrive at any point and start watching news footage until the point at which they arrived came around again. Watching images of real events was still something of a novelty, and people didn't much mind that some of the news items were days old. Within two years, Newcastle had two other news theatres. The original fought back, opening the Tyneside Coffee Rooms, a small private cinema, and a men-only smoking room. As early as 1944, the Tyneside was making a point of showing European films not shown anywhere else. By the late 1950s, the Tyneside Film Society had 1,500 members and was the largest film society in Britain. Thanks to restoration work in the 2000s, the Tyneside is still going strong, and is one of the last surviving newsreel theatres in the country. (www.tynesidecinema.co.uk)

FEBRUARY 2ND

1921: On this day, George Formby senior, father of the more famous George Formby, trod the boards for the last time, in a pantomime at Newcastle's Empire Theatre. George Formby Snr (christened James Lawler Booth) is now best known as the father to his ukulele-playing son, but he had an illustrious career in his own right, as a comic performer in the music halls of Edwardian London. Despite a weakened chest resulting from a childhood of dire poverty and street living, he began singing for his supper at thirteen, and never looked back. His big creation was John Willie, a parody of the hapless Lancashire lad, permanently puzzled by the sights of London. Plagued with tuberculosis and weakened by the influenza epidemic of 1918, it wasn't uncommon for Formby to have coughing fits on stage. He worked it into his act, recommending his favourite patent medicine 'Zambuk' and explaining that 'It's not the cough that carries you off, it's the coffin they carries you off in!' So when he collapsed on stage during a performance of *Jack and Jill* in Newcastle, no one was surprised. He was rushed to the Turk's Head Hotel, and two days later was taken by stretcher down to Newcastle Station for the journey home to Warrington. Unfortunately, a private carriage had not been properly organised. According to Eliza Formby, his wife, it was freezing cold: 'We couldn't even get a cup of tea'. George Formby senior died four days later. (www.georgeformby.co.uk / www.georgeformby.org)

February 3rd

1664: On this day, Mrs Pepper of Newcastle was accused of witchcraft by pitman's wife Margaret Pyle. Margaret said that when her husband Robert fell ill, she sent a urine sample to Mrs Pepper, who was supposed to be able to diagnose from it. Mrs Pepper, faced with a man with head and stomach pains and a trailing leg, had thrown water in his face and then placed a baby to his mouth, saying 'the breath of children would suck the evil spirit out of him, for he [is] possessed'. Unsurprisingly, Robert Pyle did not get better, but 'remained in a sad and lamentable condition'. Using animals to suck out evil spirits was not new – two women went to the church court of Durham in 1604 for using white ducks in this way. What is unique is that Mrs Pepper was also a midwife – the only midwife in the country to be tried for witchcraft. Perhaps this explains the use of a baby, rather than an animal, to inhale the evil spirit? Probably the real issue here was that Mrs Pepper was a Roman Catholic during the reign of the Protestant King James I. One original testimony identified the water involved as holy water, and also mentioned the use of a silver crucifix – for a female healer of dubious beliefs, during times of religious unease, rumour and witch trials, that proved a suspicious combination indeed! (Public Record Office)

FEBRUARY 4TH

1841: On this day, the House of Commons made a resolution that the 'Commission for enquiring into the condition of children working in mines etc' should also be extended to 'young people' (those under eighteen). Over the next few months, four men (a doctor, a statistician, and two inspectors of factories) interviewed hundreds of children and teenagers across the North East, providing a vivid picture of life for some teenage boys. Lads usually worked twelve-hour shifts, although many ended up occasionally doing a double or even a triple shift. Most were putters, or drivers (less arduous, but more dangerous). The youngest acted as trappers (operating the doors) – with the potential for a major accident if they fell asleep. Youth labour was commonplace – for instance, 144 miners in Heaton Pit were under eighteen. Among these were Joseph Taylor, a ten-year-old rolley (a wagon taking coal tubs to the shaft) driver, who did not like the pit at first as he was frightened to go into the dark; thirteen-year-old Thomas Scattery, who was off for fifteen weeks when a rolley went over his arm and he could no longer straighten it; fourteen-year-old Joseph Beaney, who was often sick in the mornings, blaming the air of the pit; and seven-year-old Joshua Stephenson, small and frail, who could not read and has never been to a school or church. (Leifchild, J.R., *Children's Employment Commission Report*, 1842)

FEBRUARY 5TH

1838: On this day, the Mayor and an Alderman met at the police station in Manors to deal with the minor cases of the day. This reveals the sorts of business that the police force – still only two years old – was handling on a daily basis:

- Agnes Watson disturbed the public peace in Sandgate – sent to the house of correction for a fortnight
- Benjamin Garland and Edward Baxter – begging on the street on a Sunday evening – discharged having promised to leave the town
- Neal Mens – stole a leg of mutton from a Sandgate butcher – a week's hard labour
- Joseph Ingham – assaulted a policeman while drunk – fined 10s and costs
- Mary Wigham picked a pocket on the Quayside and took two five pound notes and several shillings – forwarded to the assizes court
- Mary Jones and Margaret Holt – stole ribbons and other small articles – reprimanded and discharged
- George and Thomas Fethian, 'boys', broke into a master mariner's house and stole silver spoons – forwarded to assizes court

(*Newcastle Courant*)

FEBRUARY 6TH

1829: On this day, over 200 people – mostly mine workers and their wives – enjoyed a subterranean ball in the bowels of Gosforth Colliery. It was in celebration of reaching a seam of coal, after four long years of digging. This was the section known as the Brandling Pit, after its owner Reverend Brandling, and in 1827 work had also begun on the East Pit and West Pit. It shouldn't have taken this long, but the seam of coal was at a steep angle, and also shattered by another geological feature cutting across. So while coal was found higher up, it wasn't any use for mining – it consisted of seams which would normally have been lower down than the high main seam which was being sought. Once they reached the right depth they had to dig about 700 yards horizontally, often through solid rock. Over 1,000 feet down, an open space was converted into a candlelit dance hall, with a flagged floor and seats placed along the side. The entertainment was in two halves. Firstly, the guests arrived, over the space of several hours, and each one was invited to the coalface to hew their own piece of coal from a 4-foot high seam as a keepsake. Then they returned to the ballroom, the Coxlodge band started up, and the dancing began, well fuelled with biscuits and 'a whiff of malt liquor and cold punch'. Gosforth Colliery was active until 1884. (*Northern Echo* / Sykes, J., *Local Records*, Volume II, 1833)

FEBRUARY 7TH

1883: On this day, a letter was read out to the Town Council in which Lord Armstrong offered the land of Jesmond Dene to be a public park. This gift included the Banqueting Hall and several houses, as well as 62 acres of land, although the Armstrongs maintained control in their lifetime. This was a massive extension to the 26 acres of Lord Armstrong's estate already given to the city in 1878 as Armstrong Park; and further pieces of land (such as that around the medieval ruins of St Mary's Chapel) were added later. All of this land had been developed by the family, creating an idealised 'natural' landscape. The public were already well used to visiting the area, as Lord and Lady Armstrong – who had lived in a house in the Dene since they married in 1835 – allowed people to walk the paths on two days a week – for a small fee! With it now belonging to the people, they extended these hours, allowing free weekend visits 'subject to orderly conduct being maintained'. The formal opening was the following year, when the Princess of Wales planted a turkey oak – now a mature tree – near the Banqueting Hall. The Council was requested not to alter the Dene in any way which would 'render them more artificial than at present'. They agreed, and the whole proposition was met with loud applause. The park remains popular with local people to this day. (*Newcastle Courant*)

FEBRUARY 8TH

1829: On this day, Carliol Square Gaol received its first prisoner. The gaol featured a tall tower in the centre of a radiating design, so that many sections were visible from the tower's vantage point. Taking five years to build, the ominous walls around the gaol were 25 feet high and the whole building was made of strong stone and unforgiving metal. Despite this, it seems that complaints about prison luxury are nothing new. Satirical writer 'Tim Tunbelly' wrote that, 'the luxury of the age has made our old prisons unfit for modern prisoners, and [Northumberland and Newcastle], knowing how much the prisoners of the day deserve, have determined to build two good comfortable concerns. They will cost as much as palaces.' The gaol briefly opened for use a month earlier than expected, to house a minor celebrity. A week earlier, Jonathan Martin of Hexham, brother of artist John Martin, apparently disturbed by a buzzing noise from the organ, had set fire to the choir of York Minster, causing massive damage, before heading home. Now he needed to be rapidly transported from Hexham to York for trial. On the way, they passed through Newcastle – and Martin was incarcerated for two hours within Carliol Square Gaol while officials had a break! While the jury found him guilty, the judge found him merely insane (he'd already spent time in Gateshead Asylum) and he was sent to 'Bedlam' – Royal Bethlehem Hospital, London – where he died nine years later. (Redfern, B., *Shadow of the Gallows*, Tynebridge Publishing, 2003)

FEBRUARY 9TH

1723: On this day, there appeared in the *Newcastle Courant* an unusual and highly dubious advert:

> Whereas the smallpox and [a] very dangerous sort of fever have for a considerable time raged with much violence in the town of Newcastle upon Tyne and has been attended with great mortality, this is to give notice that there is a medium discovered which has never been known to fail of curing persons afflicted with either of these fatal distempers, even when all other means used for their recovery have proved ineffectual, which medicine was discovered and now prepared only by Mr Thorauld, master of mathematics and student in physick next door to the Mayor's house in Newcastle aforesaid.

In other words, come and buy our new smallpox medicine! Smallpox was a big problem in the eighteenth century, killing between 10 and 20 per cent of children, so it is not surprising people would try anything. Mothers would sometimes deliberately infect their children with an apparently mild case at an early age, because that increased their survival chances; by the late eighteenth century, doctors were doing this in relatively controlled conditions. But it was not until mass inoculation in the early nineteenth century that a real preventative was discovered; and no treatment ever did more than relieve the symptoms. (*Newcastle Courant*)

FEBRUARY 10TH

1774: On this day, the *Newcastle Courant* advertised the services of Charles Whitlock, a man leading an amazing double life. As an actor, he toured the towns of northern England, including a stay at the Turk's Head Long Room, Bigg Market. Yet he was also a dentist, practicing wherever his touring took him. Whitlock, the newspaper stated,

> ... cleans the blackest Teeth, restoring them to their natural Complexion, and the Mouth to its wonted Sweetness, without Pain. Makes and fixes artificial Teeth in so exact a Manner as not to be discernable from the natural ones. Those Ladies and Gentlemen who please to honour him with their Commands (during the stay of the Comedians) are requested to favour him with them, at Mrs Gales, in Newgate Street. Where may be had, his Tincture for the Scurvy in the Gums, and his Paste or Powder for cleaning and preserving the Teeth.

At this time, many theatre shows were technically illegal, but one trick was to make the shows free – on condition you bought a packet of tooth powder! In 1788, Whitlock was appointed the manager of the new Theatre Royal, Drury Lane. He continued to act, though a fellow actor once described him as a 'tooth-drawing reptile'. In later life he continued with both his professions in America for ten years, before returning to Newcastle – as a dentist. (Hargreaves, A.S., 'Dental Services in Newcastle from 1790-1799', *Medicine in Northumbria*, Pybus Society, 1993)

FEBRUARY 11TH

1798: On this day, St Andrew's Catholic Church opened on Percy Street. It was the first Catholic Church to open in Newcastle since the Reformation of the 1530s, and was the culmination of three years' work on the part of Father James Worswick. Worswick, aged twenty-six and newly ordained, had moved to Newcastle in 1795 with a mission to care for the increasing population of Catholic poor. His background had prepared him for almost anything – he had been studying in the Douay seminary in France when the Revolution broke out in 1789, and he was forced to make his way to the allied armies. On arrival in Newcastle, Worswick started off celebrating Mass from a run-down house in Bells Court, but finding this inadequate for the job, he bought a house in Pilgrim Street with a large garden and began building. By early 1798, his new church, St Andrew's, was ready for a congregation, and on February 11th Catholic High Mass was performed for the first time in over 250 years. But demand soon outstripped the space available, and only nine years later the church needed to be enlarged when the congregation merged with that of Westgate Chapel, the first of three extensions to the building. James Worswick died in 1843 and was buried in St Mary's Cathedral, Clayton Street, which was being built at the time. In 1933, he had a street named after him, near to his chapel. (www.st-andrews-worswick.org.uk / www.timmonet.co.uk/html/worswick.htm)

February 12th

1803: On this day, two boys were arrested for stealing a handkerchief in a small shop. Not too remarkable, one might think. But when they were examined by the Mayor, a rather strange story emerged. The lads admitted stealing the handkerchief, and indeed some other bits and bobs, not to keep or to raise cash for food, but with the specific aim of raising money for gambling. Apparently, in a private house on the Quayside, almost every night, a woman was running a raffle 'frequented entirely by children, not 14 years of age'. All lotteries and similar games had been made illegal the previous year through the Little-Go Act (a little-go was a lottery). On the basis of these boys' stories, the den of iniquity was raided, the woman tried and convicted as a rogue and vagabond and sent to the House of Correction for three months. In a way she was lucky – if the magistrate had wanted to use the full force of law, she could have been fined £500! (*Newcastle Courant*)

———— • ◆ • ————

1845: On this day, Corsair, the eight-month-old son of Iowan Native American Indians, was buried in a donated plot in Westgate Hill cemetery. His mother was part of a group who toured England, dancing and entertaining, which seems to have had a Quaker 'handler' and stayed with Quakers throughout their tour.

FEBRUARY 13TH

1813: On this day, a Newcastle sailor and his sister foiled the press gang. The impressment of able-bodied men to the navy had long been a source of anger on the Tyne (*see* April 22nd), and the Napoleonic Wars were making matters worse. But the gang had reckoned without Miss Bell of the Close, Newcastle, who had other ideas. She came to the door asking to be allowed to bid her brother – who had been literally pulled off the streets – farewell. The pair were apparently given a room to themselves, barred and bolted to prevent any possibility of escape. Seizing the moment, the pair swapped clothes. Mr Bell then walked free, in drag, wiping the 'tears' from his eyes (and so covering his face). His sister, meanwhile, awaited the wrath of the press gang. 'It would be difficult,' says a writer in the *European Magazine*, who tells the story, 'to describe the rage and disappointment of the gang on discovering how they had been duped; and crowds of persons went to see the heroine, who received several pounds from the spectators as reward for her intrepidity and affection. She was soon restored to her liberty by order of the magistrates.' (*North Country Lore and Legend*, 1891)

February 14th

1842: On this day, an Excise Officer at Newcastle Quay was amazed to uncover an unusual attempt to evade paying excise duty. He was investigating the steamer *Vesta*, which had been launched with great celebration from Hopper's shipyard, Newcastle, just over five years previously. It sailed the waters between Newcastle and Edinburgh. On this occasion, the excise officer noticed a doll, 'dressed up in the gay attire of those which are usually sold in toy shops', but notable for being extraordinarily large. On closer investigation, he discovered that the head came off with little effort, revealing the neck of nothing less than an enormous whisky bottle. Sadly it was empty, the contents presumably already extracted and sold to a welcoming Newcastle public! The whisky was probably distilled in the Scottish highlands – although whether it was done so legally or not is open to question. The 1823 Excise Act encouraged private distillers to pay a fee to produce whisky legally. Some communities, however, were known to have worked together to keep their distilleries hidden from the excise man. Whether produced within the law or not, the duty was 5*d* per bottle to move the whisky into England. The oversized doll was almost certainly an unusual method to try and avoid that! (Fordyce, T., *Local Records*, 1866)

February 15th

1944: On this day, a public inquiry into financial corruption opened in the Moot Hall. It was to last six weeks (the longest inquiry since 1939), and cost £11,000, with 128 witnesses speaking around 1,250,000 words. The cause? Irregularities within the Fire and Police Service's inventories. A mysterious 'disappearing' fire engine was the starting point for investigation – one had been bought using public money, yet had seemingly ceased to exist! A similar mysterious fate met a fire float. There were irregularities in provision of wartime rations, and the press enjoyed reporting widespread personal use of police horses and photographic equipment – the inquiry heard tales of photography at flower shows and pony trekking in the Lake District! The inquiry was set up simply to work out what had happened, but often found the paper records lacking – missing, or possibly never made? In the end, the inquiry did find out what had happened to the missing fire equipment, although their fates did nothing to alleviate the distinct whiff of corruption. The fire engine had been sold for scrap, but whether this was justified (especially as one concerned party owned the scrapyard) was unclear. The fire float was sold to the same man and then used by his scrap company, while still 'available' for fire fighting in emergencies – then repaired by the Fire Service! (Marsh, G., *Flames Across the Tyne*, Peterson, 1974)

FEBRUARY 16TH

1709: On this day, Charles Avison was baptised in St John's Church. His father, Richard, was a member of the ancient Incorporated Company of Town Waits (the official town band), receiving £4 and a uniform per year. Charles Avison moved away but returned in 1735, when he was offered the position of organist at his old parish church. The following year he moved across to St Nicholas' Church, Newcastle, for £20 a year. And here he stayed, despite being offered many more prestigious contracts further south. He became involved with the Newcastle Musical Society and its subscription concerts, becoming director in 1738. He organised musical events at the Newcastle Pleasure Gardens, and played music between the intervals of local theatre shows. He also taught, as the following announcement shows: 'He proposes to attend young ladies on the harpsichord between the hours of 9 and 1 in the forenoon; and from 2 to 6 in the evening he will teach the violin and German flute.' As well as being an accomplished composer, in 1752 Avison wrote *Essay of Musical Expression*, perhaps the first English work of musical criticism (discussing the distinctions between music which is sublime, inspiring, elegant or pleasing, for instance). Avison's death was somewhat peculiar – he was caught out by a freak snowstorm which hit Newcastle in May, 1770, and died a few days later. (www.rslade.co.uk, eighteenth-century music specialist)

February 17th

1753: On this day, a long snow ended in a sudden and dramatic thaw. In Newcastle, the water level rose 15 feet above its usual level, tearing all of the ships on the Quayside from their moorings. Ralph Jackson, a seventeen-year-old apprentice to a Quayside merchant, recorded: 'in the river there was fifteen sail of Shils besides Keels and Wherrys tore away from their Moorings, there was three large stones with rings at them tore away by the Ships ... I walked down the Key some times for the fresh had almost forced one of our Keels upon the Key. After dinner I took a walk with Billy on the Tops of the Hills of the South side above Bridge and we saw a great deluge for the water covered a great many low grounds'. Floods were not uncommon at this time (river improvements have now reduced the risk). During one such flood in late February 1826, Alexander Brodie bravely got a small boat and plied his way along the Quayside itself, 'to the amusement of numerous spectators'. Known as the oldest wherryman on the Tyne, Brodie would have been old enough to recall the massive flood of 1771, and perhaps even that of 1753, so no wonder the latest deluge didn't worry him! (Sykes, J., *Local Records*, Volume I, 1833 / *Diary of Ralph Jackson*)

FEBRUARY 18TH

1900: On this day, reformist Joseph Cowen died. His father was a brickmaker, who eventually became a mine owner and a reformist Liberal MP for Newcastle – he was knighted in 1871. In many ways, his son was to follow in his footsteps. Brought up in Ryton and educated in Edinburgh, he returned to Newcastle to take his place on the local political scene. In 1858, he was one of the founder members of the Northern Reform Union, campaigning for democratic reforms, and encouraging miners in Tyneside to campaign for better conditions as well as political representation. In 1873, when political reform still excluded most miners, he organised a protest of over 40,000 people on Town Moor. In 1859, Cowen had bought the *Newcastle Daily Chronicle* and *Weekly Chronicle*, which were transformed by campaigns for political reform and social justice. He promoted the Co-operative movement and Mechanics Institutes, and opened Newcastle Public Library and the Tyne Theatre and Opera House. He stood as Liberal MP for Newcastle from the death of his father in 1873, for thirteen years. *The Times* said that he was 'short of stature, uncouth in dress and figure, and speaking a tongue the peculiarities of which are admired only by those to the manner born [...] Among other peculiarities he introduced to Parliament the flat felt hat which forms the Sunday headgear of the Northumbrian pitman.' (www.the-nut.net)

FEBRUARY 19TH

1823: On this day, eight people were crushed to death in the Theatre Royal, Drury Lane, Newcastle. The cause was a small fire, which broke out during a pantomime. The details appeared in a letter to the *Morning Post* three days later: 'Shortly after the commencement of the second Act of *Tom and Jerry* [a play about life in London], one of the Gas-lights in the third box from the Stage, on the right side of the house, by some mischance had set fire to the wood-work that enclosed the pipe. The consequence was an immediate and very unmeasured alarm of "Fire!" pervading the house, particularly the gallery, which, unfortunately, was very much crowded. Notwithstanding it was soon apparent to the company in the boxes and the pit (both of which places were but thinly filled), that there was little or no danger to be apprehended, the people in the gallery were not to be tranquillized. Considerable efforts were made from the Stage, too, to persuade them, that if they would but patiently wait a very short time, they would see everything restored to order. All in vain: a deaf ear was turned to the judicious advice given to them, and with a tremendous rush they struggled for egress. Woefully distressing was the result: – Eight individuals were literally trodden to death!' (*Morning Post*)

FEBRUARY 20TH

1837: On this day, the Grey Street Theatre Royal had its opening night. Designed by Benjamin Green, this building replaced the 1788 Drury Lane theatre. It opened with *The Merchant of Venice*. There was an extensive report in the *Newcastle Courant* on the 24th: 'On Monday last, the New Theatre, in Grey-street, in this town, was opened for the first time under the management or Mr Montague Penley, and was attended by a very crowded audience. The boxes and gallery are beautifully embellished with richly gilt ornaments [...] The ceiling of the auditory is divided into sixteen panels, in which are, alternately, figures of dancing nymphs and groups of musical instruments. From the centre hangs a large and brilliant cut-glass chandelier. The boxes are lined with rich crimson paper, and the whole of the seats are covered with crimson moreen [...] The lighting of the Theatre is not so brilliant as might have been expected from the number of lights, but the Proprietors, it is understood, are about to introduce Argand burners into the small chandeliers instead of the imitative candles at present in use, which will obviate the defect. [...] The play selected for the opening of the theatre, no one who has read Shakspeare can fail to admire; but though Mr Young's acting throughout Shylock was scarcely in any part to be found fault with, it must be confessed that the other performers seemed hardly to have a due conception of their respective parts.' [*sic*] (*Newcastle Courant*)

FEBRUARY 21ST

2005: On this day, celebrations were held for the official opening of the ceremonial arch, or paifang, which stands at the head of Stowell Street at the entrance to Newcastle's Chinatown, one of only five in the country. The ceremony was performed by Lord Mayor George Douglas. In Chinese culture, arches like that of Newcastle's Chinatown are symbols of prosperity and success. This one took five months to build and is 11 metres tall. It is made of stone and glass, flanked by two stone guardian lions and decorated with tiles and paintings of Tyneside scenes. It was designed and manufactured in Changsu in the Jiangsu Province of China, then shipped over in November 2004 and constructed by workers from Shanghai. Chinatown itself had begun in 1972, although isolated Chinese immigrants had set up their restaurants in this area of the town centre since the Second World War. From the start, the North East Chinese Association had discussed the idea of an arch, but it took thirty years for the plan – a partnership with funding from the local Chinese community as well as the council and several other funding bodies – to come to fruition.

FEBRUARY 22ND

2008: On this day, Newcastle bank Northern Rock passed into the ownership of the government. Northern Rock was formed in the 1960s by a union of the Northern Counties Building Society, and the Rock Building Society. It did well initially, buying up several other smaller companies as it grew. With a change in government regulations, Northern Rock effectively became a bank in 1994. It focussed on its mortgage business (for instance selling its credit card organisation to the Co-operative Bank to provide more funds for the mortgage side of things), eventually becoming the largest mortgage lender in the country. But this made it more vulnerable to changes, particularly after it entered the 'sub-prime' mortgage lending market, with Lehman Brothers as underwriters of the deal. After the sub-prime crisis in America, Northern Rock began to suffer liquidity problems. Its size made the problem urgent. When it petitioned the Bank of England for financial help in 2007, shares plummeted. Voracious press coverage of the share-price drop prompted thousands of customers to queue outside the doors of local branches, ready to withdraw their money. By February 22nd 2008, Northern Rock finally reached breaking point and the government stepped in to take ownership and take on the company's debt. The company continued to function and improve its finances, and was increasingly seen as a more stable option than many of the other banks. At the time of writing, Northern Rock is once more in private hands, having been bought by Virgin Money. (www.thefinanceowl.com)

FEBRUARY 23RD

1939: On this day, Gosforth baker John Gregg opened his first bakery, little knowing that he would become a household name. For the first twelve years, John Gregg delivered yeast, eggs and confectionery on his bicycle, then, in 1951, he opened a small shop in Gosforth High Street, with a bakery in the back. When he died in 1964, there was still only one shop, but it had seven delivery vans. Under his son, Ian, the business expanded rapidly – in the 1970s it bought up several other chains of bakeries and baker's shops, initially keeping the original names but rebranding them as Greggs of Yorkshire and Greggs of the Midlands in 1999. The company now has around 1,500 outlets and a place in the FTSE 100 Index. (www.greggs.co.uk)

2011: On this day, drilling started on a geothermic borehole – the first deep excavation in Britain since the 1980s, and the deepest ever drilled in a British city – right in the centre of Newcastle, on the old Newcastle Brewery site. After passing through limestone filled with fossils, and an unexpected coal seam, the goal was reached – hot water. The plan is to use this hot water source as a cheap and environmentally friendly way to heat the Science City centre and perhaps part of Eldon Square. (www.bbc.co.uk)

FEBRUARY 24TH

1909: On this day, racing driver George Robson was born in Newcastle. Something of a 'forgotten Geordie', Robson moved with his family to Canada as a baby. The family returned to Newcastle during the First World War, when his father worked as a machinist, then moved back to Canada again (he took Canadian nationality), before settling in America in 1924. George competed in all three Indianapolis 500 races between 1939 and 1946, and was the first post-war Indy 500 winner when he finally completed the 500-mile course as the highlight of an excellent year's racing in 1946. At the time, the survival of the race itself was in question – the track, neglected during the Second World War, was bought by local businessman Tony Hulman, who made improvements just in time. Only a few months later, though, in the heavy dust clouds of the Lakewood Speedway track, Robson drove into the back of another car during the Atlanta 100-mile race. Robson and fellow competitor George Barringer were killed in the ensuing pile-up. In spite of this, his brother, Hal, also competed three times in the late 1940s. He started in the same year that George won, making them the first brothers to compete against each other in the Indy 500.

FEBRUARY 25TH

1797: On this day, the *Newcastle Chronicle* published a letter signed by the town's principal tradesmen, advertising that 'we, whose Names are hereunto subscribed, will receive the Notes of ALL the BANKS here, in Payment as usual'. This was as agreed in a meeting a few days before, and was an important step to try to minimise a growing banking crisis. There was a growing fear of a French invasion force, leading people to withdraw their cash. The Newcastle banks were running out of funds to hand over, and on February 18th, a meeting of local bankers had agreed that they would have to suspend all cash payment. On the 23rd, one of them also asked the Bank of England (large, but not yet the regulator it became) for a loan. On the 26th, the Bank of England itself stopped paying out hard cash (which was all going in payments to foreign powers because of the war). Instead, the banks all gave out notes, having first come up with the new £1 and £2 notes (even the £5 had only been around for four years). Notes, at this date, were just elaborately printed pieces of paper on which the cashier would write the payee's name. But if they could not be taken to a bank and exchanged for gold, they had no worth – unless shops said they did, hence the importance of today's announcement. (Shin, H., 'The Way to Support Credit: The Suspension Crisis in 1797 and the Declaration Movement' / www.ehs.org.uk / www.bankofengland.co.uk)

FEBRUARY 26TH

1959: On this day, Mrs Amy Barratt, a Scotswood shopkeeper, was murdered in her general store near Scotswood meat market. The shop had been broken into nearly twenty times over the previous few months (including three times in a single week) leading police to advise her to stop working there. Nearby houses were all being knocked down, and customers were few and far between. But at seventy-one years of age, and having worked there all her life, she refused to give in – and it was apparently the death of her. Her habits were so regular that when she didn't come out of the shop for her regular taxi home, the taxi driver – who had been helping her open the shop up every morning for ten years – went inside to check on her. He and a neighbour then raised the alarm. When police broke in, they found that Mrs Barratt was in front of her shop counter, dead from severe head injuries. She had been killed at some point in the mid-afternoon, and the till emptied of the few pounds it contained. Several potential weapons were examined, but the area was virtually a building site, full of possibilities. Although nearby builders gave a good description of a suspect, and one man was taken in for questioning, no one was ever charged with the murder, and despite a reward of £1,000, the case remains unsolved to this day. (*Newcastle Journal*)

FEBRUARY 27TH

1632: On this Shrove Tuesday, the apprentice population of Newcastle found something – quite why, we do not understand – to get upset about. A large group of fourteen to twenty-one-year-old lads rioted in protest over the building of a lime kiln and a ballast heap outside the Sandgate gate. This might seem an odd target, but of course there is more to it. For one thing, Shrove Tuesday was traditionally a holiday for the apprentices – and in the early seventeenth century, it was a tradition with disorder attached. For instance, in London in 1617, rioters destroyed the contents of a theatre and broke out prisoners from Wapping Gaol. There is also a suggestion that the Ballast Hills area, threatened with development, was a popular spot for lads to walk out with their lasses on a Sunday afternoon. The real answer is likely to lie in the murky depths of Newcastle's civic politics. Another traditional Shrove Tuesday activity amongst lads at the time was to tie a cockerel to a post and throw stones at it. Rector and historian John Brand, looking back from 1777, notes with relief that this custom has finally died out amongst his fellow Geordies.

FEBRUARY 28TH

1884: On this day, the local government board signed off a new set of bye-laws relating to activities in the Bigg Market – and specifically the actual market held there. Firstly, it was illegal to sell or advertise anything outside the designated market area, which would be marked out 'in legible letters of such a colour as to be clearly distinguishable from the colour of the ground whereon such letters are painted or marked'. A similarly marked area was set aside for wagons and farmers carts. All market goods had to be cleared away by 5 p.m. on Tuesday and Thursday, and by 8 p.m. on Saturday. No one could have a pitch of more than 40 square feet, and their goods couldn't project beyond it. And of course, they had to remove, or at least tidy into a suitable container, all rubbish. Most surprisingly, market stall holders were banned from causing any annoyance – including 'calling out'. Nor could they hold auctions or gather a crowd together to listen to a pitch which might obstruct the paths. Breaking any of these rules would result in a fine of 40s, unless the court decided to reduce the fine. (Gibson, J., *Newcastle-upon-Tyne Acts and Byelaws 1837-1887*, Andree Reid, 1888)

FEBRUARY 29TH

1864: On this day, Joseph Swan patented a new method which was to revolutionise photography. Before this point, photographs were not well fixed to paper, and tended to fade. Swan's new 'carbon process' took a thin sheet of gelatine containing particles of carbon, which were sensitised by exposure to potassium chromate. When the gelatine was placed on a paper support, it was ready for use – when light was shone through a negative onto the paper, a permanent image was created. As soon as the patent was granted, Swan and his business partner, John Mawson, started selling elegant images. Soon they were also selling ready-made tissue to allow photographers to produce their own work, in black, sepia, and purple-brown. The Mawson and Swan Company also sold rights to make the paper to different companies around the world, including the Autotype Printing and Publishing Company of London, who gained the English rights in 1868. Carbon process photographs became known as autotype, and lasted, with some improvements, well into the twentieth century. Meanwhile, Swan went on to make other discoveries in photographic processing. In 1871, he realised that heat affected the photographic emulsion, and worked out how to dry it to make the first 'dry plate', and two years later he patented bromide paper, still widely used in printing photographs. (Seaborn, S., Linsohn, P. and Godding, D., *Celebration of Innovation: A History of Autotype 1868-2005*, Autotype International Ltd, 2005)

MARCH 1ST

1942: On this day, yachtsman and polar explorer David Scott Cowper was born in Newcastle. As a youth Cowper was prone to seasickness and was banned from sailing class because he could not swim, yet he became one of the greatest sailors of the twentieth century. In 1980, he first sailed around the world in 225 days, beating the previous world record (in terms of time spent at sea) by a single day, and smashing the total time (including land stops) by twenty-three days. Two years later, he circumnavigated the world in the opposite direction in 231 days – beating the world record by an incredible seventy-one days and becoming the first person to sail around the world in both directions. At this point he still couldn't swim, arguing that if you fell overboard into rough seas, being able to swim wouldn't help! In 1984, Cowper was the first person to circumnavigate the world solo in a motorboat (a converted lifeboat), as he failed to gain enough sponsorship to pay for top-of-the-range equipment. And the records continue – he was the first to circumnavigate the world via the North West Passage, although it took him several years (having to abandon his ship in the ice for long periods). By the end of 2011, he had sailed around the world six times. David Scott Cowper still lives in Newcastle. (Gibson, J., *Spirit of Tyneside*, John Donald, 1990 / www.wikipedia.org)

MARCH 2ND

1923: On this day, George Hume, son of a specialist heart surgeon living in Jesmond, was born. His father was Anglican, but his mother was a Catholic Frenchwoman – the couple met while William Hume was billeted in Wimereux during the First World War, and they became determined to marry even though he was twice her age. Back in Newcastle, Marie Hume continued to speak French to her children, and took them to Mass while her husband was at work. As a child, George helped his father hand out food in the wards of the Royal Victoria Hospital on Christmas Day. At ten years old, George met a Dominican priest, under whose tutelage his faith, and his desire to help the poor, grew stronger. He later attended Ampleforth College, Yorkshire, and trained to become a priest. It was here that he took his new Catholic name, the name by which he has become famous – Father Basil Hume. In 1976, he was appointed Catholic Archbishop of Westminster – the first monk to be given the position in 125 years. Later that year he became a Cardinal. In 1980, Cardinal Hume was made a Freeman of Newcastle – alongside Jackie Milburn. He had always been a football fan, and the two Freemen became firm friends – something which would have pleased his father, who had hoped he would become a footballer. He remained in the post until his death in 1999. (Castle, T., *Basil Hume: A Portrait*, Fount, 1987)

MARCH 3RD

1745: On this day, John Wesley was attacked on Pilgrim Street. Hearing that his attacker, Robert Young, habitually threw stones at Methodists, Wesley sent him a letter asking for an apology, 'Otherwise, in pity to your soul, I shall be obliged to inform the magistrates of your assaulting me.' Young turned up a few hours later and promised to change his ways. Wesley concludes: 'So did this gentle reproof, if not save a soul from death, yet prevent a multitude of sins.' (www.visionofbritain. org.uk)

———— •◆• ————

1877: On this day, football in Tyneside was born! A group of local enthusiasts put together two teams – one with eight men, the other with nine – for the first local match under associated rules. The starting point was Elswick Rugby Club, at Mill Inn, Westgate – and a lot of the players were club members. The teams were simply called 'Team A' and 'Team B'; Team A won 2-0 (despite being the team with one man short). A few weeks later they formed a football club, Tyne AFC, and started encouraging other local rugby clubs to put up a side. Confusingly, in the same year, Elswick Rugby Club changed its name to Northern Football Club, while continuing to play rugby. Tyne AFC weren't the first north-eastern club though – that honour goes to Middlesbrough, or to South Bank in Teesside, depending on who you ask. (Joannou, P, *Pioneers of the North*, Breedon Publishing, 2009)

MARCH 4TH

1976: On this day, Eldon Square Shopping centre – which had cost £60 million – opened to the public for the first time. Crowds gathered outside, keen to be among the first to see the future of shopping in Tyneside. Only the first half of the centre was complete; the second half opened six months later, including what was then the world's biggest Boots store. Indeed at this point, Eldon Square was Europe's biggest indoor shopping centre. With over a million square feet of retail space, and around 175 stores, it is still in the top ten overall, and the largest in a city centre. An extension in 2010 added a further 300,000 square feet of space, and another twenty-five stores. Even from the start, Eldon Square had more than its share of the big names in local retail, being helped massively by the relocation of Bainbridges, which included a 'UFO' design café, and a sculpture/children's play area made from giant pencils. However, Eldon Square's success had not come without controversy, in particular due to the demolition of two thirds of the original Eldon Square, now known as Old Eldon Square, an attractive set of 1820s terraces. (icnewcastle)

MARCH 5TH

1921: On this day, an act of terrorism was averted by a most unlikely source. A mere five years after the 1916 Easter Rising in Ireland, Irish Republican activists, under cloak of darkness, entered an oil refining works on Forth Banks, drilled holes in two oil barrels and lit the contents. Westgate Fire Station had a report of fire in the yard of Messrs Goodall, Bates and Co. Ltd and rushed to the scene, but were initially puzzled to find that the flames were already extinguished. It turned out that the refinery was close to a Sea Scout headquarters. Upon seeing smoke pouring their way, the Sea Scouts not only climbed an 8-foot hoarding to get into the yard, but also succeeded in beating down the fire. Earlier that same evening, three men had attracted suspicion by lurking around a bonded warehouse. Unfortunately, only a single policeman arrived; he arrested one man, Owen Salmon, but the others escaped, perhaps moving on to Forth Banks. Salmon was found to be carrying explosives, a detonator, and a pamphlet from the Irish Self-Determination League. He later joined the Garda. Another arson attack was carried out in Tyne Dock on the same night, and a few months later an aircraft assembly shed was burnt to the ground in Gosforth. (*Evening Chronicle* / Brennan, P., *The IRA in Jarrow* / www.donmouth.co.uk)

MARCH 6TH

1867: On this day, Charles Dickens, whilst visiting Newcastle during one of his long lecture tours, wrote to his sister-in-law Georgina Hogarth: 'The readings have made an immense effect in this place, and it is remarkable that although the people are individually rough, collectively they are an unusually tender and sympathetic audience; while their comic perception is quite up to the high London standard.' He goes on to speak approvingly of the rest of his visit to the North East, even enjoying a wet walk through rainy Tynemouth. Indeed, Dickens was quite the walker – on at least one occasion he walked to Newcastle from his previous performance venue in Sunderland. He said, 'a finer audience there is not in England; for while they can laugh till they shake the roof, they have a very unusual sympathy with what is pathetic or passionate.' But it wasn't all good. On November 22nd 1861, his recitation from *Oliver Twist* at the Lecture Room of the Music Hall in Nelson Street had been packed out. But his 'gas batten' (a gas-powered personal lighting rig) fell, mid-recitation. A woman screamed in panic and ran towards him. Dickens feared a lethal stampede developing. His own staff were more fearful of a deadly blaze erupting! Fortunately, calling on his masterful powers of oratory, he was able to calm the crowd and avert any danger. Still, Dickens must have enjoyed his 'warm' reception in Newcastle, performing to appreciative audiences six times in total. (www.opencorrespondence.org)

MARCH 7TH

1829: On this day, thirty-year-old fishwife Jane Jameson was hanged for matricide before a crowd of around 20,000, half of them women. She was the first woman to be hanged in the town for over fifty years – and the last hanged in the town at all. The *Newcastle Weekly Chronicle* described the scene: 'Mr. Scott having sung two verses of *The Sinner's Lament*, the cord was adjusted, and in a few seconds the world closed upon her forever'. Jane had visited her mother at the Keelman's Hospital, and, while drunk, stabbed her with a hot poker. Although her mother claimed to the end that she had fallen and tripped on the poker, all the evidence suggested otherwise, and in a packed court, the accusation of murder stuck. Rumours spread that Jane had already killed her father and two bastard babies. As an additional punishment, her body was sent to the Barber-Surgeons for dissection – the last criminal to suffer this fate in Newcastle. Surgeon's apprentice Thomas Giordani Wright was there, and wrote: 'Mr John Fife on Monday noon gave a very good demonstration on the brain of [Jameson] … and had good opportunity, from the freshness of the brain before him, to exhibit its parts and structure in a clear manner. The audience altogether might be about 50, of whom almost one third were non-professionals'. It seems that some locals enjoyed the hanging so much that they also turned out for the dissection …
(*Newcastle Weekly Chronicle* / Wright, T.G., *Diary of a Doctor*, (ed. Johnson, A.), Tynebridge Publishing, 1998)

MARCH 8TH

1830: On this day, an Egyptian mummy from around 700 BC was unwrapped by three surgeons in the lecture room of the Newcastle Literary and Philosophical Society. The mummy, with an inner and outer coffin, was uncovered in 1798 by Baron Dominique-Vivant Denon, the Louvre's first director. The mummy was bought in Paris by John Bowes Wright in 1826, and given to the Lit & Phil soon afterwards. Underneath 50lbs of bandages, the surgeons found a well-preserved specimen, 'sepia brown' and with perfect teeth, 'pendulous' breasts, long red hair, and 'some mobility' in the limbs, all filled with embalming oil. They also found, wrapped within her bandages, six gilded wooden amulets around her neck, blue glazed tubular beads at her waist, and a silver embalming plate, engraved with an eye. The mummy was varnished, placed back in her coffin, and displayed in the gallery of the library room, the Lit & Phil charging a penny per view. In 1964, hieroglyphics were deciphered, identifying the mummy as Irt-irw, daughter of Pedamenope. Mysteries surround Irt-irw – her coffin is elaborate, but her mummification cheap and crude. Also, the fingernails on one hand are longer than on the other – perhaps she was a musician? She is now in the care of Tyne and Wear Museums. (Gray, P., 'Two mummies of Ancient Egyptians in the Hancock Museum Newcastle', *The Journal of Egyptian Archaeology*, December 1967)

MARCH 9TH

1912: On this day, the suffrage campaign in the North East took a turn for the explosive. The campaign for votes for women was already well established in the region, and direct action had its supporters, mostly members of the Women's Social and Political Union (WSPU). For instance, in October 1909, Jane Brailsford was arrested for chopping through a street barricade in Newcastle, near where Lloyd George was trying to give a speech. She was jailed for a month. But arson was something new to the campaign. In the early hours of the morning, someone took a perforated pail, full of burning material, into the pavilion and bowls house of Heaton Park. The building caught fire, and completely burned down. Between the railings was a warning card: 'No peace until women get the vote'. Things escalated as the WSPU gained followers. In February 1913, acid was poured into letterboxes, and telephone wires cut. After the Heaton arson attack, there were attempts to set fire to the Newcastle Labour Exchange and Gosforth Golf Club, among other establishments. Church services were disrupted with prayers for Emmeline Pankhurst, then in prison. The biggest incident was probably that of September 18th, when Kenton Railway Station was destroyed. (Neville, D., *To Make their Mark*, North East Labour History, 1997)

MARCH 10TH

1967: On this day, Jimi Hendrix played in Newcastle for the first time. This was no isolated visit – his manager, Chas Chandler, was local, and they stayed with Chas' mother in Heaton. Kathy Etchingham, then Jimi's girlfriend, described the house as a tiny back-to-back terrace with no running water, adding that, for the sake of Chas' mother's sensibilities, the men and women slept in separate rooms. It is claimed that Jimi busked on Chillingham Road, though there is no evidence to support this. Hendrix played two gigs at the Club-a-Go-Go. 'The Young Set' was at 8 p.m. in the under-18s room. The other was in the Jazz Lounge at 2 a.m. Watching that night were at least two people who went on to find fame of their own. Singer and actor Jimmy Nail, who was then just thirteen, recalled, 'I hadn't seen anything like it … but get this, he let [the guitar] go, and continued playing while it hung from the ceiling'. Also watching was fifteen-year-old Gordon Sumner, later to become Sting, who recalled: 'I think I remember snatches of "Hey Joe" and "Foxy Lady", but that event remains a blur of noise and breathtaking virtuosity, of Afro'd hair, wild clothes, and towers of Marshall amplifiers. It was also the first time I'd ever seen a black man. I lay in my bed that night with my ears ringing and my worldview significantly altered.' (Sting, *Broken Music*, Simon & Schuster Ltd, 2003 / www.hendrixnortheast.pwp. blueyonder.co.uk)

MARCH 11TH

1861: On this day, the 'Garibaldi panorama' was exhibited in Newcastle. A panorama was a series of images that were gradually revealed within a frame by the use of rollers. A narrator described the action, while vividly painted scenes – full of action, war, and exotic locations – were unrolled to a fee-paying audience. The one in Newcastle was one of the smaller moving versions of this uniquely Victorian entertainment. In 1861, Garibaldi was at the height of his fame thanks to press reports about the wars in Italy. More than one panorama telling his story was made to take advantage of this. It may be hard to believe now, but this was the equivalent of going to see an epic film at the cinema! This day was the start of an eleven-day run at the Assembly rooms, with afternoon and evening showings. They must have expected to do well with their depiction of 'the most interesting events in the great struggles for freedom', since Garibaldi had personally visited Newcastle in 1854. On that occasion, he was presented with a sword and telescope 'by the people of Tyneside, friends of European freedom'. Capitalising on his local celebrity, the papers somewhat cannily advertised 'Garibaldi is coming!' Public reaction – and indeed, if he ever heard of it, the reaction of Garibaldi himself – to such a misleading advertisement has sadly not survived the passage of time. (Sutcliffe, M.P., 'Negotiating the 'Garibaldi moment' in Newcastle-upon-Tyne (1854-1861)', *Modern Italy*, May 2010)

March 12th

1776: On this day, writer James Boswell made a second visit to his brother John, who suffered bouts of insanity and withdrawal, and several times was placed in a private asylum in Spital Tongues, St Luke's House (later called Belle Grove Retreat). Reflecting on this experience in his journals, he wondered whether it was in fact better to have one's mind obscured, than to be unhappy. He was pleased to find that John recognised him, but upset by his asking, 'take me with you' – even though James knew that his brother was well looked after. St Luke's House was one of two mental hospitals in Newcastle at that time, both the brainchild of one man, Dr John Hall. The other facility was the Pauper Hospital for Lunatics – public, much bigger, and largely serving the workhouses. The surgeon and physician attended three times a week, and nurses were to behave at all times with 'tenderness to the patients'. At some point later, things deteriorated: an 1824 report found that the Pauper Hospital contained 'chains, iron bars, dungeon-like cells, many close, cold, dark holes, less comfortable than cow houses. There was no separation of the sexes, no classification, and for medical treatment the old exploded system of restraint and coercion'. This scandal prompted the building of a new facility in Bath Lane. Belle Grove Lunatic Asylum was enlarged and remained in use until 1857; the house still stands, but is today a private residence. (Le Gassicke, J., 'The Early History of Psychiatry in Newcastle upon Tyne', British Journal of Psychiatry, April 1972)

March 13th

1940: At one minute to midnight on this day, Kenton Bar Bunker was declared operational. This was the headquarters for RAF 13 Group Fighter Command, one of the four regional centres of operation, the Newcastle location chosen because it was roughly in the middle of the region from Humberside to Scotland. The bunker was 15 feet below ground. Above it were a range of related buildings, from housing to a NAAFI, a decontamination centre, and grocery store. The whole thing was under the command of Air Vice Marshall Saul, who ran everything from the comfortable surroundings of Kenton Hall. Kenton Bar bunker's finest hour was August 15th 1940 – the Battle of Britain. The northern response to the Battle of Britain was co-ordinated from here, as was the general air defence for the remainder of the Second World War. Although the bunker was retired from use after the war, it was temporarily called into precautionary service again in 1952, when the Cold War was gathering pace. It became a Regional War Room, the only one to use an existing structure rather than being purpose-built. The revival of the Kenton Bar Bunker proved short-lived, however. After a few years it became superfluous under a new system of larger command posts – the Regional Seats of Government. The bunker still exists, forgotten except by enthusiasts and some locals, with many of its original fittings and equipment intact. (websitedcm.com/bunker/)

MARCH 14TH

1863: On this day, Newcastle residents were able to witness an execution for the last time, when nineteen-year-old George Vass went to the gallows for the murder of Margaret Jane Docherty. The gallows were specially erected on top of the jail wall, at the south-west corner of Carliol Square. This is what eyewitness Archibald Reed later recalled of the event, in his book *Bruce's School*:

> Vass was tried and condemned to death for the murder and outrage of an old woman near the West Walls. The whole length of the street from the Arcade Steps to Carliol Street was barricaded strongly at short intervals, forming pens, to avoid accidents through the enormous crowds anticipated, and well it was so, for every available space was filled [...] looking down as far as the eye could carry, the whole thoroughfare had the appearance of a street paved with human heads. These people assembled as early as 5.30 a.m. By 8 o'clock the crowd was so dense that dozens of people had fainted; and these were passed over the heads of the multitude to the outside. The story of the execution is soon told; the condemned man was under a minute in view before he disappeared from the gaze of the bloodthirsty mob.

(Redfern, B., *The Shadow of the Gallows*, Tynebridge Publishing, 2003)

March 15th

1899: On this day, in a matinee performance at 11 a.m., Newcastle's Theatre Royal staged the first ever performance of George Bernard Shaw's play, *Caesar and Cleopatra*. It is a five-act chronicle, loosely based on – and serving as a sort of prelude to – Shakespeare's *Anthony and Cleopatra*. Here, though, the mood is not melodramatic but sad and wry, with Cleopatra not so much a temptress as a capricious child, and Caesar world-weary and isolated. *Caesar and Cleopatra* is often considered one of Shaw's finest works. (www.theatrehistory.com)

●◆●

1977: Sticking with the theatrical theme, on this day the Royal Shakespeare Company (RSC) continued its very first Newcastle season with a production of *Romeo and Juliet*, having opened on the 10th with *Much Ado About Nothing*. Over the next month, the public were treated to eighteen different plays, performed either at the Theatre Royal or the Gulbenkian. *Romeo and Juliet* was directed by Trevor Nunn and starred Ian McKellen (who was with the RSC for two years) and Francesca Annis. In the same season, McKellen also brought *Macbeth* to the Theatre Royal, starring opposite Judi Dench. Since then, the RSC has continued to bring plays from all eras to Newcastle. Although the 2011/12 season was controversially cancelled in the face of funding cuts, 2012/13 saw business as usual. (Royal Shakespeare Company archive catalogue)

MARCH 16TH

1866: On this day, the *Newcastle Courant* reported on a rather odd story. 'For some time past, a horse, the property of Mr John Brewis of this town, exhibited symptoms of illness. The poor animal gradually became worse, and at length it was found necessary to call in the services of Mr Richardson, veterinary surgeon of this town; and strange to relate, after it had been under the treatment of that gentleman for a short time, it voided a quantity of worms and [...] a fully grown frog. The horse had been out at grass last summer.' The story was taken up by *Punch* magazine, which added that the frog in question was preserved in spirit so that people could look at it and be sure that it was indeed a frog. It cynically noted that while stories of frogs or toads inside oak trees were not uncommon during the 'silly season' – the summer Parliamentary recess – for such a story to be published during a session of Parliament suggested a lack of interest in the Reform Bill. (*Punch / Newcastle Courant*)

MARCH 17TH

1911: On this day, the Clarion Drama Club – which was to develop into the People's Theatre – was formed. It aimed to raise money for the Newcastle branch of the British Socialist Party, who met in Leazes Park Road (in what is now Magic Box). Early in 1911 they started running dances, but this was considered to be too lowbrow by some members, who sought a more high-minded route to funds. Well-known local reciter Wilf Armstrong was the ringleader; another key member was Colin Veitch, captain of the FA-Cup winning Newcastle United team. Their first performances – on July 11th – were *The Bishop's Candlesticks* (an excerpt from *Les Miserables*) by Norman McKinnen, and *Pot Luck* by Gertrude Jennings. They followed this with George Bernard Shaw's *The Shewing Up of Blanco Posnet* – even though this had been banned by the Lord Chamberlain. In 1915, the Clarion Drama Club formally separated from the British Socialist Party, taking premises in the Royal Arcade, Pilgrim Street, but retaining its politics, and its connection with Bernard Shaw. Their Rye Hill premises even saw his last appearance on stage, in 1936, after a performance of *Candida*. Apparently, he remarked that the stage was cleaner than the last time he had been! The People's Theatre is still active, and, among others, has supported the early career of actor Kevin Whately, Neil Tennant of the Pet Shop Boys and comedian Ross Noble. (Armstrong, K., 'People's Theatre: People's Education', *North East History*, 2008)

MARCH 18TH

1775: On this day, it rained. This was not unusual. What *was* unusual was that it hardly rained again for months! Elizabeth Montagu was in Denton and reported in July that: 'Hay here will be at an excessive price … Cows are oblig'd to be driven to the rivers to drink – our little streams are all dry'd. The Tyne Vale, where I live, used to look green and pleasant. The whole country is now a brown crust with, here and there, a black hole or a coal pit, so that I cannot boast of the beauty of our prospects.' (Doran, J., *A Lady of the Last Century*, R. Bentley & Son, 1873)

———— • ◆ • ————

1901: On this day, Matt Kingsley became the first Newcastle United footballer to play for England. Kingsley was not local, but had been playing in goal for United since 1898. He had a distinctive playing style, continually swinging his arms around as he waited for the ball to come his way. At 14 stone, he was heavier than most footballers and put his bulk to good use. He was a master at punching the ball away from the goal – catching it risked the goalie being bundled back over the goal line, which counted as a goal in those days. Kingsley justified his selection, as England beat Wales 6-0. Mysteriously, it was his only international cap. He continued with Newcastle until 1904. (Joannou, P., *United: The First 100 Years*, Polar Print Group, 2000)

MARCH 19TH

1885: On this day, Newcastle saw the birth of an almost-forgotten star of stage and screen. Norman Todd Slaughter grew up in Newcastle as the eldest of twelve surviving children. He first took to the stage at twenty years old, treading the boards up and down the country and soon managing his own company. After the First World War, he brought Victorian penny dreadfuls (cheaply-made sensationalist fiction) to the stages of London. Todd Slaughter did not appear on camera until he was forty-nine years old, but when he did, he instantly found his calling – appropriately for a man of his surname – playing cackling and hammy English villains. The first such part, 1935's *Murder in the Red Barn*, was really a filming of a Victorian melodrama. He carried on in the same vein, appearing in cheaply-produced seat-fillers featuring characters like Sweeney Todd and Spring-Heeled Jack. He married Jenny Lynn, who played alongside him in *The Ticket of Leave Man* (true to form, he played a crazed killer called The Tiger). Eventually Slaughter's acting style fell out of favour and parts came less frequently. He was declared bankrupt in 1953, although he continued in theatre and occasional film appearances to the end. When he died, aged seventy, he was once more performing in *Murder in the Red Barn*. Slaughter's performances have a verve all of their own and have recently received critical acclaim as being in the same tradition as Hammer Horror. (www.imdb.com)

MARCH 20TH

1804: On this day, the people of Newcastle took part in a city-wide alarm drill. This was necessary due to a huge false alarm earlier in the year. On February 1st, many people were convinced that Newcastle was being invaded by Napoleon's armies. The city militia were mustering, the static forces were milling around, guards were posted and messengers dispatched. The panic had spread from Berwick, where the troops and volunteers were placed on garrison duty. But eventually, as no invasion force appeared, it became increasingly clear that the whole thing was a mistake; probably started when someone mistook the burning of gorse on Lammermuir hills for the lighting of signal fires! This was obviously very embarrassing. The Corporation wanted to make sure the signals were unmistakable. So today, the people of Newcastle were warned that between 12 noon and 1 p.m., and 8 p.m. and 9 p.m., the new signals were to be tested. A signal was shown at certain high spots – the Castle Keep, the churches of St Nicholas, All Saints' and St Andrew's, and the tower at the Westgate. A red flag was used by day, and a light by night. At the same time, the town guns were fired for five minutes. These new signals served their purpose, though you do have to feel sorry for all those who hadn't read the warning notices, and so wouldn't have had a clue what was going on! (Sykes, J., *Local Records*, Vol. I)

MARCH 21ST

1831: On this day, around 20,000 miners gathered on the Town Moor, as part of a long-running period of worsening relationships between workers and coal owners. It all started with miner Thomas Hepburn, who essentially began unionism in North East mining communities. In 1831 things were tough for the miners, who had suffered in a time of recession. Miners were forced to buy their groceries and essentials from shops approved by mine owners, often paying for them directly from their wages at exorbitant rates. Working days were up to eighteen hours long. So Hepburn formed the Northern Union of Pitmen (the so-called Hepburn Union), striking against the rules of his employers. This mass meeting on Newcastle's Town Moor was intended to show strength and solidarity. The Union successfully campaigned for a twelve-hour working day and payment in cash. They declared that they would refuse to sign up to be 'bound' labour for the forthcoming year. If the employers would not take them unbound, they would refuse to work. Across the region, things then became nasty, with lock-outs, strikes, evictions, and even deaths. Things dragged on into 1832, with Hepburn, now elected a full-time paid official of the Union, attempting to keep order as the pitmen increasingly favoured violence. But by the end of it, the Union had crumbled, and the leaders of the strike – including Hepburn – were banned from working on the coalfield. (www.hettonlocalhistory.com)

MARCH 22ND

1919: On this day, 10,000 spectators gathered at St James' Park to watch the second and last Cup Final of the Munitionettes league. This was the first ever league for women's football, launched in 1917 as the Tyne Wear and Tees Alfred Wood Munition Girls' Cup. As the name suggests, the league was for teams of female munitions workers. With so many local men involved in conflict, it was left to women to work in the factories and supply the ammunition and machines needed for the war effort. On this day, Palmer's of Jarrow beat Brown's of West Hartlepool 1-0 on a snow-covered pitch in a closely contested match. Palmer's player Mary Lyons already had a remarkable career behind her. Nine months earlier she had played in an England *v.* Northern Ireland match (the return game for an earlier Tyneside Internationals *v.* Belfast Ladies match, the first ever women's international). Not only did she score two goals, helping England to a 5-2 win, she was only fourteen years old, making her the youngest ever footballer – male or female – to play for England! Nonetheless, these women's teams were not always taken seriously, sometimes being pitted against men (who had their hands tied behind their back, or with some war-induced disability) – but at least it was for charity.

After the war, as women left the factories, their football teams faded away and by late 1919 Munitionettes matches were stopped. (Brennan, P., *Football on Tyneside 1914-1919* / www. donmouth.co.uk)

MARCH 23RD

1882: On this day, John James Fenwick – a mantle maker and furrier – opened a shop at no. 5 Northumberland Street. Although Northumberland Street is now a busy shopping street, the scene at the time would have been very different, as the street was a semi-residential area. Fenwick paid £181 4s to convert what had been a doctor's house into a space where he could sell fashionable ladies' clothing. This was a substantial outlay at the time, but the gamble paid off. Hiring two shop assistants, he sold mantles, dresses, silk items, fabric and trimmings, with healthy sales from the outset. Three years on, he bought and moved to numbers 37 and 38 Northumberland Street, before adding no. 40 in 1890. Incredibly, this is the shop frontage still held by Fenwick today. While the clothing continued to do well, what really set Fenwick's shop apart was its early adoption of the 'department store' model, with different types of goods sold under one roof in separate departments. Fred Fenwick, John's eldest son, picked up on this concept when he was training in retail in Paris – home of the world's oldest department stores – and brought the model back to Newcastle with great success. Fenwick's shop still thrives in the same premises today – particularly in December when its festive window displays are an integral part of the Geordie Christmas. (www.fenwick.co.uk)

MARCH 24TH

1881: On this day, organised hare coursing began in Gosforth Park. The High Gosforth Park Company had enclosed 52 acres of ground, to prevent the escape of 200 imported hares. They built thirty kennels nearby for the greyhounds, which would try to catch released hares in what was considered the ultimate test of their performance. It was one of five enclosed hare-coursing grounds across the country, and the best known greyhounds would travel to compete for the major titles – in this case the Gosforth Gold Cup. Betting was heavy, involving complex assessments of form, weather conditions and so on. While there were already voices raised in protest at the 'sport', others argued that the hares were well fed, and most escaped the dogs, making it less cruel than the non-enclosed equivalent. The 1884 edition of *The Illustrated Sporting and Dramatic News* includes a sketch of hounds 'Britain' and 'Nimrod' chasing the hare, 'Mr Bettony raising the white flag' for the start of the contest, and 'a clever kill' in which the dog has bowled the hare over so fast that both have gone into a somersault. Gate takings were good for the first few years, and the quality of the contests top-notch, but numbers declined as the novelty wore off. In 1889, the directors called a halt to the event. Fortunately this didn't really matter as from 1882 horse racing provided a bigger and better attraction. (Cox, H., *Coursing and Falconry*, Longmans Green and Co., 1899)

MARCH 25TH

1412: On this day, the on-going battle between the Corporation of Newcastle and the Bishop of Durham, over activities on the River Tyne, took a new turn. The Bishop of Durham complained to the Court of Chancery that, after years of peaceful co-existence, in 1383 Newcastle had begun to build a tower on the Gateshead third of the Tyne Bridge. By the early fifteenth century, the tower was built, and the border markers between the two counties had been removed. The Bishop said that since this point, Newcastle Corporation had been claiming the whole bridge for themselves, and trying to claim the various rents and fees that went along with it. He challenged the burgesses of Newcastle to decide on a point on the bridge, and swear not to go beyond it, at which point the Bishop would do the same – and on this day in 1412 the burgesses appeared in Durham to do just that, swearing that the Palatinate of Durham extended to a point on the bridge called 'Jargon Hole'. But the Court of Chancery were not satisfied that this would end the matter, and indeed it was only one exchange in the continuing conflict. Eventually a blue stone was added to the bridging point, indicating the boundaries of the two rival towns. That stone is currently displayed in the Castle Keep. (Welford, R., *History of Newcastle and Gateshead*, 1884)

MARCH 26TH

1649: On this day, the puritan Corporation of Newcastle sent a petition northward with a peculiar aim. Left to deal with capital crimes themselves because of the chaos of the Civil War, and worried about witchcraft, the Corporation sent for a renowned Scottish witchfinder, who was at that time working in Berwick. Thirty women were dragged to the Guildhall, where the witchfinder – whose name we will sadly never know – used a pin to search for the 'witch's mark' on their bodies. He 'discovered' twenty-eight witches that day – it is rumoured with the help of a retractable pin. A cynic might suggest that his eagerness to 'find' witches was also encouraged by the 20 shillings he would be paid for each one! According to Ralph Gardiner, writing in 1655, one young and attractive woman avoided accusation because it was decided that she must have blushed – the pin did not cause her to bleed simply because all the blood had rushed to her face! Over the next few months, some of the alleged witches were set free (probably due to good references from local dignitaries). Nonetheless, on August 21st 1650, fourteen women and one man were led to a specially constructed scaffold on the Town Moor and hanged, watched by a crowd of thousands. (Gardiner, R, *England's Grievance Discovered*, 1655 / Rushton, P., 'Crazes and Quarrels: The Character of Witchcraft in the Northeast of England, 1649-80', *Bulletin of the Durham County Local History Society*, 1983)

MARCH 27TH

1834: On this day, Richard Grainger set his plans out before the Town Council. He was planning to buy Anderson Place, a magnificent stately home in the heart of Newcastle, and 12 acres of grounds for £50,000. But he would also have to knock down a series of other properties, including the (still quite new) Butcher and Vegetable Markets. For that, he needed council permission, so they requested that a lithographed plan be circulated to the council members. The same plans were later exhibited in Mr Small's sale room, in the Royal Arcade (one of Grainger's earlier architectural triumphs) two months. There were always going to be voices against the plans, from those worried about property prices or due to lose their own homes, to the stall holders of the doomed Butcher Market. Nonetheless, 5,000 signatures were signed in favour of the plans, with only 300 against. The *Newcastle Journal* was strongly in favour: 'the merits of this case are so obvious'. On June 12th, the council agreed the plans, and Grainger concluded his land purchases. The agreement was sealed on the 15th, and 'the bells of the churches in Newcastle rang several merry peals'. The only downside was that, fuelled with free celebratory ale, some of Grainger's workmen broke into Anderson Place and destroyed the staircase, starting off the demolition process a little sooner than expected ... (Ayris, I, *A City of Palaces*, Tynebridge Publishing, 1997)

MARCH 28TH

1944: On this day, the Tyneside Apprentices Strike began. It is often forgotten that the Second World War was a time of relatively high levels of industrial action. Pay was poor, and basic working rights often eroded by wartime conditions, leaving many wondering what they were fighting for. The government was running short of coal, and while coal owners grew richer, safety levels worsened. The unpopular Bevin scheme aimed to conscript 10 per cent of apprentices to the coalface. Tyneside apprentices had been working for very low pay to achieve a skilled status, and were unhappy about being pushed into the pits with no guarantee that they would be able to return to their trade. In the absence of an official trade union, they formed the Tyne Apprentices' Guild – 'the government of the apprentices, by the apprentices, for the apprentices'. They demanded exemption from the 'pit compulsion plot', linking up with apprentices in other areas and securing support wherever they could. Twenty-six thousand apprentices – firstly in Tyneside, then in Glasgow, Huddersfield and Teesside – came out on strike, calling, 'Bevin won't climb down, so we'll pull him down'. In the end, the strike lasted only two weeks. Three men and one woman from the Communist Party were charged with inciting and furthering of an illegal dispute, and went to jail. Nonetheless, in the end no more Tyneside apprentices were in fact sent to the pits. (Dabb, T., 'Official Secrets: The Hidden Strikes of the Second World War', *Socialist Review*, 1995)

MARCH 29TH

1810: On or around this day, workmen digging a sewer to reach a house being built in Collingwood Street for tallow-chandler John Arnett were surprised to stumble upon a previously unknown section of Roman wall. Interestingly, some sort of internment was found as well – a hollowed out stone, built into the structure of the wall, and containing bones and ashes. The wall followed, more or less, the route of Westgate Road for some distance (the road was built along the old defensive ditch). We can't be sure of the whole route, but it seems to have gone fairly straight down to a fort near the Tyne, which guarded the first bridge over the river. Both fort and bridge were called *Pons Aelius*, meaning the the Bridge of Hadrian (Aelius was his family name). The wood and stone bridge, on the site of the modern Swing Bridge, seems to have survived into Norman times, perhaps until a great fire in 1248. As late as the mid-1980s sections of the wall were being found in the city centre, such as part of 'Milecastle 4', which lies underneath part of the Newcastle Arts Centre on Westgate Road. Other fragments of Rome might yet lie undiscovered under Newcastle's streets. (Mackenzie, E., *A Descriptive and Historical Account of the Town and County of Newcastle upon Tyne: Including the Borough of Gateshead, 1827*)

MARCH 30TH

1925: On this day, thirty-eight lives were lost in Montagu Pit, Scotswood. It was 10.30 in the morning when workers on the Robson's Board Flat inadvertently brought disaster down on their own heads. The trouble was, the Brockwell Seam which they followed went dangerously close to the old Paradise Pit, abandoned in 1848. In the meantime, the Paradise Pit had flooded, and when three shots were fired against the dividing wall, the water crashed through into the Montagu Pit. Most of the 150-odd miners in the pit were able to get out, but some were cut off in the rising waters. Thousands gathered at the pithead to try to help, and rescue parties were sent down, but were hindered by flooded tunnels and bad air. It took a long time to pump all the water out, and the last body was not recovered until October. Thirty-eight men died. The first associated funeral was for twenty-three men and boys, and the line of mourners stretched for three miles. Although set in the fictional north-eastern coal mining city of 'Tynecastle', Archibald Cronin's 1935 novel, *The Stars Look Down*, was clearly based on this tragic event. Cronin knew what he was talking about, having been a medical mines inspector for Northumberland, and involved in the Montagu's rescue work. It was turned into a film in 1940 starring Michael Redgrave and directed by Carol Reed (of *The Third Man* fame). (*Newcastle Chronicle* / Myers, A., *Myers' Literary Guide*, Carcanet, 1995 / www.dmm.org.uk)

MARCH 31ST

1838: On this day, boatman John Gordon died after falling into the River Tyne while mooring his steamer, the *Duke of Wellington*, at Newcastle Quay. What makes this particularly poignant is that Gordon was mooring up having just returned from the 'dead house', where he had dropped off the body of a drowned wherryman that he himself had picked out of the river earlier that morning. He is said to have remarked, while delivering the corpse, on the uncertainty of life. (Fordyce, T., *Historic Register of Remarkable Events*, 1866)

———— • ◆ • ————

1925: On this day, the Borough Gaol in Carliol Square – the last prison within central Newcastle – was closed. For nearly 100 years it served as a prison for all levels of crime, with both a gallows and a house of correction, before it was demolished and Telephone House built on the site. Coincidentally, it was also in 1925 that Newcastle got its first police boxes. They began in Sunderland, where, in 1923, Frederick Crawley came up with design – wooden boxes rather like sentry boxes as mobile bases for constables on the beat, with a telephone and first aid box on the outside for public use. When he moved to Newcastle two years later, he brought the idea with him – it didn't reach London for another three years. (www.policeboxes.com)

April 1st

1801: On this day, the *London Courier* fell foul of an April Fool joke, publishing a spurious letter concerning recent events in Newcastle. Allegedly, a storm on March 29th had devastated the town. The detailed account tells of the falling of St Nicholas' Church steeple – first a few stones injuring a young woman and causing the meat market to close down, and then the collapse of the whole steeple into the Flesh Market, causing the destruction of a public house and the death of at least seven townsfolk. Meanwhile, a second letter had been sent to the *Edinburgh Courant* – in this account, on the 27th 'the spire of that modern-built church, called All Saints', suddenly fell to the ground, on the south side, at about half-past 5 o'clock this morning. The cause of this accident is generally attributed to the impropriety of building the spire so high, it being known that the tower on which it was built had considerably shrunk.' (*London Courier / Edinburgh Courant*)

1997: On this day, the courts sentenced seventeen-year-old Anthony Kennedy to a four-year jail term, following a six-year burglary spree. He had become nationally famous as 'Ratboy', because, whenever he ran away from council care, he would apparently hide within the heating and ventilation shafts of the Byker Wall flats. (*Newcastle Chronicle*)

APRIL 2ND

1812: On this day, John Forster, often called the first professional biographer, was born in Fenkle Street to a family of butchers and cattle dealers. He was brought up a Unitarian – then a newly legalised sect – and educated at Newcastle Grammar School. As a teenager he had already involved himself in the town's literary and theatrical scene, writing his first play at sixteen. This Civil War melodrama, *Charles at Tunbridge*, saw its one and only performance at the Theatre Royal. A few months later Forster left town, first for Cambridge and soon after, London, where one of his companions described him as 'a raw, oddly-dressed, energetic, impetuous youth from the provinces'. He gave up a promising legal career to throw himself into the literary scene, writing poetry, articles, reviews and more. Eventually he moved into biography, writing volumes on the lives of figures of the Commonwealth, and what were to become the standard biographies of Charles Dickens and Jonathan Swift. Dickens, in turn, immortalised him as Mr Podsnap in *Our Mutual Friend*. Forster also persuaded Tennyson to restore the lines: 'Half a league, half a league / Half a league onward … ' to the beginning of 'The Charge of the Light Brigade'. When he died in 1864, the literary fashions of London had already moved on, but the *Newcastle Weekly Chronicle* wrote that Forster had had a 'kind of talent which only just fell short of genius'. (Davies, J.A., *John Forster: A Literary Life*, Leicester University Press, 1983)

April 3rd

1837: On this day, notorious 'cunning man' Black Jacky Johnson died, while in the process of reading tarot cards for a customer. Fortune telling was only one of the many claims he made to the public. He claimed his 'magic mirror', supposedly a relic of an ancient Greek magus, could find stolen property, interpret dreams and identify future husbands. He also knew a particular spell for making someone invisible. According to Johnson, all that was needed was to find a black cat (without a single white hair) which then must be boiled for three hours during Sunday service. Its heart should then be dried in a new oven, crushed into a powder, and over the course of seven nights, distributed in pinches over a churchyard. On the seventh night, the caster of the spell would meet a stranger at the entrance to the churchyard. He should then give the stranger half the powder. From that moment on, whenever the caster carried the other half with him, he would become invisible! The idea that black cats are the key to invisibility also appears in African-American voodoo tradition, in which black cats are thought to have a single bone somewhere in their body which, if correctly obtained, can render the wearer invisible (once you have worked out which one it is, using a mirror). Whether the two traditions are connected is not known. (Histon, V., *Nightmare on Grey Street*, Tynebridge Publishing, 2000)

APRIL 4TH

1550: On this day, John Knox preached from the pulpit of St Nicholas' Church. The Scots preacher had had a colourful life, including watching his mentor burned at the stake, and serving as a galley slave. Exiled to England, his preaching in Berwick alarmed the conservative Bishop of Durham. Knox was summoned to Newcastle to defend his opinions in front of the Council of the North – which he did, on this day, in rousing style. It is one of only two of his sermons to survive. A year later he returned to Newcastle and preached in St Nicholas' Church on and off until 1553, encouraging regular public religious services without the official authorisation of the organised Church. (Myers, A., *Myers' Literary Guide*, Carcanet, 1995 / Newton, D. and Pollard, A., *Newcastle and Gateshead Before 1700*, Phillimore & Co., 2009)

1827: On this day, visionary William Martin – brother of artist John and arsonist Jonathan (*see* February 8th) – gave a lecture. He wandered Newcastle in a hat made from a tortoise shell and was constantly inventing – a new velocipede, an improved suspension bridge, a lifejacket, anything. He even claimed George Stephenson stole his idea for a safety lamp *and* his 'invention' of railways. (Martin, J., *The Life of Jonathan Martin*, 1826 / Morden, B., *John Martin: Apocalypse Now!*, Northumbria Press, 2010)

APRIL 5TH

1901: On this day, the rivalry between Newcastle and Sunderland football teams led to disaster. The traditional Good Friday encounter was held in St James' Park, which had capacity for 30,000 supporters. But so many gathered that an hour before kick-off the stands were already packed out. The decision was made to lock the gates, but that didn't have the intended effect. Instead, as the local papers reported, fans 'clambered over the rails like cats' and perched in their hundreds on the stand roof, much to the alarm of those sitting below. Overall it was estimated that between 50,000 and 70,000 people tried to pack into the space. With only twenty-five policemen, it was impossible to even clear the playing area, and although the teams attempted to get onto the pitch, this idea was soon abandoned. That turned a good-humoured mob into an angry one, and thousands of young men went on the rampage, throwing bottles, destroying the goalposts, and using the barriers as weapons. Eventually, wagonloads of police arrived, and, as the *Guardian* puts it, 'had to make a number of baton charges before order could be partially restored.' Amazingly, only twelve people received treatment for their injuries. One Sunderland fan sued Newcastle United over his ticket money, and, in an important test case, not only failed but also had to pay legal fees. (Joannou, P., *United: The First 100 Years*, Polar Print Group, 2000)

APRIL 6TH

1750: On this day, diarist Ralph Jackson recorded a visit to see 'a fine sculpture in the Bigg Market'. This sculpture depicted the life of Christ, and was huge and complicated, featuring over 400 figures. The *Newcastle Chronicle* claimed that the sculpture had been captured by British privateers in the Channel, and had originally been intended for France, and a place in the gardens of Versailles. The public could see it for between 3*d* and 1*s*. There was a lot going on in the market area at that time. For instance, also in 1750, Leigh Smith opened a grocers and possibly also a coffee house on the Flesh Market. The business is still going strong today, though it is now called Pumphrey's. The names in this area of town are interesting, often changing with the goods sold. In 1723, there were named areas for the selling of iron, wool, cloth, butter, poultry, and meal. A century later, only the Groat Market, Flesh Market and Middle Market survived – and one area has changed its name between Cloth Market and Flesh Market on several occasions depending on the provision available elsewhere. The Bigg Market is slightly to the north, and until the sixteenth century was called the Bere (pronounced 'beer') Market. This isn't a wondrous piece of foresight – both words relate to types of barley. (*Diary of Ralph Jackson* / www.pumphreys-coffee.co.uk / archaeologydataservice.ac.uk)

APRIL 7TH

1842: On this day, world-champion rower James Renforth was born. While usually thought of as a child of Gateshead, Renforth was actually born in New Pandon Street, Newcastle, and moved across the river at around a year old. In his early twenties, Renforth worked rowing materials and men out to the Tyne Bridge, which was being demolished. He took up sculling at twenty-four and was soon beating all-comers. Just two years after first rowing competitively, he beat Londoner Henry Kelley on the Thames, and became Champion Sculler of the World. He retained this title until he died. Renforth began to race in pairs and fours, and the Tyne team was soon known as the best in the country and perhaps the world. Meanwhile, he also became landlord of the Belted Will Inn, Scotswood, and then in 1870, the Sir Charles Napier Inn, Queen Street. Early the next year, his crew of four – including his old rival Henry Kelly – travelled to Canada for a challenge race. But early on in the race it became clear that something was wrong. The Tyne boat gradually fell behind, and then Renforth's oar dropped from his hand. His fellows helped him to his bed, but he died that evening, aged just twenty-nine. Although his death was probably caused by heart failure following an epileptic fit, rumours persisted for years that he might have been poisoned. (Whitehead, I., *James Renforth of Gateshead*, Tynebridge Publishing, 2004)

APRIL 8TH

1884: On this day, classical violinist Marie Hall was born. Despite violin playing being seen as unfeminine in Victorian times, she became the foremost player in the country. Her claim to being a Geordie is down to an accident of birth. Her father, Edmund, was harpist in the Carl Rosa English Opera Company, and he travelled all over England with them, taking his wife with him, even when she was pregnant. After Marie was born, the family settled in Newcastle. But as she grew up, her father lost his job and she was soon sent into the streets to play the violin for a few pennies. The struggling family moved away in 1895, and Hall's next eight years were to be a struggle of genius and determination (with the help of several famous musicians) against poverty. In the end, genius won and she went on to have a long and successful concert career. (songofthelark. wordpress.com)

———◆———

1887: On this day, stage carpenter Robert Crowther died following a most unfortunate accident. The previous night, he had been working at the Tyne Theatre during a production of the opera *Nordisa*. He was standing in the wings when a cannonball – usually rolled on boards 20 feet above the scenes to produce the effect of a roll of thunder – fell on his head. The inquest judged that the chute used for the effect was fundamentally unsafe. (*Newcastle Weekly Courant*)

APRIL 9TH

1953: On this day, the *Evening Chronicle* included an interesting advert for a 3D experience – as the poster had it, 'a thrilling new dimension has been added to screen entertainment!' The Newcastle Stoll was to show the fifteen-minute film *A Day in the Country*, which had been flown across from America a few days before. As one might expect, the film had been made with the intention of shocking an audience with no previous experience of 3D (although a range of technologies had been tried since the 1920s, they rarely reached England). There would be, for instance, the appearance of a bucket of water being thrown at the audience. Most films in this first 3D golden era were shown using Polaroid lenses, and a pair of projectors synched up to project images for the left and right eye at the same time, onto a silver screen. But *A Day in the Country*, narrated by Joe Besser and composed mostly of test footage jammed together without much attempt at a logical flow, was an anaglyph film – there was a red version and a green one, and the viewer wore cardboard spectacles with red and green plastic sheets for a lens. Both methods need two projectors in perfect synchronicity. *A Day in the Country* was believed lost, but has recently been discovered and restored to a watchable form. It is described as 'a bumpkin family vacation, with misadventures and lots of slapstick … complete with ham-handed sound effects.' (*Newcastle Evening Chronicle* / Wikipedia)

APRIL 10TH

1941: In the early hours of this day, more than fifty German bombers reached Newcastle and dropped a large number of incendiary bombs. The sixty-eight fires that were started caused widespread damage in the west and north of the city. Sixty-five homes were damaged, along with a Boys' Club, a school, the Regal Cinema in Fenham, and the Roman Catholic Church of St Michael on Westmorland Road. Here, priests helped the fire fighters tackle the blaze, but the roof was still destroyed. One of the targets must have been Vickers-Armstrongs, but the fire fighters were quick off the mark and little damage was done. Only two weeks later, on April 25th, another intense air raid hit the city, this time with a wider mix of explosive and incendiary types. Bombs fell in Jesmond (two fell on vacant land here, causing craters 30 feet wide and 15 feet deep) and right across Heaton. Two gas mains were broken and in several places rescue workers struggled to get survivors and bodies from collapsed buildings. Thirty-five people died at Guildford Place, Heaton, and another twelve nearby. Bodies were still being found five days later, some of whom could not be identified. Fire fighters were rushed off their feet trying to put out fires with sand and stirrup pumps. But they had help – two civilians scaled a drainpipe and threw bombs out of the window to the ground, where they were put out with sand. (www.ne-diary.bpears.org.uk)

APRIL 11TH

1759: On this day, Susannah Fleming suffered a near-fatal punishment on the pillory, at White Cross, Newgate Street. She was an elderly lady, sentenced to stand for one hour, once a quarter for a year, with her hands and head strapped in place by a wooden board, as a punishment for fortune telling. The *Newcastle Journal* reports: 'Tho' not molested by the Populace, she was nearly strangled before the Time was expired, occasioned either by fainting and shrinking down, or some say by tying too much about her Neck, and being thereby straitened in the Hole. It is believed that she would not have got down alive, had it not been for the Activity of a Sailor, who out of Charity, run up the Ladder and brought her down on his back.' Fleming wrote a letter to Sir William Blackett's wife, arguing that she had character references from people who had known her for thirty years, and that she had been convicted on the evidence of 'two wicked abandoned women'. She describes herself as over eighty, 'of tender constitution and ... a very bad state of health', and worried that she would not survive another turn in the pillory. The Blacketts must have acted on her behalf, because, as far as we know, Susannah Fleming did not reappear in the pillory. (Redfern, B., *The Shadow of the Gallows*, Tynebridge Publishing, 2003)

April 12th

1941: On this day, one Mass Observation Diary gives us a good insight into leisure activities of the time. It was the writer's twenty-fourth birthday, and also Easter Saturday. He 'travelled to Newcastle on the 9.57, fare 5/3 – pre-war 4/2. Train was punctual and full, but not overcrowded. Number in uniform fewer than I had anticipated. Only paper available "Daily Mirror"... Newcastle very busy under its balloon barrage. Visited news cinema at 11.13, nearly empty. Programme included glass-making, a village in India, 3 news reels, 2 coloured cartoons, and an anti-aircraft film. Back into crowds and warm sunshine. Many daffodils and a few tulips obtainable, but no chocolate or cigarettes. Lunch in crowded Garrick's cafe. Fish cake and chips, brown bread and tea, 1/1. Menu advertised boxes of vitamin B available a 2/0 per box ... Entered Leazes Park, where a middle aged man showed us two bomb craters with almost paternal pride. Both had fallen after "all-clear". Gentleman volunteered that "he" was probably trying for nearby barracks. Small crowd outside St James' Park before gates opened. Eventually 20,000 inside, gas masks a novelty. Very little war talk, but one man from Coventry inclined to talk down local raids. Crowd slow to warm up, but enthusiasm high after Newcastle scored after 48 minutes and very great as the scored mounted to 4-0. Tried to tea at Co-op, but queue waiting outside café door ...' [*sic*] (*Mass Observation Diary*)

APRIL 13TH

1916: On this day, Russian novelist Yevgeni Zamyatin arrived in Newcastle after forty hours on rough seas, for a stay of eighteen months. His career was just taking off at this point, and his main interest was in the ice-breaking ships (Russia had to find a new way to the west since Germany had cut routes through the Baltic, and yet did not build their own icebreakers until the 1930s). From his house on Sanderson Road, he spent most of his time working and visiting shipyards. He also wrote *The Islanders*, a sharp satire on the English middle classes and their constrained, respectable lives: 'By Sunday, the stone doorsteps of the Jesmond houses had been scrubbed to a dazzling whiteness. The houses were of a certain age and smoke-begrimed, but the steps were gleaming rows of white, like the Sunday gentlemens' false teeth. The Sunday gentlemen were produced at one of the Jesmond factories and on Sunday mornings, thousands of them appeared on the streets with the Sunday edition of the St Enoch parish newspaper. Sporting identical canes and identical top-hats, the Sunday gentlemen strolled in dignified fashion along the street and greeted their doubles.' Zamyatin wasn't impressed with Newcastle, feeling isolated and hating the food. He wrote home: 'All the streets, all the houses are identical, like the grain barns in Petersburg near the Alexander Nevsky monastery. As we went past, I asked: "What are those storehouses?" "They're houses that people live in."' (Myers, A., *Myers' Literary Guide*, Carcanet, 1995)

APRIL 14TH

1915: On and around this day, the 50th (Northumbrian) Division of the Territorial Army were mobilising for the Western Front. One of several new forces created in 1914 by the Newcastle and Gateshead Chamber of Commerce, this one is particularly remembered because it is thought to be the inspiration for the city's war memorial, *The Response - 1914,* near St Thomas' Church, Haymarket. A group of Northumberland Fusiliers are shown marching from their camp in Gosforth Park, down the Great North Road towards the station, led by drummer boys. One description has it: 'Their route was lined by well-wishers and their parents, wives and children, some cheering, some weeping, as the flower of their youth went out to sacrifice itself on Europe's battlefield.' There is a realism in the expressions of the soldiers, their wives and children, torn between fear and patriotism, crushed together around the flag and drawn ever forward by the figure of 'Renown', flying about the crowd with trumpet raised. *The Response* was unveiled by the Prince of Wales on July 5th 1923. A high relief bronze sculpture by Sir John Goscombe, on a granite base, it has been commended by the Imperial War Museum as one of the finest sculptural gatherings on any British monument. (*National Monuments Record*)

APRIL 15TH

1915: On this day, Private Fred Appleton wrote a letter to his sweetheart, Mary, the day before he set off for the Western Front. A Yorkshireman, he was stationed in Elswick school at the time. He writes: 'We are all ready packed up for off. When and where I don't know. But I think it is tomorrow night. I was very pleased to see you dearest one. How I loved those few kisses I had. How sweet they seemed. When I was looking out of the window in the afternoon and saw you I could even see your eyes dear sparkle with love when you saw me … I shall always be true to you, Mary dear, while I'm away. This will be the last letter you will get from me from Newcastle. I am going to tell you something now, dearest. I was going to ask you to become engaged to me, then I thought perhaps I'd better not as I may not have the luck to come back, but I am hoping so. I thought it was no use fashing you like that dearie. When I do come back then I would not be with you five minutes before I asked you for your hand.' In fact he did propose before the end of the war, and the two married in early 1918. Frank survived to the end of the war, and the couple had three children together. (www.ww1-yorkshires.org.uk)

APRIL 16TH

1813: On this day, George Wilson, for a bet, walked 50 miles in the space of just seven hours and twenty minutes. What made this particularly remarkable was where he did it – inside Newgate Gaol, where he was imprisoned as a debtor! Walking over 2,500 times around a yard only 33 metres by 25½ metres, he did vastly better than the initial bet – £3 1s if he could walk it in twelve hours. Released from prison, Wilson continued his hobby. 'Pedestrianism' was a popular spectator sport of the time, and Wilson was its first nationally famous practitioner. But his most famous walk was left incomplete. He set out on a 1,000-mile walk in September 1815 from Blackheath, London, intending to walk fifty miles each day for twenty days. But so many people gathered to watch that the authorities feared a riot and had George arrested. In 1822, aged fifty-six, Wilson returned to Newcastle and walked 90 miles in twenty-four hours, covering a half-mile stretch of the Town Moor. He was followed by others, like John Simpson, whose bid to walk 96 miles ended in stomach pains – it was quickly rumoured that his tea had been poisoned – and 'Russell the Pedestrian', who walked 101 miles in twenty-four hours. (Sykes, J., *Local Records*, Volume II, 1833 / www.folknortheast.com)

APRIL 17TH

1751: On this day, Newcastle apprentice Ralph Jackson wrote in his diary: 'I got a letter from my Mother with four of my Uncle Ward's Pills, and I went to Mr Harrisons for one Pound of Capers, and went up to the stables to help them get in the Hay.' Posterity has left us nothing about Mr Harrison's capers, but he would have been well advised to leave the pills alone, even if they were sent by his mother. Uncle Joshua Ward was one of the most notorious quacks in the country. Ward had an amazing life – born in Cleveland, in 1717 he was elected MP for Marlborough, until it was noticed that no one had actually voted for him and he had forged the Mayor's signature! After a spell in prison he moved to France, where he embezzled £70,000 from the Duke of Buckingham, and invented 'Ward's Pills' and 'Ward's Drops', using such ingredients as antimony, mercury, ipecac and nitric acid. Returning to England in 1734, with a pardon from George II, he began to trade his inventions, claiming they cured everything from syphilis to cancer. Alexander Pope noted that they had 'several surprising effects' (true enough, as the body tried to expel the toxins by any means possible). It was said that 'before you take his drop or pill, take leave of your friends and make your will!' (Tyerman, D., 'Health and Disease in the Eighteenth Century' / www.greatayton.wikidot.com, 2007)

APRIL 18TH

1804: On this day, a deal was reached between the Incorporated Companies of Newcastle and the government to rent 11 acres of land near Spital Tongues for £55 a year. The aim was to build a large military barracks, complete with stables, storehouses, etc. The army were a big presence in the town in Napoleonic times – by 1812, a ceremony for King George III's birthday celebrations involved a Brigade of the Royal Artillery, the 2nd Dragoon Guards (based at the barracks) and ten regiments of volunteers. The barracks cost £40,000 to build and housed 274 men, although conditions were ripe for disease and discomfort. Horses lived on the ground floor and the soldiers on the first. Each barrack room shared two copper boilers for cooking meat and vegetables. They did not have adequate washing and toilet facilities: at night, the soldiers had to rely on a urine tub on the outside landing, and washing was done at a tap. To make matters worse, soldiers' wives and children were expected to live in a corner of the barrack room, partitioned off with a blanket! In 1822, instructions were issued to soldiers about health problems and disease, which were blamed on dampness after floor washing. It is tempting to suggest that the authorities had missed the bigger picture … (Hewitson, T., *A Soldier's Life: The Story of Newcastle Barracks*, Tynebridge Publishing, 1999)

April 19th

1858: On this day, excise officer Thomas Davis went to 'coffee roaster and mustard manufacturer' Thomas Scrivener's Croft Stairs shop, and bought 2lb of coffee, 2lb of ground pepper, and 2lb of 'P.D.', an imitation pepper made with mustard. Not remarkable in itself – except that Davis was trying to catch Scrivener doing something illegal. And it worked – indeed he said in court that he'd never seen a case before which required the involvement of the relevant laws as much as this one, to protect honest traders and the public. Firstly, Scrivener didn't have a licence to sell coffee in the first place, and he needed one. Secondly, when the products were sent to an analytical chemist, the coffee was found to be half chicory, and the pepper to be 10 per cent mustard dust. But things were a bit more complicated. The man who had actually sold the coffee and pepper was Joseph Jameson, a dissatisfied apprentice. He knew that he was selling to an excise man, and didn't mind. He'd fallen out with the Scriveners after Mrs Scrivener had accused him of insolence when he commented on her desire to sell mustard adulterated with plaster of Paris! The defence argued that the adulteration had been done by Jameson himself as a way to get revenge on his master, who wasn't even there at the time. But the courts disagreed, and fined Scrivener £300. (*Newcastle Courant*)

APRIL 20TH

1895: On this day, the British Ladies' Football Club played in Newcastle, only a month after its formation. Tickets were not sold in advance, but the gates were opened early and 8,000 spectators – more than double the average attendance for a match – packed into St James' Park. The crowd were apparently 'delighted by the spectacle', although the *Sporting Man* reporter was more interested in the women's clothing: 'The orthodox jerseys were made the basis of the attire, but it was seen that a great deal had been left to the coquetry and taste of the wearers. In many instances they were made loose after the manner of blouses and were relieved at the edges by a little white embroidering. There was the same variety in the make of the knickers. Several of them, probably more advanced in reformed dress ideas than their sisters, wore the lower garments in the ordinary football fashion. Others, probably from feelings of modesty, had made a compromise by wearing the trousers of such wide dimensions as almost to resemble an ample divided skirt. Despite this difference in the cut of the garments, however, the young women presented a pretty appearance on the field, and this was in a great measure due to the nice assortment of colours, as well as the dainty way in which the women set them off.' (www.spartacus.schoolnet.co.uk)

APRIL 21ST

1998: On this day, the *Newcastle Journal* reported the unveiling of the refurbished Rutherford Fountain to the Bigg Market. The red sandstone fountain was originally built to the memory of Dr Rutherford, a preacher, public health campaigner and philanthropist. He had supported the anti-alcohol Band of Hope Union, a popular movement in an era when pubs were on every street corner and alcohol was seen as the scourge of the working class. When he died in 1890, the Band of Hope commissioned the fountain, bearing the legend 'water is best', and set it up in front of St Nicholas' Cathedral in 1894. It was moved to the Bigg Market – which had been home to public houses since at least the sixteenth century – in 1901, but over the years became very weathered, and also eventually had to be turned off. The 1990s facelift involved replacing some of the more weathered panels – the complex design has seventy-four sections – and moving it slightly up the road to provide an entrance feature for the market area. It was also connected to the mains, making it the cheapest pint in the street, even if most of those who walk (or stagger) past it are oblivious to its message! (*Newcastle Journal*)

APRIL 22ND

1804: On this day, twenty-four-year-old ship's carpenter John Stoddart died at the hands of the press gang. Naval press gangs had the job of forcing sailors to join the Navy (impressment) and Stoddart had never had much luck with them. In 1801, when he turned twenty-one, his apprenticeship ended and he was first impressed to the navy for a short stint fighting Napoleon's forces, though he was legally too young. Returning to Tyneside, he joined a whaling ship bound for Greenland – only to have seven of his fellow crew impressed as they passed Shields. When he returned, in 1803, he was impressed at Nore, near London, because he could not produce the paperwork relating to his apprenticeship. He wrote to his mother, who sent the necessary documents, and he was released. However, as soon as he reached Newcastle, the press gang got their eye on him yet again. Pushed too far, Stoddart ran for it – down Broad Chare, and into the fast-flowing Tyne, where he started swimming for Gateshead. One of the press gang took aim, and shot him dead. The subsequent inquest concluded that this was death by misadventure – 'he lost his presence of mind, and was drowned'!

APRIL 23RD

1837: On this day, two of the last ships of Newcastle's whaling fleet met. The previous winter, both ships had been trapped in the Davis Strait. Eventually the *Grenville Bay* had limped home, but the *Lady Jane* was stuck for another six weeks. It was so cold that ice penetrated the timbers and the blankets froze to the sides of the ship. According to the *Newcastle Chronicle*, when she made it to Orkney just eight men, of a crew of sixty-four, were capable of work. Twenty-seven men died. But at a public inquiry, held in the Peacock Inn on the Quayside, Captain Leask was found innocent of endangering the crew and hoarding raisins and currants rather than giving them to the sick. The following year, both ships headed out again – and this time it was the *Grenville Bay* which became stuck. Several ships closed in to give spare provisions, and one of these – on this day – was the *Lady Jane*, still under Captain Leask. But again, by the time the *Grenville Bay* had broken free and made it back to Britain, twenty men had died. It was clear that whaling in the area was becoming too risky. Soon there were only two whalers, and then one – *Lady Jane* soldiering on alone for four years. She last left the Tyne in 1849. Three months later she was crushed in ice, though the crew trekked 500 miles back to civilisation and no lives were lost. (Barrow, T., *The Whaling Trade of North East England, 1750-1850*, University of Sunderland Press, 2001)

April 24th

1827: On this day, apprentice surgeon Thomas Giordani Wright was an extremely busy man. As he recorded in his diary, at 7 a.m. he was called out to a man who had bruised his foot, in Benwell. He'd just gone home and had breakfast when a woman came to ask him to see a man who had bruised his side the night before, in Heaton. As she left, word came in that two men were 'desperately hurt' in the Middle Pit, Heaton. Wright found the bruised man was basically fine, and hurried on to the next – a man whose thumb tip was nearly separated, and who was insistent that, if it needed to be removed, he wanted it done immediately. Wright avoided that, carefully binding it up. In his diary for this day, he also describes some cases of the last few days – splinting a leg of another Middle Pit miner, and stitching up the hand of a lad who had a rolley (a wagon transporting several tubs to the shaft) run over it. Then there was the woman who accidentally drank a sip of caustic lye (used for making soap). His master dealt with her stomach and throat inflammation by bleeding her with leeches, apparently successfully as 'she is almost well again today'. (Johnson, A. (ed.), *The Diary of Thomas Giordani Wright*, Surtees Society, 2001)

APRIL 25TH

1927: On this day, Newcastle Brown Ale was first launched. It had been three years since Barrass Ramsey, the chairman of Scottish and Newcastle Breweries, had identified an increased demand for bottled beer and set his star brewer, Colonel Jim Porter, to blending one for the company. He was confident that the resulting beer would be a big success. Certainly one (perhaps apocryphal) story says that the day after it went on sale, the police requested the strength be reduced as so many people had drunk it and ended up in the cells.

This was such a popular new brand that the following year it won several prizes at the prestigious International Brewers' Exposition in London. These are the gold medals still featured on the label. In the same year, the blue star logo was added, the five points representing the five founding breweries of Tyneside. Newcastle Brown Ale soon went into full-scale production on the Tyne Brewery site, which Newcastle Breweries had owned since 1890. When Newcastle Brown was introduced, the style of beer known as a 'brown ale' – historically a porter or stout – was on its last legs, beaten by the popularity of new malt roasters and the resulting 'pale ale'. Although not really a brown ale by the old definitions, Newcastle Brown Ale at least kept the name going and re-invented it.

APRIL 26TH

1312: On this day, Edward II was in Newcastle. Many of the nobles were unhappy with his rule, and his apparent obsession with his favourite, Piers Gaveston, Earl of Cornwall. One writer at the time said that, 'I do not remember to have heard that one man so loved another', and Edward chose to spend most of his wedding banquet with Gaveston, rather than his new wife. He also seemed to get too many titles. Soon the nobles were refusing to have anything to do with Gaveston. In early 1312 the Earl of Lancaster, with his own private army, marched on York, forcing the pair to flee north, arriving in Newcastle on April 11th. Edward's pregnant wife, Isabella, followed soon after. Edward's accounts show that on this day physician William Burntoft and a Tynemouth monk, Robert of Bermygham, were both paid handsomely for treating Gaveston for an unnamed illness. On May 4th, Lancaster's army caught up. Some chroniclers report that Edward and Gaveston left together, leaving a tearful Isabella behind, but this is disputed. Either way they were forced to leave Gaveston's belongings behind in Newcastle. These possessions were listed in three large books, and include such items as 'another belt of lion skin, decorated in gold with a cameo', and 'a buckle of gold with two emeralds, two rubies, two sapphires, and eleven pearls', as well as more than sixty horses. A few months later Gaveston was caught and executed.

APRIL 27TH

1870: On this day, Newcastle man T.A. Brewis died far from home. He was a commission merchant who had worked for some years for Hulsenbus, Harrison and Co. in Broad Chare. He had moved to Virginia, America, and was visiting the Senate Chamber when catastrophe struck. The Virginia Supreme Court of Appeals was due to announce its decision in a highly controversial and complicated case concerning the legitimacy of Richmond's mayoral elections. This was a tumultuous time in the politics of the southern states, with race a massive issue. A large crowd had gathered in the courtroom, built in the upper floor of the Capitol building. Suddenly the girder supporting the viewers' gallery collapsed, tipping the gallery and its occupants down onto the main courtroom floor – which in turn collapsed under the additional sudden strain. This sent around 350 people, black and white alike, tumbling down 25 feet into the Hall of Delegates below, along with furniture and building materials. Fifty-eight people died, including Brewis. Four more later died of their injuries and around 250 people were injured. A few managed to cling to window frames and the metal rails surrounding the judge's area, but most of those who survived were buried alive amongst the rubble and corpses until rescue workers could get to them through thick plaster dust. Most of the dead were found to have suffocated. (Christian, G., 'The Capitol Disaster' / www26.us.archive.org, 1926)

APRIL 28TH

1910: On this day, Newcastle United replayed Barnsley in the FA Cup final. Newcastle United were one of the dominant teams of Edwardian England, frequently providing players for the England squad and winning the League in 1905, 1907 and 1909. But the FA Cup eluded them. They were losing finalists in 1905, 1906 and 1908, to the great disappointment of the many fans who had travelled down to Crystal Palace on special steamers which ran from Tyne to Thames. In 1908, their loss was so unexpected that it led to accusations of corruption, especially after two players were transferred within weeks. In 1910, the upcoming final was again on everyone's lips – could United finally bring the Cup to the North East? Their first attempt, five days earlier, was a good-humoured affair – one observer reported, 'each side quipping in turn and each wishing the other good luck before parting'. United grabbed a draw with an equaliser eight minutes before time. The stage was set for a monumental replay, with 70,000 boisterous spectators gathering in the heavy rain at Goodison Park, Liverpool. Newcastle were on much better form, or at least playing a more aggressive game – so much so that the press even labelled them 'Dirty Newcastle'. After a string of near misses, centre forward Albert Shephard scored a second-half brace. Interestingly, his second was courtesy of the first ever penalty scored in an FA Cup final. (Joannou, P., *United: The First 100 Years*, Polar Print Group, 2000)

APRIL 29TH

1942: On this day, the philosopher Ludwig Wittgenstein arrived in Newcastle. He had been working as a porter in Guy's Hospital, and became interested in the work of Doctors Grant and Reeve into the effects of shock. When the pair moved to the Royal Victoria Hospital in November 1942, apparently looking for the victims of industrial accidents, they invited Wittgenstein to join them as a lab assistant for £4 a week. They lodged together at 28 Brandling Park, West Jesmond. A trained engineer as well as a philosopher, Wittgenstein worked on methods of measuring symptoms and improving equipment for studying breathing and pulse. Scruffy, quiet and intense, with a strong foreign accent, he didn't make friends easily. Indeed, when this was suggested, he replied, 'It is obvious to me that you are becoming thoughtless and stupid. How could you imagine that I would ever have "lots of friends"?' He annoyed his colleagues with chatter in the mornings, then retreated into himself in the evenings, spending many nights alone at the cinema. Unsurprisingly, they declined to invite him on their regular social rambles along Hadrian's Wall. In January 1944, Grant and Reeve left Newcastle for the battlefields of Italy. Wittgenstein's last words to Reeve were, 'You're not such a nice person as I first thought.' Although their successor would have kept him on, Wittgenstein instead headed south to Cambridge to return to his philosophical studies. (Schardt, B., 'Wittgenstein on Tyne' / www.newphilsoc.org.uk)

APRIL 30TH

1781: On this day, the Georgian Tyne Bridge was officially opened for wheeled traffic (pedestrians could cross the previous day). After the flood of 1771 washed away the medieval Tyne Bridge, ferrymen were very busy. Within ten days, a free ferry service had been established for the post, although it was some months before ferries could – very slowly – transport carriages across the river. Prices ranged from half a penny for a person and one penny for a sheep, to one shilling and sixpence for a broad-wheeled wagon. Soon, a very narrow temporary structure was built over the Tyne. This bridge was auctioned just before the new one was opened. George Stephenson won, presumably wanting scrap materials. The new stone bridge was on the site of the old one, and took five years and £60,000 to build. It was of unusually varied dimensions – probably due to a combination of disagreements between the Newcastle and the Gateshead engineers, as well as the poor quality riverbed and remnants of the medieval bridge. It was widened in 1800 and had a toll attached until 1818, when all the debts incurred in building it were finally repaid. But the problem remained that the bridge was at low level, forcing land traffic to use steep slopes. It also allowed nothing bigger than keelboats underneath, and this of course hindered the development of industry upriver. This problem eventually led to the bridge being demolished, in 1866. (www.bridgesonthetyne.co.uk / Manders, F. and Potts, R., *Crossing the Tyne*, Tynebridge Publishing, 2001)

MAY 1ST

1930: On this day, Peter Taylor – later Chief Justice, and Baron Taylor of Gosforth – was born at 242 Westgate Road. Both his parents were Jews whose ancestors had settled in Leeds; his father was a doctor. While he was growing up they moved to a bigger house they had had built in Kenton Road, Gosforth – they named it Roundhay after the Leeds suburb. On the outbreak of war, Taylor was evacuated to Penrith. Soon after his return he won a place at the Royal Grammar School. Upon leaving, he nearly entered the Royal College of Music, but a summer school persuaded him that he would never be a true virtuoso – so instead he went to Cambridge to study law. Even after being called to the bar in 1954, he still lived in Newcastle, only moving away when appointed to the High Court Bench in the 1980s. Cases he dealt with in this time included the trial of former Liberal Party leader Jeremy Thorpe, for murder, and John Ryman, MP for Blyth Valley, for mishandling his election expenses. In Taylor's later career, he is perhaps best known for heading the inquiry into the Hillsborough disaster. He eventually became Lord Chief Justice of England and Wales – one of only two people to do so having started life in Newcastle (the other, Harry Woolf, held the position in the early 2000s but moved from Newcastle at five years old). (*The Independent*)

MAY 2ND

1836: On this day, the twenty men of the Newcastle police force went on duty for the first time (unless we count the abortive attempt of 1832, *see* November 3rd). They were all aged between twenty-five and forty-five, of good character, and able to read, write, and pay £4 towards a uniform. Some people, however, weren't convinced. In a council meeting on the 5th, Mr Doubleday said that most people seemed to be against the 'day-police'. He did accept that a small 'day-watch' (avoiding that French p-word) might be useful on Saturday market days, and on Sundays to prevent drinking in public houses. (*Newcastle Courant*)

———— • ◆ • ————

1903: On this day, Benwell heavyweight boxer Jack Palmer fought Ben Taylor to effectively become English champion. Palmer repeatedly floored Taylor and it was incredible that he was able to continue to fight strongly. But in the twelfth round Palmer put Taylor down for the full count. He was still around, if past his prime, in 1908, when he was one of several boxers defeated by the touring world champion, Canadian Tommy Burns.

MAY 3RD

1815: On this day, a dreadful accident occurred at Heaton Pit. An older section of workings, long abandoned, had filled up with water. A deafening crash was heard and a strong gust of wind signalled a massive inrush of water. There was just enough notice for eighteen men and boys, close to the exit, to escape. Still, by the time the last survivor made it out, he was wading through water up to his waist. Because the flood was at the deepest point of the mine and the tunnels beyond it went upwards, it meant that there was a large section of mine left dry, but inaccessible. Seventy-five men and boys were still alive, but trapped. And there they remained, as attempts were made to work out where they were, and reach the spot via other tunnels. Hampered by primitive equipment, collapsing tunnels, flammable gas and the rising water, hopes soon faded for the survival of the trapped men. Attempts to reach them continued without success until early in 1816, when they were found. Tragically, all those trapped had long since died. It seems that they had spent many weeks trying in vain to work through to a tunnel from which they could have escaped. In the end they starved to death. The oldest was eighty-two; the youngest just seven. (Richardson, M.A., *The Local Historian's Table Book*, 1843)

MAY 4TH

1997: On this day, Leazes Park hosted the first of its annual Green Festivals. Green Fairs had been held in Newcastle Student Union the previous two summers, but these were on a much smaller scale and have largely been lost to memory. It was only when the Friends of Leazes Park, spurred on by Newcastle United's plans to build a new stadium in the park, invited the Green Society to run an event there that things really took off. There was an outdoor sound stage, stalls and craft workshops. The beautiful weather on this first day has largely held (with a few exceptions) over the years. The following year, there were three stages, a bar, and more family activities added; the one after that was extended over the whole weekend, with the Saturday intended to be more family-friendly in tone. The Festival was temporarily hosted by Exhibition Park in 2003 due to improvement works and the draining of the lake in Leazes Park, and was temporarily cancelled in 2009. Nonetheless, it goes from strength to strength as a flagship environmental event for the region and is probably the biggest free environment festival in the country. (www.newcastlegreenfestival.org.uk)

MAY 5TH

1798: On this day, the *Newcastle Courant* published the obituary of architect William Newton. Given the many buildings that Newton was involved in designing, in Newcastle and beyond, he really deserves to be better known. Born in December 1730, Newton learned the trade of a shipwright under his father. By twenty-three he had begun to be employed as an architect on small jobs around County Durham, and by twenty-nine he was considered established enough to be placed in charge of altering the courtroom in the Moot Hall, where the assizes met. As well as many large projects (often country houses) across the region, he designed St Ann's Church (serving the population of Sandgate), Newcastle Infirmary, and new wings for Fenham Hall. He must have liked his own designs – he built Charlotte Square, where he lived for over twenty-five years and brought up twelve children. The building which made his name, though, was the 1776 Newcastle Assembly Rooms. He suffered a long illness and died aged sixty-seven; as the *Courant* stated, 'His memory will be perpetuated by the various edifices he planned and built in this town and adjacent counties'. (Wills, M., 'William Newton: An Elusive Practitioner', *Archaeologia Aeliana*, 2007)

MAY 6TH

1975: On this day, Rollermania came to Newcastle. When the Bay City Rollers played City Hall, thirty-two policemen, eight St John Ambulance staff and fifty stewards were on hand. But they struggled to control the 2,000 fans who gathered outside the hall without tickets, screaming hysterically. Inside, fans rushed the stage to get closer to their idols. Although only a handful of girls were taken to hospital, scores more were treated when they fainted or collapsed in hysterics, and the gig had to be stopped less than halfway through. There was much debate as to whether the band should, in this circumstance, contribute towards the additional cost of policing. (*Newcastle Chronicle*)

———◆———

1983: Exactly eight years later, a rather different singer was also on a Newcastle stage. The Tyne Theatre had been around since 1867, but had been shut during restoration. For the grand re-opening they wanted something special, so they hired Plácido Domingo, then probably the best tenor in the world, to perform for one night only. The production was Tosca, and the co-stars were Mara Zampieri, a professional soprano performing in Britain for the first time, and the sixty-strong Northern Sinfonia – and a group of local amateurs. The theatre was packed, with an audience of 1,200. During the sixth curtain call, a lady passed something to the conductor – it was passed through to Domingo and Zampieri – an empty bottle of Newcastle Brown Ale, with a single red rose! (Mackintosh, I., 'Tonight Only', *Theatres: The Magazine of The Theatres Trust*, 2006)

MAY 7TH

1935: On this day, Newcastle-built technology reached for the stars, with the opening of the David Dunlap Observatory in Toronto, Canada. Two years before, a huge disc of Pyrex had been cast at Corning's Glassworks, New York. This disc weighed 2½ tons, and measured 76 inches across. It was then sent to Parson's Optical Works, Newcastle, who built the mechanical parts of the telescope and then ground and polished the disc to fit. They had the unenviable task of shaping the disc so that no part of it was more than 2 millionths of an inch off its theoretical contour. The roof of the erecting shop was rolled back to allow the disc to be tested on real stars before it was shipped back across the Atlantic. What Parsons had helped build was, at the time, the second largest telescope in the world. The largest – the Hooker Telescope at Mount Wilson Observatory in Los Angeles – had a mirror 100 inches across, but its yoke mounting prevented it from looking towards the North Pole. Hence, the Dunlap telescope was the biggest *fully moveable* telescope in the world. Cyril Young, the General Manager of Sir Howard Grubb, Parsons and Co., was present at the opening ceremony. (Hogg, F.S. & Hogg, H.S., 'The Official Opening of the David Dunlap Observatory', *Journal of the Royal Astronomical Society of* Canada, 1935)

MAY 8TH

1636: Around this date, the plague hit Newcastle – and hit hard. It is impossible to be sure when the first death came, but it was probably May the 7th or 8th – certainly this is the first day that the parish clerk of St Nicholas' had to write 'pl' alongside the deceased's name in the parish records. The following week, fifty-nine people succumbed. What followed was catastrophic. At the height of the plague, there were 400 deaths in a week. By the time it was killed off by cold weather in December, at least 5,600 had died in the town. That amounts to almost half the population and made it, in proportional terms, the most devastating plague death toll in any English town or city of the sixteenth and seventeenth centuries. Ordinary life ground to a halt. Captain Fenwick said the town was 'almost desolate, thy streets grown green with grass, thy treasury wasted, thy trading departed'. Some were quarantined in 'lodges' on the Town Moor. Others were shut up in infected houses for a period of six weeks, with wooden beams nailed across the doors (though this was more effective in some cases than others, and often people found ways to pass food in). Once the danger had passed, the houses were cleansed and fumigated by burning a variety of substances – broom and frankincense, sulphur or simply coal. (Wrightson, K., *Ralph Tailor's Summer*, Yale University Press, 2011)

MAY 9TH

1639: On this day, King Charles I was staying in Newcastle, as his army manoeuvred during the Bishop's War. Courtier John Aston recorded the stay in a diary. He arrived on May 4th and lodged at a woollen drapers in Side, leaving his horses at a 'poor man's stable without Newgate'. On the 5th, in a proclamation during divine service, the Scots were given eight days to surrender – and preparations for war began. The King, with much of his army, arrived a day later, and was greeted by the Mayor – salt merchant Sir Alexander Davison – and Aldermen in the market place on Sandhill, and given 'a purse of gold'. He lodged with Mr Lyddall of Pilgrim Street. On this day, 900 Yorkshire soldiers marched through town, and the King went to watch. That evening, wined and dined by the Mayor, the King gave both him and the town clerk knighthoods. This didn't do Mayor Davison much good – a staunch Royalist, he was still in the town (then aged around eighty) during the siege of 1644. One of his sons spent time in the Scottish camp as a guarantee for the safe return of negotiators, and the other died in the bombardment. A few days afterwards Davison himself, perhaps careless in grief, was mortally wounded. He was buried in St Nicholas' Church, which still has a large wall-mounted monument to him. (Hodgson, J.C. (ed.), *Six North Country Diaries, Vol. I*, Surtees Society, 1910)

MAY 10TH

1895: On this day, Israel Brodie, future Chief Rabbi, was born in Newcastle. His parents were Aaron and Sheina Brodie, immigrants from Kovno, Lithuania. Never wealthy, his father was a tradesman, travelling around the pit villages of Durham and Northumberland and selling drapery and other goods from a pack on his back. His mother was apparently determined that Brodie should be a rabbi, and from an early age he attended a Talmud Torah school twice a day, learning the Hebrew language, prayers, scriptures and the practice of Jewish faith, as well as talking with the rabbi that lodged with them. He later studied at Rutherford College. After higher education, he spent fourteen years working as rabbi for a congregation in Melbourne, Australia, and eight years as rabbi to the British Armed Forces (this was not a desk job – he was sent to Dunkirk!). Brodie was appointed Chief Rabbi of Britain and the Commonwealth in 1948. He remained in post until he retired in 1965. He was the first Chief Rabbi to be born and educated in Britain, and also the first to receive a knighthood. (Kopelowitz, L., 'Who was Chief Rabbi Brodie?', *St John's Wood Synagogue Magazine*)

MAY 11TH

1851: On this day, Sandgate erupted in violence between the Irish workmen and native-born residents. At this point, over 8 per cent of Newcastle's population were Irish-born; and most of them were keelmen. According to the *Newcastle Courant*, many of them enjoyed hanging around in the area, 'the worse sink of profligacy and vice in the town'. There were many theories as to the riot's cause, from an accidental fall or a street preacher's words, to the throwing of oyster shells! For about two hours in the late afternoon, groups of Irishmen 'occupied' the streets, threatening anyone who came near. At 6.30 p.m., two policemen tried to make them move on, and 'about 200 Irishmen turn[ed] out suddenly and simultaneously out of different alleys and lanes, armed with sticks, iron rods, tongs, pokers, coal rakes and other offensive weapons'. The ringleader was shouting, 'By Jasus we'll take Sandgate tonight, and be revenged on every English ___ in it.' But as more police arrived, and the area's other inhabitants became more organised, the tide turned. More than forty Irishmen were dragged to the police station, and the rest evaporated into the vandalised streets. One man received a month's hard labour and a dozen were fined. A popular dialect song, 'The Horrid War i'Sangeyt' was written in commemoration. (*Newcastle Courant*)

MAY 12TH

1937: On this day, most people would have been busy celebrating the Coronation of George VI, with street parties and merriment. But for the Stern family it had another significance – in an upstairs room in Philip Street, Arthurs Hill, Jenny Stern was in labour. This was a stroke of luck – every child born on that day was given £5 by the Crown. There were only two newborns in Newcastle that day, and Miriam Stern – later Dr Miriam Stoppard – was one. Her mother recalled, 'The Lord Mayor of Newcastle presented us with our £5, a lot of money then, and we bought a pram with beautiful high wheels for four guineas.' Miriam was brought up in a poor, strictly Jewish household. She was encouraged to read classical literature. She spent the war as an evacuee, first near Morecambe Bay, and then at Bamburgh, before returning to Newcastle, attending Wingrove Road Senior School, Fenham. Her intelligence and drive were rewarded in a scholarship to Newcastle Central High School, before she moved away from the area to study as a doctor. She was married to playwright Tom Stoppard between 1972 and 1992. She later forged a successful television and writing career as an expert on medical issues. She says she gained a lot 'from being brought up a Geordie. It's just grit that got me where I am'. (Gibson, J., *Spirit of Tyneside*, John Donald, 1990)

MAY 13TH

1934: On this day, a fascist meeting was broken up by demonstrators. In 1934, fascism was on the rise and Sir Oswald Mosley, leading the blackshirted British Union of Fascists (BUF), was gaining support in England, aided by rallies and aggressive propaganda. In the North East, the BUF had financial support and the organisational skills of several ex-army officers. They aimed to appeal to the workers – and masses of unemployed men – of the industrial and mining districts. As meetings and parades got larger, local clashes were inevitable. Confrontation in Gateshead led to the formation of the Anti-Fascist League, who held many open-air meetings in Newcastle and across Tyneside. While the Labour Party were recommending leaving it to the police, and even the Communist Party were favouring ridicule (calling the Blackshirts 'Mickey Mouse') above conflict, the Anti-Fascist League favoured a more direct approach. The BUF soon found that they were not welcome on the streets of working-class Newcastle. On May 13th, a fascist meeting was broken up by a large crowd of demonstrators, and the Blackshirt leaders were besieged in their own Newcastle headquarters. The Anti-Fascist League were based in the Smith's Hall, Blackfriars, and held physical training sessions in the enclosed square. Mosley began to feel the pressure, and in the summer he voluntarily cancelled a rally on the Sunday of Town Moor's Race Week. Over the next few weeks BUF support in Tyneside dwindled and died. (Todd, N., *In Excited Times*, Bewick Press, 1995)

MAY 14TH

1929: On this day, the North East Coast Exhibition was opened by the future King Edward VIII. The intention was to showcase the industries of the North East, and especially Tyneside, to the world. There were three 'palaces' (for engineering, industry and the arts), a festival hall, a hall for artisans and another for women, as well as a 20,000-seater stadium. Outside was a massive amusement park, with rifle ranges and water chutes, and the Himalayan Railway (over 80 feet high and over a mile long). You could see the Bluebird train and a Supermarine Seaplane, both record-breakers for speed. There was an African village – a group of mud huts housing 100 men and women described by the press as 'dusky visitors ... awfully mischievous rascals'. They lived a sanitised pastiche of tribal life, with animals, dancing, and open fire cooking. When the exhibition closed in late October, over 4 million people had visited, an average of around 30,000 per day! However, three days after its closure came the Wall Street Crash, and the start of the Great Depression. While most of the structures of the exhibition were dismantled, the Palace of Arts, a steel-framed concrete-clad building, still survives. The only other remnant of the 1929 exhibition is the name of the area where it took place – Exhibition Park. (Baglee, C., *The North East Coast Exhibition*, 1979)

MAY 15TH

1993: On this day, Jesmond Dene was the site of the 'Celebrate the Trees and Save the Dene!' demonstration. The threat came from road developers intent on creating a shorter route between Newcastle and the Coast Road – the Cradlewell Bypass. Developers' claims that the road would cut travel times were met with scepticism. Although the details are contested, local planning enquiries were not favourable. Things were especially difficult because this was land given by Lord Armstrong to the people of Newcastle *in perpetuity*. On this day, the first demonstration was held on Armstrong Bridge, with scores of people tying ribbons and drawings to the threatened trees. This was all relatively calm – but things changed when the bulldozers moved in, inspiring a four-month direct action live-in, one of the key campaigns in the anti-road protest movement of the mid-1990s. By mid-June, the 'Flowerpot tribe' had set up camp and clashes were starting to get violent. By mid-July, court injunctions were in force and several protesters were sleeping in hammocks slung between the trees – and even in tree houses, thought to be the first of the movement. But it was, in the end, a losing battle, and as the weather grew worse and more legal and physical pressure was brought to bear, the bypass was eventually built. Traffic remains slow at peak times, but there are fewer accidents. (*The Independent* / www.eco-action.org)

MAY 16TH

1639: On this day, the King's Printer published the *Laws and Ordinances of War* while stationed in Newcastle. At this point, King Charles was marching north towards Scotland. While the Civil War had not begun, the Scots, in defence of their ways of worship, had raised troops and the King was responding with force. The King's Printer travelled up the Great North Road with his press, type, and other equipment on a wagon, changing horses frequently in an attempt to keep up. He brought the first printing press to the area around May 8th. The following day he printed a requisition for butter. Stocking the town with food was part of a bigger plan: to prepare the town for a siege. The next publication was a copy of a sermon which had been preached at Durham Cathedral to the King and his men a few days earlier. The subject, no doubt pleasing to King Charles' ears, was the divine right of kings to rule, and the solemn duty of subjects to obey. The *Laws and Ordnances of War* was the fourth and final document to be printed. Produced by the army's general, the Earl of Arundel and Surrey, it included an oath for all soldiers binding them to a strict moral and religious code. (Philipson, J. and Sessions, W., 'The King's Printer at Newcastle upon Tyne in 1639', *Archaeologia Aeliana*, 1984)

MAY 17TH

1464: On this day, captured Lancastrian leaders were executed for their part in the Battle of Hexham, two days earlier. The battle had not been big – indeed, some say that more were executed in the following days than actually died on the battlefield. Still, it was a turning point in the topsy-turvy internal conflicts of the Wars of the Roses. Henry VI's Lancastrian forces had been routed near Wooler; he had camped out at Bywell Castle, leaving much of his army at Hexham. The Yorkist opposition were encamped in Newcastle, and set out to strike a decisive blow. They stormed through Bywell – the King escaped leaving his helmet behind – and met the Lancastrian forces near Hexham, sweeping them aside and capturing their general, the Duke of Somerset. Somerset met a headsman's axe in Hexham the following day, but the executions had only just begun. Those executed in Newcastle included the 3rd Baron Hungerford, who had already spent most of the 1450s as a prisoner in France, and Lord Roos, a close friend of the Lancastrian Royals. Also executed was Sir William Tailboys, a former treasurer to Henry VI, who had escaped the field of battle only to be found the next day hiding in a coal pit near Newcastle with some 3,000 marks (£2,000) of money intended to pay the Lancastrian forces! The prisoners had been held in the Castle Keep and were beheaded a short walk away at Sandhill. (Sadler, J. and Spiers, A., *The Battle of Hexham in its Place*, Ergo Press, 2007 / www.lordburghsretinue.co.uk)

May 18th

1908: On this day, the Hippodrome cinema opened in Northumberland Street. The building had never been meant to be permanent – from 1890 it was a circus, and from 1893 a lowbrow theatre called the Amphitheatre. In theory, it was keeping up with the times when Harry Taft leased it and began showing 'Animated Pictures of All Nations' every evening at 8 p.m., plus a special Saturday matinee. Tickets cost between from 3*d* and 1*s*. But it was a very large building and never seemed to get the audience it needed. On June 12th, managerial desperation resorted to hosting a 'funny face' competition! Exactly one month after the Hippodrome opened, it closed – making it the shortest lived cinema in the city. It was demolished the following year, and the far more successful Olympia cinema was built on the same site. (Manders, F., *Cinemas of Newcastle*, Tynebridge Publishing, 2005)

———— ◆ ————

1997: Also on this day, rowers from Newcastle University and Durham University competed for the first time in the Northumbrian Universities Boat Race. The races – there are six, for experienced rowers, freshmen and school teams of each gender – take place over 1,800 metres and finish near the Millennium Bridge. Both teams have produced international competitors over the years, demonstrating the high standard of the contestants. (*Newcastle Chronicle*)

MAY 19TH

1801: Around this time, reformist Reverend William Turner published a vivid description of his hometown for the *Monthly Magazine*. 'To the stranger who arrives from the south [...] a precipitous eminence presents itself, which extends along the river westward leaving only room for a narrow street, very properly denominated The Close; but clustered all the way to the very summit of its almost perpendicular banks with houses and [...] with an unsightly mass of miserable tenements, five storeys high, which seems to threaten destruction to the houses and streets below'. He continues that the Quayside, 'is occupied by no less than twenty-one wynds or alleys (here called chares), only one of which, the Broad Chare, will admit the passage of carts. All the rest may easily be reached across by the extended arms of a middle-sized man, and many even with a single arm'. Further up, he contrasts the Quayside with the spaciousness of Pilgrim and Northumberland Streets, but even here is not wholly positive: 'The grey colour, however, of the bricks, and the general (though not now universal) covering of bright red pan-tile roofs, certainly taken much off from their appearance. The pavements are in general very good, but it must be acknowledged that too little attention is paid to [...] keeping them clean and neat. Nor can it be said that it is well lighted; the few lamps scattered here and there, serving [...] only to make "darkness visible".' (Hardbottle, S., *The Reverend William Turner*, Northern Universities Press, 1997)

MAY 20TH

1884: On this day, the stamps of the Newcastle Assay office on Dean Street were handed over to the Inland Revenue. Newcastle, a centre of gold and silver work since the thirteenth century, had been one of the few cities with the right to assess the quality of precious metal. Run by the Company of Goldsmiths, from 1702 onward the assay office would test the metal, then punch into it a purity mark to signify the metal type, a year mark, a maker's mark and the three castles of Newcastle. Sadly, at this time production of local silver fell into steep decline and the decision was made to shut the office. Their last work was to assay thirty gold rings on May 2nd. Twenty-one punches were handed over and eleven local ones destroyed. (Hallmarks Database and Silver Research forum)

— ◆ —

1977: On this day, The Clash played Newcastle University. Punk bands have something of a reputation for smashing up hotel furniture, but what The Clash apparently did in their Seaton Burn hotel was pilfer. Singer Joe Strummer nicked £26-worth of pillows and towels, which were later found in their tour coach, while drummer Topper Headon was charged with taking a hotel key and keyring. The pair failed to turn up to their court hearing, so they were brought to Morpeth and spent two nights in custody before a new hearing, where the two men were fined £60 and £40 respectively. (*Evening News*)

MAY 21ST

1965: On this day, retired Benwell bus driver Kempton Bunton posted a left-luggage office ticket to the *Sunday Mirror*. The story begins four years earlier, when a priceless portrait of the Duke of Wellington by Goya was stolen. Sixty-one-year-old retired bus driver Bunton went to the National Gallery and started talking to the guards, who boasted about the hi-tech security surrounding the painting. They then told him that it was switched off every morning for the cleaners! He climbed into a toilet window using ladders left by builders and took the painting. There was great speculation about its whereabouts – a fictional version even turned up in an arch-villain's lair in *Dr No*! In reality Bunton just locked the painting in a cupboard. A long-standing campaigner for free television licences for the elderly, he had been enraged that the government spent money buying the painting. So, he held it to ransom, offering to return it if £140,000 was found to finance poor people's television licences. Eventually it got too much for Bunton's conscience. He left the painting in a cloakroom in Birmingham railway station and handed himself in. He was never found guilty of stealing the painting, because he had returned it and had no intention of keeping it (the law has since changed as a direct result of this case). He was, however, punished for the theft of the frame, and sentenced to three months in jail. (*Evening Chronicle*)

MAY 22ND

1838: On this day, a bare-knuckle boxing contest between whitesmith John Brown and engine-wright Robert Forbister, over £20, ended with a fatal punch. At this date, bare-knuckle boxing was usually fought until one participant was simply unable to continue. It is said that the fight was begun at the border between Northumberland and Durham, on one of the islands in the Tyne. When a Durham magistrate arrived, business was resumed on the northern side, at Hedley Common, roughly opposite Ryton. This was no spur of the moment match – a 24-foot ring had been marked out with ropes, with spectators gathered to watch and to bet. Brown got first blood, and first knock-down, despite being 20lb lighter than his opponent. But he also tired more quickly (neither was a big man – Forbister was 5 feet 10 inches, and Brown a mere 5 feet 6 inches and 9 stone 6 pounds). Still, it took thirty-seven rounds of gruelling slog until Forbister gave him a knock to the neck from which he did not get up. Brown was carried to a nearby public house where he died that evening. Apparently, Reverend Dodd refused to allow him to be buried in St Andrew's. Forbister, meanwhile, was charged with murder. The jury found him guilty but recommended leniency, and his sentence was commuted to four months' hard labour for manslaughter. (Fordyce, T., *Local Records*, 1867)

MAY 23RD

1640: On this day, Lord Conway, deputy-general of the English Army, wrote to Archbishop Laud to explain events of the previous week. In anticipation of a fight with the Scottish, a knight with the glorious name of Sir Fulke Huncks had arrived in Newcastle on April 29th, with seventy mounted men, reluctant conscripts and ill-prepared for battle. When two pennies were taken from their pay, for equipment costs, a group complained. Conway arrested the ringleader. The next day, twenty came to his door to protest – and again, he arrested the ringleader. He decided that the death of either one for mutiny would be enough. He didn't care which one it was, and so, bizarrely, made them roll dice for it. The loser was Anthony Viccars. A gallows was set up in the Bigg Market, right in front of Thomas Malaber's front door. The soldiers all refused to be the one to hang Viccars, so Conway made six of the mutineers into a firing squad. Oddly, Conway actually had some sympathy for the mutineers, writing the same day to the Earl of Northumberland that gunners pay too much for gunpowder and repairing their own guns, and that anyone who thought the King's interests were served by giving the soldiers poor quality arms was deceiving themselves. (Clephan, J., 'The Bigg Market Military Execution', *Archaeologia Aeliana*, 1887)

MAY 24TH

1138: On or around this day, a Scottish occupation of Newcastle began which was to last nearly twenty years. King David I of Scotland was repeatedly campaigning southward, to support the claim to the throne of his niece, Matilda, over that of her cousin, Stephen. He seems to have been particularly keen to take Newcastle. There were family ties – in 1093 (when he was nine) his parents were killed, and his grandmother and aunt fled to Newcastle, where they founded the town's first religious house, the Benedictine nunnery of St Bartholomew. By 1139, Stephen had little choice but to make peace, so the Earldom of Northumberland was revived and given to David's eldest son, Henry. David certainly saw Northumberland as a new and permanent addition to Scotland, and perhaps he even saw Newcastle as an alternative capital. He certainly spent a lot of time there, issuing laws, and borrowed some of its administrative methods for the *Leges Burgorum* which governed four Scottish towns. He refounded St Bartholomew's nunnery, and rebuilt the old English church in Newgate Street – this might be why it is dedicated to St Andrew. But by the early 1150s all the Scottish leaders had died, and in 1157 England recovered the North. (exlaodicea.wordpress.com)

MAY 25TH

1928: On this day, the *Italia* airship crashed in the high Arctic. Several groups tried to rescue the crew with hi-tech aeroplanes, including the famous explorer Roald Amundsen, who died in the attempt. Seven weeks later hope was fading, when into the fray came the *Krassin*, an icebreaker built at Armstrong, Whitworth and Co.'s Low Walker docks in 1916. *Krassin* not only rescued the survivors, but went back and rescued three would-be rescuers. Nearly 100 metres long, the *Krassin* was the most powerful icebreaker in the world for almost forty years. She is now a floating museum in St Petersburg. (www.portoftyne.co.uk)

———◆———

1970: On this day, film director Neil Marshall was born in Newcastle. As a child, Marshall saw *Raiders of the Lost Ark* at Newcastle's Odeon, and later said, 'Walking out of the cinema I knew then that I needed to make films'. Fascinated by the process of directing, he began to take home movies on his mother's Super-8 camera, before studying film at Newcastle Polytechnic in 1989. After years as a film editor, his directorial début came in 2002 with the soldiers *v.* werewolves horror/black comedy *Dog Soldiers*. He has continued to direct films, often making the most of a small budget to exploit a confined situation, notably the award-winning *The Descent* (2005). (*The Observer*)

MAY 26TH

1878: On this day, William Campbell 'the Scottish Giant', died in the upstairs room of his pub, The Duke of Wellington on High Bridge. He was just twenty-two, but was around 6 feet 4 inches tall, and also 6 feet 4 inches in circumference around his chest, although all accounts suggest that he only ate moderately. Weighing in at 54 stone, for many years he held the record of Britain's heaviest man. He had lived in Newcastle for less than a year, but was not shy about promoting himself and hence advertising his pub. When he died, there were immediate logistical problems. The coffin was specially constructed from thick wood lined with lead, and so many people gathered to watch it being made that the carpenter had to call in the police to keep order. Even more gathered as the coffin was removed from Campbell's house. Undertakers had to remove not only the window, but also some of the surrounding brickwork with block and tackle in order to lower the coffin to the ground three floors below; the combined weight being more than a ton. The streets were packed tight along the route of his funeral procession, the band were rushed and scattered, several people were injured in the crush, and in the cemetery itself things became so bad that some were actually pushed into the awaiting grave. (*Queanbeyan*)

MAY 27TH

2000: On this day, the Centre for Life was opened. Part funded by the Millennium Fund, this ground-breaking space houses several different institutes with interests in biochemistry, genetics and related fields under one roof – combining to form the £10m Life Knowledge Park. Partners include the Newcastle Fertility Centre (one of the largest centres of fertility treatment in the country, which has aided more than 3,000 births), Newcastle Human Embryonic Stem Cell Group, North East England Stem Cell Institute, the Institute of Human Genetics (one of Europe's largest human genetics research centres) and a group dedicated to the ethics of medicine. It is a centre for the management of muscular dystrophy, and has produced several significant – and much-discussed – breakthroughs in genetics and stem cell research, including a stem cell treatment for some forms of blindness. Most controversially, in 2005 research on therapeutic cloning led to the announcement that scientists at the Centre for Life in Newcastle were the first group in the world to successfully clone a human embryo. Also within the Centre for Life is a museum dedicated to engaging the public with science. It includes the North's largest planetarium. The open space between the buildings is converted into an ice rink each winter. (www.life.org.uk)

MAY 28TH

1838: On this day was held the annual 'Barge Day'. In the early nineteenth century, on every Ascension Day, the Mayor would formally perambulate the boundaries of Newcastle, including (in his Mayoral Barge) the parts accessible by water. This was a big local celebration, with crowds rushing down to the river to watch an amateur regatta and race, or play games on King's Meadows. King's Meadows was an island in the Tyne, near Elswick. It had its own pub called the Countess of Coventry, horse racing, and a field of cows. At least this year Newcastle successfully avoided a repeat of 1812's Barge Day, when a celebratory cannon exploded and its unfortunate gunner was knocked from the castle wall to his death! On Barge Day in 1822, Ascension Day coincided with the King's birthday, so there was all the more reason for a party. This was begun with a rifle salute, the firing of cannon from the castle and the ringing of church bells, followed by the usual trip to King's Meadows for sports and races. Less usual was Mr Kent's exhibition of a 'marine velocipede'! A few years later, control of the river moved from the Council to the Tyne Improvement Commission, so the council's enthusiasm understandably dimmed and Barge Days began their decline. King's Meadows was dredged away in the 1870s. (*Newcastle Courant*)

MAY 29TH

1969: On this day, Newcastle United played Hungarian team Ujpest Dozsa at home in the first leg of the final of the Fairs Cup. They won 3-0, and after a return match on June 11th, were declared overall champions. What made their victory particularly remarkable was that it was their first shot at a Europe-wide competition. Amazingly, they had got a place despite coming 10th in the League during a season in which they had lost more games than they had won! The Fairs Cup had odd entry rules, one of which was that only one team per city could compete, which ruled out several teams above them. This and other complexities allowed Newcastle to sneak in – but they were hardly expected to lift the trophy. In fact, they stormed past Feyenoord, beat a Sporting Lisbon team in turmoil over the resignation of their manager, were tested by Real Zaragoza and confused Vitoria Setubal (who weren't used to playing in the snow). That took them to a semi-final win against Glasgow Rangers – a victory somewhat overshadowed by hooliganism as unhappy Glaswegian fans took out their disappointment on the streets of Newcastle. Finally, on this day, United faced Ujpest, who had just beaten the champions, Leeds. Nearly 60,000 tickets were sold, despite heavy rain. United was able to go to their final match three goals ahead, and retain a two-goal lead – fittingly, on team manager Joe Harvey's birthday. (Jeffrey, J., *Newcastle United: The 1968-9 Fairs Cup Story*, DB Publishing, 2012)

MAY 30TH

1756: On this day Elizabeth Elstob, an unusual lady born and brought up on the Quayside, died. Her mother, a widow with eight children, had nonetheless taught her daughter the basics of Latin before she died in 1764. Elstob moved away, to live with her uncle in Canterbury, and then with her brother William, who supported her intellectually even though she could not study at Oxford University alongside him. She helped him on the Anglo-Saxon *Homily of St Gregory*, and they even taught the tongue to the servant boy so that he could help. Elstob said that she picked up Anglo-Saxon easily through having grown up in the North East, where the language retained Saxon influences. She prided herself in being probably the first – and for many years the only – woman to speak the tongue in the modern era, although she could not help being drawn into debates about whether this was appropriate for a woman. In 1715, she produced an important Saxon grammar book; she was the toast of liberal intellectual Oxford society. After her brother died, she spent fifteen years as a schoolteacher, before being 'rediscovered' in old age by a new generation of feminists and intellectuals. She died comfortably, 'surrounded by books and dirt,' but prevented by her gender from fully making her own way and living up to her potential. (Clarke, N., 'Elizabeth Elstob (1674–1752): England's First Professional Woman Historian?' *Gender & History*, 2005)

MAY 31ST

1925: On this day, Joe Robinson, 'the Blond Beefcake', was born in Newcastle. Wrestling was in the blood – his father and grandfather had both been champion Cumberland wrestlers. He quickly followed in their footsteps as 'Tiger' Joe Robinson, winning the European heavyweight championship in 1952. After injuring his back, he turned to acting. He had studied at RADA and had a few bit parts before he was spotted playing Harry 'Muscles' Green in the musical *Wish You Were Here*. He landed the role of Sam, a wrestling gentle giant who becomes Mr World in *A Kid for Two Farthings* – with Diana Dors as his love interest. Several roles followed – he claims he was even offered the chance to hit the gong on the Rank Cinema advert, but turned it down, fearing typecasting. He was running a martial arts centre (he co-wrote a book on judo with Honor Blackman) when he was offered his most well-known part. As diamond smuggler Peter Franks, he wrestles Sean Connery (who in real life had trained at his gym years before) in the James Bond film *Diamonds are Forever*. In all, he appeared in around nineteen films, performing alongside the likes of Roger Moore (in *The Saint*) and Errol Flynn. (*The Visitor magazine*)

June 1st

1774: On this day, the Town Moor Act clarified the rights of Freemen of the Town. The exact area and location of the moor had shifted over time since it had been given to the Freemen centuries earlier, and most of it was in a rough condition and poorly drained. In 1771, the Common Council enclosed an area south-west of the current Barrack Road and Ponteland Road. They then let it to Joshua Hopper, a farmer who planned to cultivate it. Unfortunately, they hadn't consulted the Freemen, who fought back by physically breaking part of the enclosure fence, knowing that this would provoke a legal response. Hopper started a lawsuit for trespass, backed by the council. The case began on August 10th 1773. The counsel for the Freemen admitted trespass, but argued eloquently on the evils of rampant land enclosure. The counsel for the Corporation only said, 'How can I reply? He has pounded me in a common [i.e., trapped me with his argument] and I cannot get out.' This led to the Town Moor Act, whereby any lease would be decided by the Freemen, and could not be for more than 100 acres in size or seven years in length. Extra measures were put in place to preserve the quality of the grass. The Freemen and their widows were granted the right to graze two milk cows on the moor. Indeed, their right to graze cattle on the Town Moor remains to this day. (www.freemenofnewcastle.com / Journals of the House of Commons, Volume 24)

JUNE 2ND

1908: On this day, Tommy Watson was born in Byker. Brought up locally, he took up boxing at fifteen, training in Jimmy Britt's Gym. Two years later, after serving in the Royal Navy, he returned home for his first bout at St James Hall. He adopted the name 'Seaman' Tommy Watson, which would stay with him throughout his career. At nineteen, he began to box seriously; buying his way out of the Navy once convinced he had genuine potential. He was British featherweight champion, and is widely thought of as one of the best featherweights Britain has produced, only losing nine of his 123 fights. And yet, though he came very close, he never quite managed to grasp a world championship title. His first attempt was cancelled when the Cuban all-time-great Kid Chocolate was unexpectedly deported from America for not having the right paperwork for the fight. Watson instead fought Fidel La Barba, returning home in triumph with one of his greatest scalps. The following year he did meet Kid Chocolate, in a tough fight which Chocolate won, retaining the championship by a narrow decision on points. Tommy Watson retired at the age of twenty-seven, saying he didn't want to lose his sight through further damage to his eyes. (checkhookboxing.com)

JUNE 3RD

1816: On this evening, Signor de Montfort – who had advised on pyrotechnics for the grand events of the Prince Regent in previous years – ran an exhibition of fireworks in the Spital Field, Newcastle. Unfortunately, he underestimated the strength of the wind. A spark from a Catherine Wheel landed on the stage amongst four rockets. They caught light and shot off in four different directions; several people were injured, and one, fifteen-year-old John Price, was killed when a rocket struck him in the chest. Calamity did not stop de Montfort, however. Far from his career 'fizzling out', Signor De Montfort turned up again as 'fireworks manager' in London and Bath in the 1820s, connected to the Vauxhall Gardens. He was one of only a handful of itinerant Georgian firework masters, usually French or Italian, who travelled from town to town, putting on shows in pleasure gardens. The types of fireworks they used were similar to modern ones. There were Roman Candles, Sky Rockets, Javelin Wheels and Sunflower Wheels, Fixed Suns (which sent out sparks in all directions from a fixed hexagonal frame), Fountains of Chinese Fire (gunpowder and iron filings), Pigeons (small rockets which were propelled along a rope), a Battery of Maroons (each of which made a flash and a loud bang) and Pots de Bruin (pasteboard rolls filled with gunpowder). (Sykes, J., *Local Records*, Volume II, 1833 / austenonly.com)

JUNE 4TH

1312: On this day, the Dominican Friary of Newcastle solved a problem. The Dominicans, or Black Friars, had been in the town since about 1260. In 1264, they got a Royal grant to extend their grounds and build an aqueduct from a fountain outside their courtyard, piping running water into the building and then beyond it into the town. The following year work began on the town wall. Pretty soon it had separated the Dominicans from their gardens! In 1280, they were granted a Royal licence to build a special postern gate in the town wall, allowing the friars to walk to their gardens. Thirty-two years later, the problem re-emerged with the digging of the King's Dyke, a dry moat of 11 metres wide and 4.5 metres deep, right around the town. On this day, the monks were given permission to build a 5-foot-wide wooden drawbridge over the moat. It was allowed on the condition that as soon as there was any sign of danger, the drawbridge would be entirely removed. Spare a thought for the nearby Hospital of St Mary the Virgin at Westgate. The monks there did even worse out of the building of the town wall – which was built right through the middle of their courtyard, with several buildings on the wrong side!

JUNE 5TH

1812: On this day, disaster struck at the racecourse. Racing was very popular and the spectators were packed in to watch from temporary wooden stands. At the end of one race, one of the stands, built for patrons of the White Hart Inn, near the Flesh Market, collapsed under the strain. The whole middle section gave way, and around a hundred people fell into the wreckage (and into the barrels of drink which were being stored underneath). It is thought that about forty people were seriously hurt (including a pitman who called himself 'the Duke'). Two later died from their wounds. (Sykes, J., *Local Records*, Vol. 2)

———— • ◆ • ————

1862: On this day, singer-songwriter Geordie Ridley first performed 'The Blaydon Races'. The venue was Tyneside's most popular music hall venue, the Wheatsheaf pub in the Cloth Market, which had an extra 'singing room' built on the back. It became known as Balmbra's after its owner, and is immortalised in the song itself: 'I took the bus from Balmbra's, and she was heavy laden / Away we went along Collingwood Street – that's on the way to Blaydon'. Ridley was twenty-eight at this point, and recently crippled by a runaway wagon (he'd been working down the mine since he was eight). Incapable of manual labour, he turned to music, making his debut in the old Grainger Music Hall earlier that year with 'Joey Jones' – a tribute to that year's winner of the Northumberland Plate. He died two years later. (Mellor, G., *The Northern Music Hall*, Frank Graham, 1970)

JUNE 6TH

1887: On this day, the mortal remains of two sailors were buried in St John's cemetery, Elswick. What makes this unusual is that the two men were Lien Chin Yuen and Chin Shou-Fu, two sailors who had come in with the Chinese transport ship *Too Nan*, which was there to collect two cruisers built in Elswick yard for the Imperial Chinese Navy. They died in Newcastle Infirmary. At 4 a.m., forty of their crewmates arrived. They wrapped the bodies in white sheets and placed them in black wooden coffins, varnished and lead-lined. After the tricky job of placing the heavy coffins in the waiting hearses, they were accompanied by a procession of their shipmates up the hill to the cemetery. As the *Newcastle Courant* put it, 'The idle curiosity which in Newcastle follows all the walks abroad of the wanderers from the Flowery Land was not allowed to lapse even in the instance where death intervened'. Despite the early hour, about 200 people gathered to watch the ceremony, which involved ritual bows and the burning of joss paper. They were buried near to two Chinese soldiers who had died in similar circumstances six years before. Another man – who had watched the coffins leave the Infirmary from his room there – joined them six days later. (Keys, R. and Smith, K., *Armstrong's River Empire*, Tynebridge Publishing, 2010)

JUNE 7TH

1849: On this day, the Mayor of Gateshead, George Hawks, ceremonially hammered in the last key to tension the chain of the last arch of the new High Level Bridge. Designers had long suggested a high level crossing, but it became more important after 1837, when the railway line from London could reach Gateshead, but no further. The design is Robert Stephenson's, although William Martin previously published a very similar design – with added giant sculptures. He claimed Stephenson had stolen the idea from him (*see* April 4th). In total, around 800 families were displaced as their homes were knocked down during construction. Work began in April 1846, helped by a newly patented pile driver which replaced much of the hand-work. Impressively, a temporary wooden bridge – strong enough to carry locomotives – was built on the foundation pillars, and then gradually replaced. After testing, the first passengers crossed the Tyne on August 15th (*see* September 28th). Originally the whole thing was painted stone-coloured, but after smoke pollution turned it black, they settled for repainting in black, and later, dark grey. Although in theory the two-level system benefited walkers, in practice the ceiling of their layer leaked badly in spite of its asphalt roof. That didn't put everyone off – in 1859, the *Illustrated London News* reported that this quarter mile of straight covered track, which could easily be blocked at both ends, was proving popular for dog racing! (Manders, F. and Potts, R., *Crossing the Tyne*, Tynebridge Publishing, 2001)

JUNE 8TH

1808: On this day, the first meeting of the Killingworth, Longbenton and Weetslade Association for the Prosecution of Felons was held. This was effectively an early neighbourhood watch/private police. People of the Weetslade and Gosforth district paid into a fund each year – initially 10 shillings. The fund was then used to fund prosecution of crimes committed in the area, and to put up rewards for criminals' identification via adverts in the *Newcastle Courant*. The idea was to catch anyone who stole from the members. Initially these were private individuals, but in 1859 the fifty-or-so members agreed to allow in companies, collieries and the like. The property covered stretched as far as Haddricks Mill and Walker. In 1812, they successfully paid for the apprehension of two highway robbers. There were also more mundane tasks, like catching those who drove carriages recklessly and paying a constable to clear the streets of vagrants. The prosecutions the society paid for included the theft of grass, turnips, potatoes, pigeons and lead. This was an era when the law was very harsh, particularly on property crime, and punishments reflected this – the system's flexibility came from adjusting the details of the offence, or through pardons. The Association was responsible for at least one sentence of seven years' hard labour in Australia – for stealing a workman's tools. (Tyne and Wear Archives)

JUNE 9TH

1662: On this day, a tragic tale unfolded in Newcastle Gaol. Anne Mennin was accused of witchcraft, and not for the first time. She had been imprisoned at least three times before, found not guilty, then released. Because of her history of temporary imprisonments, every time a mysterious illness came around, fingers of accusation would point at her. John Mennin, her husband, not liking the effect on her reputation, had already thrown her out of their house. Anne had resorted to begging on the streets, which made things worse. On this occasion, it would seem that John had had enough. His housekeeper, Jane Akaman, had almost certainly taken Anne's place in his bed, and they both wanted Anne out of the way. They sent their servant girl with a bowl of oatmeal, which must have been gratefully received given prison conditions. But this gift contained arsenic. Her death throes were watched by Emma Gaskin, who was also in jail awaiting trial for witchcraft. Suspicions raised, two Newcastle barber surgeons were brought in. They opened Anne's stomach, and confirmed that arsenic was the cause of her death. Meanwhile the gaoler's wife had sifted through the remains of the meal, and also found traces of arsenic. This was one of the earliest examples of forensic science in the North East. John was tried for murder, but we do not know if he was found guilty. (Public Record Office)

JUNE 10TH

1726: On this day, two men were whipped and pilloried in Newcastle market for the attempted murder of Gateshead coal owner William Cotesworth exactly a year before. The two men were his butler and his gardener – the butler had dosed Cotesworth's morning cup of hot chocolate with a substantial quantity of arsenic, which he had talked the gardener into supplying. Arsenic was easy to get hold of from any apothecary's shop at the time, as it was the standard method of poisoning rats. It was also relatively cheap and virtually tasteless. Doctors considered Cotesworth lucky to have survived. The motive was all down to the rivalries between the coal owners of the era – Cotesworth was an energetic self-made man who had made enemies through aggressive legal suits. Sir Ralph Carr had had him beaten up and subsequently threatened over a land dispute not long before. Another man entangled in complex legal wrangles with Cotesworth was Richard Ridley – the butler's previous employer. He also supported the two men during their imprisonment. Although this involvement was never proved, the Durham judge argued that they must have been prompted into action from outside, as 'so great and so vile an attempt was not the produce of the fellows' own brains'. (Ellis, J., 'The poisoning of William Cotesworth, 1725', *History Today*, November 1978)

JUNE 11TH

1835: On this day, the construction of Richard Grainger's grand scheme for the centre of Newcastle suffered a setback. The houses lining the south side of Market Street were nearly built to their full height, when at three o'clock in the afternoon, without warning, three of them suddenly fell. Mr Grainger himself had been looking at the buildings only a few minutes before, and was actually next door when it happened. Given that over 100 men were working in, or very near to, the buildings at the time, it is surprising that only twenty-one men were trapped. Immediately, all 700 workmen in the area rushed to the scene to try to dig the survivors free. This was a difficult task – the rubble was precarious and likely to slip further on top of the trapped men or those around it. Soldiers were placed around the Nuns' Field to keep back the crowds. Work continued for almost twelve hours until all the missing men were accounted for. Two were already dead, and three more (including John Kilgour, the foreman) died either on the scene or in the Infirmary. Another thirteen had suffered serious injury. It was never established why the buildings fell, although the weather had been stormy so there were suspicions it had been struck by lightning. (Latimer, J., *Local Records*, 1853)

June 12th

1913: On this day, painter Ralph Hedley died at his home in Belle Grove Terrace, Spital Tongues. He was born in Richmond around 1850 (dates vary), but the family moved to Newcastle when he was a child. His father was a carpenter, and perhaps this is where he developed his love of woodworking – as a young man, he built up a wood carving and architectural sculpture business in New Bridge Street. By thirty-two, he employed nine men, one woman, and five boys. His carvings grace St Andrew's, St Mary's and the chancel of St Nicholas' Cathedral. He later passed the business to his sons. But Hedley had a second career, as a painter, exhibiting twenty-two times at the Royal Academy from the age of thirty until shortly before his death. He'd attended evening classes run by Pre-Raphaelite William Bell Scott, but he soon found his own realist style, depicting everyday life in Tyneside; the labourers, sailors and children at work. When he died, his obituary in the *Newcastle Daily Chronicle* stated, 'What Burns did for the peasantry of Scotland with his pen, Ralph Hedley with his brush and palette had done for the Northumberland miner and labouring man.' Among his best-known images are *Cat in a Cottage Window*, *Last in Market* (in which a tired lad and his dog sit in the back of a wagon), and *The Newsboy*. ('Ralph Hedley', *Mapping the Practice and Profession of Sculpture in Britain and Ireland 1851-1951* / sculpture.gla.ac.uk)

JUNE 13TH

1885: On this day, the Austro-Hungarian torpedo-cruiser *Panther* was launched from Armstrong Mitchell's shipyard, Elswick. In 1882, Armstrong's arms manufacturers and Mitchell's shipbuilders had merged to build – appropriately – warships. The building of the Swing Bridge had allowed large ships to be built further upriver than before, so they decided on Elswick, where munitions were already made, as a site. *Panther* was the first ship to be built there. Indeed, when they first laid down her keel in October 1884, the yard itself wasn't even finished – ship and yard grew together. *Panther* was an early example of the new torpedo cruiser class, which at the time caused consternation with their combination of speed and deadly weaponry. *Panther* managed 18 knots in speed trials. Rather than also being fitted locally, *Panther* was supplied to the Austro-Hungarian navy intact apart from the weaponry, then went to Pola on the Adriatic, where she was fitted with guns made by rivals Krupp of Essen. Although impressive at the time, *Panther* was soon eclipsed by new generations of torpedoes. She fought for Austro-Hungary during the First World War, then was handed to the British as a war reparation. Later she was sold to Italy for scrap. Armstrong Mitchell, meanwhile, went from strength to strength, taking orders from almost all the world's major navies and producing ninety armed vessels in the next thirty-three years. (Keys, R. and Smith, K., *Armstrong's River Empire*, Tynebridge Publishing, 2010)

JUNE 14TH

1954: On this day, English Heritage listing was established for hundreds of buildings and structures in and around Newcastle. These ranged from the very well known – Earl Grey's Monument, the Castle Keep, Grainger Market, the town walls – to the less well known. For instance, King John's Palace is the remains of a fortified medieval hall house, now on the edge of Heaton Park. Also known as Adam of Jesmond's Camera, it was probably connected to the Sheriff of Newcastle in the 1260s. Other interesting listed structures from this day include a single arch of the fourteenth-century medieval bridge across the Tyne (visible underneath the Newcastle side of the Swing Bridge); the remains of the twelfth-century chapel of St Mary, standing beside Jesmond Dene Road; and a sixteenth-century tower for storing munitions, which lurks next to the Holy Jesus Hospital. Many more structures have been added since – forty per cent of Graingertown's buildings are listed – and the reader interested in the hidden treasures of Newcastle would be well advised to take a look at the English Heritage register of listed buildings. (www.english-heritage.org.uk)

JUNE 15TH

1858: On this day, poet Christina Rossetti got on a train in Newcastle and headed home after visiting painter William Bell Scott and his wife. While on that train she wrote the bittersweet lament 'Written in the train from Newcastle'. It is more often called 'Parting after parting', for these lines – 'Parting after parting/ All one's life long/ It's a bitter pang, parting/ While life and love are strong.' Several of her poems of this period are tinged with frustrated passion, and some biographers argue that Scott was its object. But her reflections on time in the North East were not all melancholy – she wrote a cheerful poem about a picnic trip out towards Sunderland in which 'grimed streets were changed for meadows soon'. (Marsh, J., *Christina Rossetti*, Pimlico, 1996)

❖

2006: On this day, walkers on the Tyne were surprised by a new temporary art installation – a series of partially submerged cars in convoy between the Millennium and Tyne Bridges, gently bobbing in the water and apparently attempting to head for the sea. At night, they were lit up from within. This was Michael Pinsky's 'Come Hell or High Water', designed as a comment on congested roads and climate change. As it happened, the Tyne got the better of the art – after a few days, the river's strong currents dragged the cars fully underwater. Pinsky argued that this only underscored his point about the unstable nature of the planet, and redesigned the cars for a second, more successful launch on the 27th. (www.michaelpinsky.com)

JUNE 16TH

1911: On this day, one of Newcastle's most exotic residents died. The Andean Condor had been brought from Chile in 1886 – although nobody now seems to know how or why – and caused a great stir when it was exhibited. It remained, caged in a back room of the Hancock Museum, for over twenty-five years: a good innings for a captive condor. It was famous enough that, when it died, it was given an obituary in the local papers. Afterwards, it was stuffed and continued to attract visitors, although the fact that it had spent its life, as well as its afterlife, in the museum was almost forgotten. A recent campaign to get it a commemorative plaque failed, but did add to public knowledge. (*Newcastle Journal*)

1964: On this day, Morden Tower saw its first poetry recital. The medieval tower had housed the Company of Plumbers, Bricklayers and Glaziers for many years, and so arrived in the twentieth century in reasonably good shape. In 1964, Tom and Connie Pickard took on its lease, and began to organise a series of live poetry readings. Over the years, the tower has been host to most of the key figures in modern British and American poetry (including Beat poetry), as well as nurturing new talent. The intimate space is considered exceptional for poetry readings. (www.mordentower.org)

JUNE 17TH

1817: On this day, civil engineer John Rennie presented the Corporation with his proposals for improvement of the River Tyne. This was sorely needed. Despite the high flow of river traffic and Newcastle's position as one of the premier ports of the country, conditions for navigation were gradually getting worse. In theory, this was the responsibility of the Corporation, but – much to the dismay of the Shields ship owners and others – they seemed content to at best maintain a status quo. In 1774, Parliamentary candidate Captain Phipps said that ignorance and avarice had turned a fine river into a 'cursed horsepond'. Eventually, Rennie was appointed to carry out a survey and suggest a course of action. The Corporation were probably relieved that the process took him several years, but may well have been unhappy with the final cost of his recommendations. Ranging from new jetties on Newcastle Quay to widening some sections of the river, the improvements would cost over £500,000 (about £15 million today). The Corporation was content to discuss the suggestions, but cared only that ships could get to and from Newcastle itself. A River Jury, appointed to investigate nuisances to river traffic, was described by Eneas MacKenzie as 'a standing jest' composed of company men and incompetents. Indeed, anyone appointed to look into developments was never given enough money to do anything effective. It took until the formation of the Tyne Improvement Commission in the 1850s for the tide to turn. (Archer, D., *Tyne and Tide*, Smith Settle, 2003 / Mackenzie, E., *A Descriptive and Historical Account of the Town and County of Newcastle upon Tyne: Including the Borough of Gateshead*, 1827)

JUNE 18TH

1856: On this day, Seghill Colliery saw an unusual visitor: Napoleon III, the nephew of Napoleon Bonaparte. At this point Britain and France were allies against Russia in the Crimea. Prince Napoleon came to Tynemouth in the early hours and visited the Priory, then took a train into Newcastle for breakfast at the Queen's Head Inn. It is unclear why he decided to follow this with a visit to a pit on the Newcastle/Northumberland border, but Seghill's employees were quite happy to demonstrate mining procedure. As seems to be traditional for visitors to the coalface, Napoleon took a pick and had a go at hewing the coal for himself. Apparently, after a few minutes he looked at his blistered hands and said that he 'could not work like that for six shillings a day if he were starving'. It's worth saying that a significant proportion of locals would have happily seen him starving, as the more politically radical saw him as a despot and oppressor. The *Newcastle Daily Chronicle*'s political stance was so strongly against him that in 1862 the paper was banned in France. Prince Napoleon then went back to Tynemouth via Hartley and Seaton Delaval, before sailing off to Scotland to the sound of a Royal Salute from Tynemouth Castle. (www.dmm.org.uk)

JUNE 19TH

1838: On this day, the first train from Carlisle finally made it to Newcastle. The planned opening of the Newcastle to Carlisle route featured processional trains running from Newcastle to Carlisle and back on the 18th, but things went wrong from the start. A gangway collapsed as passengers were alighting a steamer to attend the opening ceremony, dumping a dozen of them into the river. VIPs found that their carriages were occupied by other people, leaving them to seek space elsewhere – the 'Chief Magistrate obliged to look for refuge in a pig cart'. The first train – which had a steam organ fitted to its front – did not set off until 12.30 p.m. and was slowed by heavy rain. Then the occasion descended into farce. By the time the trains arrived in Carlisle, there was no time for the planned ceremony or parade, just a rush for refreshments and then a squash back on board. As events turned out, there was more time than first thought – while passengers shivered in light, summer clothing, it took three hours to get the engines turned! On the way back, two of the trains collided, causing further delays and injuries. The trains stopped to allow some gentlemen to seek relief in the bushes, but then the whistle blew, making them come running back! Many hours late, the first train did not get in to Newcastle until 3 p.m. and the last until 6 a.m.! (Guy, A., *Steam and Speed*, Tynebridge Publishing, 2003)

JUNE 20TH

1511: On this day, the Office of Chamberlains – the finance department of Newcastle Corporation, which among other things worked out tolls for import and export – recorded the following ships and cargoes docking at the Quayside. The early Office of Chamberlains records only survive for a few years but tell us a lot about the sort of business that went on at the Quayside. Coal was by far the biggest export, most ships leaving with little or nothing else. The imports were a much more varied lot – many different foodstuffs, but also timber goods and other building materials. The *Lennert*, from King's Lynn, brought in 9 tons of ballast, and left with 12 chaldrons of coal. The *Kattrin*, of 'Sellikse', brought in 3 barrals of soap, salt, pike, 8 hundredweight of madder, wine (and 'terr' and 'lynttis'), and took 80 chaldrons of coal, and a wainload of lead. The *James*, of Antwerp, brought in 10 tons of ballast, along with 5 half-barrels of soap, 8 hundredweight of hops, ash wood, and 200 earthenware pots, and also left with coal and lead. And the *Jesus*, also of Antwerp, brought nothing in, but left with coal and 5 chaldrons of grindstones. (Fraser, C. (ed.), *Newcastle Chamberlain's Accounts 1508-1511*, Society of Antiquaries of London, 1986)

JUNE 21ST

1676: On this day, the Corporation accepted the petition of one John Stobbs and granted him the Freedom of the Town. According to John Brand's *The History and Antiquities of the Town and County of the Town of Newcastle upon Tyne*, he was represented as 'particularly skilful in the making and tempering of steel – making water-engines against the accidents of fire and the like – making wind-guns, speaking trumpets, glazier's vices, and several mathematical instruments.' It is a shame that nothing survives of any of this, as Stobbs was clearly an exceptional man: in particular, the ability to design 'water-engines' would have made a difference in a town full of wooden houses facing very narrow passageways. (Brand, J., *The History and Antiquities of the Town and County of the Town of Newcastle upon Tyne*, White & Son, 1789)

———— • ◆ • ————

1836: Also on this day, an Act was passed to allow the construction of a 7-mile stretch of railway line between Newcastle and North Shields, including the building of viaducts over the Ouseburn valley and Willington Dene beyond Wallsend. In the 1840s, trains went on the hour from Carliol Square, and on the half hour back from North Shields. It cost 9d to travel first class and 6d in second class, with fares for doing part of the journey set at 6d and 4d. The line was extended to Tynemouth in 1882 and a hundred years later converted into a major part of the Metro system. (www.lner.info)

JUNE 22ND

1492: On this day, the 'Guild of the Blessed Trinity of Newcastle upon Tyne' came into being. Originally a charitable guild, which aimed to support the growing maritime community, it grew into much more than this. On June 22nd, they signed a lease for land on the Quayside, for a 'peppercorn' (nominal) rent. In this case it could be called a 'rose' rent, as every midsummer's day they had to – if asked – give one red rose to the landowner, Ralph Hebburn. On this day, they also began making plans for the building of a hall, chapel and lodgings on the site, and appointed a priest to sing Mass. The new building would take in poor mariners and their relatives. They would have to pray for the souls of the Hebburn family and also the brethren of the guild, past and present. In 1524, Ralph Hebburn's son followed in his father's footsteps, giving the land next door in exchange for a half gallon of wine per year. Gradually the brethren became known as the go-to experts in navigating the Tyne's sand banks. In 1536, the charity became a 'company', by Royal Charter, with the right to levy dues on ships trading in the Tyne. In exchange they had to build two fortified towers, as lighthouses, at North Shields – the original High and Low Lights. (www.trinityhouse.co.uk)

JUNE 23RD

1635: On this day, Sir William Brereton visited Newcastle as part of a tour of the north of England and Scotland. His diary tells us something about what the town was like at the time. 'This is beyond all compare the fairest and richest towne in England, inferiour for wealth and building to noe cittie save London and Bristow. This towne of Newcastle is governed by a maieor, a recorder, a sheriffe, and 12 aldermen: Itt hath great revenewes belonging unto itt (as I was informed) att least 5,000/. or 6,000/. per annum. [...] There is every day a markett here kept; and in a daintie markett place. Tuesday and Saturday a mightye markett and much provision comes out of Northumberlands infinite store of poultrye. This towne placed upon the highest and the steepest hills, that I have found in any great towne. These soe steepe as horses cannott stand upon the pavements : therefore the daintiest flagged channells are in every streete that I have seen : hereupon may horse or man goe without danger of slideing. Here att New-castle is the fairest key in England I have mett withall, from Tine-bridge all along towne-wall and allmost to the glass-workes where is made window glass. This towne is allsoe famous for the walls which compass round the towne, about which you may walke : and which is strengthened with strong towres placed upon the wall noe great distance.' [*sic*] (Brereton, W., 'The Journal of Sir William Brereton', *Surtees Society*, 1914)

JUNE 24TH

1776: On this day, the Newcastle Assembly Rooms opened with a flourish. Their aim, as carved into the foundation stone, was to provide a space 'dedicated to the most elegant recreation'. They did it in style, hosting the balls and soirées of the great and good of the North East. In size it was thought to be second only to the House of Assembly in Bath, with a huge ballroom, a dining room for nearly 500 people, card rooms, and a library and newsroom. Its elegant neo-classical design was thought a triumph of William Newton, though some did regret the lack of a portico under which guests could alight from their carriages in the dry. (Mackenzie, E., *A Descriptive and Historical Account of the Town and County of Newcastle upon Tyne: Including the Borough of Gateshead*, 1827)

* ◆ *

1839: On this day, Newcastle gained another 'civilising' influence in the form of public baths. Designed by John Dobson with an elegant portico and still standing today, for a small fee the inhabitants of Newcastle could enjoy hot water all year round as well as warm shower and vapour rooms. However, the fee was still too much for some, and the site – Saville Row – too far from the crowds of Sandgate. Six years later a report suggested building a second facility, with at least tepid water available all year, for the poor – not only to get them clean, but also to help keep them off the streets. This was opened on New Road in 1848. (Latimer, J., *Local Records*, 1853)

JUNE 25TH

1876: On this day, the Swing Bridge was opened to traffic. Its unusual swing design was intended to allow large ships to reach the Armstrong works in Elswick. Its first opening was for the Italian ship the *Europa* three weeks later, there to pick up a 100-ton Armstrong gun (at the time the largest piece of ordnance ever made). Government permission for a bridge had been granted in 1861, but other plans were suggested. Some wanted another higher level bridge; others favoured one with a single section that tilted up. Alternatives included a new ferry network and plans were even drawn up for a tunnel. The first planned swing bridge was eventually discarded when someone realised it would, at the extreme of its turn, hit the High Level Bridge! Eventually the current design was settled on. When the previous bridge was being dismantled, it was found that on one pier the foundations of all three previous bridges – Roman, medieval and Georgian – could be seen on the same site. Apparently the Roman carpentry was the best! The machinery was made at Armstrong's, and although it needed forty-five minutes notice to get up to steam, it took only ninety seconds to rotate through 90 degrees. It allows room for ships 31.7 metres wide, which at the time made it the largest swing bridge ever built. Though it is now powered by electricity rather than steam, much of its machinery is original. (Manders, F. and Potts, R., *Crossing the Tyne*, Tynebridge Publishing, 2001)

JUNE 26TH

1740: On this day, the keelmen and labourers of the town systematically wrecked everything they could in the town's Guildhall. After a hard winter and poor weather patterns for sea trade, the cost of grain had doubled in six months. But merchants were tantalisingly taking grain up through starving Newcastle towards the more lucrative Scottish market. All across the North East disturbances were breaking out. A week earlier, a gathering was begun by pitmen demonstrating with horn, drum and flag on Sandhill. This semi-formalised demonstration achieved its aim – a promise of lower grain prices at the next market. But there still wasn't enough to go around. On the 26th, the keelmen stopped all river traffic and around 3,000 men gathered. Inevitably, as the Corporation men made their way through the crowd, a fight broke out; panicked, a soldier fired into the crowd and killed a man. Then all hell let loose as the crowd rampaged across Sandhill, broke into the Council Chambers, destroyed papers and stole hard cash. Interestingly, there was little violence against people – any seized guns were thrown into the river, not turned against the magistrates. After eight hours of chaos, it took the footsore arrival of three companies of troops to bring calm. While many were prosecuted, the penalties were more lenient than you might think, the harshest being transportation. (Ellis, J., 'Urban Conflict and Popular Violence in the Guildhall Riots of 1740', *International Review of Social History*, 1980)

JUNE 27TH

1866: On this day, the annual race meet on the Town Moor descended into riot as Irishmen clashed with locals. The Fenian movement – agitating for British forces to withdraw from Ireland – was gathering speed, and at the same time increasing numbers of Irishmen were coming to the North East looking for work. In the afternoon there had been some trouble from Irishmen running around with shillelaghs, shouting out, 'May the Pope get to heaven'. Some were likely Fenians, others militant Roman Catholics, or perhaps both. And then, just after the last race of the day, as people began to head home, around 300 Irishmen made a rush through the crowd. It is unclear how exactly this turned into a fight, but the Irish, it was reported, had turned on the crowd and attacked anyone to hand with theirs sticks, sending many – including several policemen – to hospital. When a larger police force arrived the Irish scattered, but eighteen were arrested over the course of the evening. Eleven men were tried, and ten sentenced to twelve months' hard labour. It should be noted, though, that this was an exceptional event, and most local Irishmen were peaceful enough. (Baron, F., *The Town Moor Hoppings*, Lovell Baines, 1984)

JUNE 28TH

1882: On this day, at 2 p.m., the first Newcastle Temperance Festival was opened, with speeches given by various dignitaries from a stand on the Town Moor. Supporters of the event included the YMCA and the Gospel Society. No alcohol was available for sale, and there was a competition for best anti-alcohol speech. There were sporting contests in cycling, football and cricket, a brass band competition, military displays and an array of sideshows, including 'high flyers and galvanic batteries' (but no gambling!). One thousand poor children were given a free tea. Unfortunately, low wind kept the kite-flying contest from getting off the ground. The 150,000 or so attendees made it the biggest English Temperance festival to date, and inspired the organisers to greater things ... though they might turn in their graves to see The Hoppings – the direct descendant of the festival – today! (Baron, F., *The Town Moor Hoppings*, Lovell Baines, 1984)

———— • ◆ • ————

1981: On this day, the Great North Run was held for the first time. It was devised by Brendan Foster and initially advertised as a small local event. Still, 12,000 runners turned up to complete the half-marathon course. This first race was won in 1:03:23 by Mike MacLeod, who went on to win an Olympic silver medal for Britain in the 10,000-metre race in 1984. Today, the Great North Run is the largest athletic event in the country and one of the largest in the world, with over 50,000 entrants. (www.greatrun.org)

JUNE 29TH

1859: On this day, prizes were handed out at the world's first dog show. This two-day event was held in Newcastle Corn Exchange and was organised by Messrs Shorthouse and Pape. Pape was a gun-maker and enthusiast of gun dogs, breeding world-famous black pointers in centrally heated stone kennels near his home in Amble. The event attracted fifty-nine male dogs and comprised two classes – one for pointers and one for setters. The show was judged by the editor of *The Field* magazine, and the prizes were guns, made by Pape and valued at 15 guineas each. The two winners were Mr Murrel's 'Spot', and Mr Brown's 'Venus' (this was, of course, before the idea of the registration of unique competition names – the Kennel Club came up with this idea in the 1870s, when they tried to make sense of the winners of the previous fifteen years). The intention had been to hold another contest the following year, but there were complaints that the first one had made a mess of the floor and had made the venue smell bad, although supporters argued that the smell was from the floor cleaner, not the dogs! (Prahms, W., *Animals in Newcastle*, The History Press, 2008 / www.thekennelclub.org.uk)

JUNE 30TH

1882: On this day, Newcastle was made a city. Many people think that this was the first time that Newcastle parted from the diocese of Durham, but that's not entirely true. In 1553, the Duke of Northumberland, a powerful man, was pushing hard for the dissolution of the Diocese of Durham, largely because he disagreed with the relatively conservative Bishop Cuthbert Tunstall. An Act of Parliament in 1553 dissolved the old Diocese. Rather than dividing it into two, as the Duke wanted, it allowed for new bishoprics to be created by Letters Patent. Plans were going forward to do this – including a scheme sponsored by the burgesses of Newcastle – but they were never completed. In July, Mary I took the throne, and by spring 1554, Durham Diocese was back in business. For over a year, the area had had no bishopric at all! After this, Newcastle remained part of Durham Diocese until 1882. As the Victorian city swelled, this became inadequate, and a new diocese was created, with a new bishop – Ernest Wilberforce. St Nicholas' Church was reborn as a cathedral. In the next few years it was given a facelift to match, with new wood and stone features and stained-glass windows. (Pollard, A. and Newton, D., *Newcastle and Gateshead Before 1700*, Phillimore & Co., 2009 / www.stnicholascathedral.co.uk)

JULY 1ST

1941: On this day, diarist 5165 in the Mass Observation project (which encouraged thousands of people to keep a diary for posterity) had a half day. In theory he should have been able to leave at one o'clock, but he was kept busy until three o'clock by the need to deal with 'secret ammunition returns' that his boss, an army quartermaster, had forgotten about. He wrote: 'Newcastle was terribly crowded. People seemed to fill the shops to capacity and more. Fenwick's was like a funfair, and crowds of women did their best not to trample on the show dresses spread all over the floors. The stuff in the shops was rather poor. In Fenwick's the prices struck us as very high ...' He went to the French Café for tea, but 'the lettuce was so tough that it tasted more like cabbage, and the cucumber seemed to have been cut at least a week before. No tomato sandwiches, no eggs. There was nothing either fresh or appetising ... The teapot was half filled, and when we added the hot water what came out wasn't drinkable. In the streets we saw hundreds of people of all kinds, coming from work. Most of them looked overcome by the heat. The papers carried headings about Russia inflicting heavy casualties on the enemy, and they were selling quickly. I bought one, and found very little in it ...' (Mass Observation Archive)

JULY 2ND

1902: On this day, Newcastle gained its own Wimbledon Champion – in rather odd circumstances. Muriel Robb was born in Jesmond in 1878 and began playing tennis as a child, before developing her talent at Cheltenham Ladies' College. She was also a member of the Jesmond Lawn Tennis Club. Aged twenty, Robb competed in the English National Championships at Wimbledon, losing in the quarterfinals. Over the next two years she won the Irish, Scottish and Welsh Championships, but Wimbledon eluded her until 1902. That year, Robb played brilliantly through the tournament and played Charlotte Sterry, the defending champion, in a rain-soaked final on July 1st. Robb lost the first set 4-6 before taking the second at 13-11 (the longest set in the ladies' final until 1970). At this point rain stopped the match. For some reason the committee decided that the next day, rather than starting from the last point, both players should start afresh! This was a unique decision, and has never been explained. So it was that on July 2nd, Robb and Sterry replayed the final, with blank scorecards. Robb won comfortably, 7-5, 6-1. At fifty-three games in total over the two days, this was the longest women's Wimbledon final ever. Sadly, after her Wimbledon victory, Robb only played one more tournament before retiring with ill heath, aged just twenty-four. She returned home to Jesmond, and died two years later of unknown causes, still the youngest Wimbledon singles winner to die. (*Wimbledon Archive* / www.clcguild.org)

JULY 3RD

1827: On this day, trainee doctor Thomas Wright enjoyed a day at the races. Every July since 1751, a week of races had been held on the Town Moor, for which a grandstand had been built in 1800. Thomas Giordani Wright's diary offers an insight into the thrills and spills of Georgian horseracing, which provided 'a little gaiety in the town'. The previous day had seen 'the Tyro Stakes', which a son of the renowned Dr Syntax won. The last race, the 'Gosforth stakes', was a neck-and-neck matter from the distancing post – only two horses ran. Today, Wright began to bet, with mixed fortunes! He reveals that 'Mr Powlett's Gazebo (a horse I bet upon by chance for the Plate) won the Kings £100, which is a four mile job and with very heavy weights.' He bet all profits from this day on the next day, and did well (though in one 'race' only one horse took part!) On the last day, he did the same and, inevitably, lost – 'with all my winnings, however, I am not a farthing the richer'. (Johnson, A. (ed.), *The Diary of Thomas Giordani Wright*, Surtees Society, 2001)

———◆———

1953: Also on this day, the *Chronicle* reported on a council enquiry into women's public toilets. Amazingly, there were only sixteen in the city. The cost of 'spending a penny' was, naturally, one penny! Plans were drawn up to make them free – at a loss of income to the council of £5,500 per annum – and to build new ones at ten sites, including Haymarket, Marlborough Crescent, and Cross Street. (*Newcastle Chronicle*)

JULY 4TH

1838: On this day, an agreement was reached for the building of Newcastle's first synagogue, in Temple Street. In October 1830, seven Jewish residents started paying regular money into a fund towards buying a cemetery plot and a surrounding wall – this is the first really clear documentary evidence that survives for Jews in Newcastle. On September 8th 1831, we hear of a service being held in someone's house for the Jewish New Year, conducted by Martin Valintine of Poland. By October 1832, a congregation was formally established and seven Jews (at least two from the earlier group) agreed to meet its expenses. The group rented a room, initially in Pilgrim Street, though it moved around a lot – sometimes even being held in pubs. Every member agreed to attend all Sabbaths and festivals, or be fined a shilling. It was another six years before they were able to borrow enough money to begin establishing a purpose-built synagogue. Costing £360, it was a 60-foot-square building in stone, with a polished ashlar front. It was sited near the cemetery, with a narrow railed walkway between the two. The community enjoyed support from its non-Jewish neighbours – when the foundation stone was laid on July 11th, the Cathedral bells rang in celebration. On the 13th, the *Newcastle Courant* even published a headline in Hebrew. (Olsover, L., *The Jewish Community of North East England*, Ashley Mark Publishing Co., 1980)

JULY 5TH

2007: On this day, the Byker Wall estate was granted grade II* listed status by English Heritage. It is unusual for modern buildings to be listed – but then, Byker Wall is itself unusual. In the 1960s, several rows of terraced houses were demolished and award-winning architect Ralph Erskine hired to design a new estate. His intention was to maintain a sense of community cohesion in the area (in contrast to some other developments of the time), and he frequently consulted locals about what they wanted. The distinctive 'wall' itself is half a mile long, multi-coloured, and contains 620 flats. It rises to between eight and twelve storeys tall but remains only one flat wide throughout. Behind the wall, Erskine designed pubs, churches, green space, swimming baths (now converted into a climbing wall) and enough lower-rise buildings for 9,000 residents. Often considered Erskine's finest work, the estate won several prestigious awards for its innovative approaches to social housing. Inevitably, Byker Wall still saw problems with anti-social behaviour, leading to the installation of an extensive CCTV system. The listing status might be viewed as a statement of faith in the estate's future and its architectural merit, but was controversial, and took several years to secure. (*Daily Telegraph*)

JULY 6TH

1912: On this day, the various suffrage groups of the region – the Women's Social and Political Union, North Eastern Federation, and Church League for Women's Suffrage – put aside their differences and staged a great procession, themed 'great women of history'. The magazine *Votes for Women* described it like this: 'Nuns, prisoners, nurses, wounded soldiers, Greek maidens, at first sight forming up seems like the prince's task in the old fairy tale … Joan of Arc leads the way, her graceful bearing and soldier-like control of her splendid white charger giving the keynote of the pageant. The Prisoner's Car preceded by "modern crusaders" with broad arrows is placed between the Warrior Maid and Boadicea … Abbess Hilda and her group of nuns followed by Nightingale with her nurses show how great is woman's power to help and comfort, while the huge Greek Car with its living statues typifies the beauty women have given to the world of art. Grace Darling heads the representation of the famous rescue of the sinking ship. Then comes a long procession of women "in plain clothes".' No wonder the crowds gathered to watch! Later, around 6,000 people listened to the speeches on the Town Moor. (Neville, D., *To Make their Mark*, Centre for Northern Studies, 1997)

JULY 7TH

1752: On this day, the first ship of the fleet of Newcastle Whale Fishing Company returned home triumphantly for the first time. Things were set in motion the previous November when Newcastle newspapers ran adverts calling for subscriptions to the company's foundation. Evidently this was thought to be a good plan by Newcastle's leaders. Subscribers included the town's MP, Sir Walter Blackett, the Mayor and most of the Aldermen. In December, the newly-formed company bought a second-hand whaling ship, *The Swallow*, for around £2,000.

The Swallow headed out to Greenland in March and returned on this day, having caught four whales – a great first catch! Apparently, the church bells were rung in celebration. This inspired the company to buy another ship that winter, while a rival Newcastle-based operation bought a third. Within a few years, five ships were sailing from the Tyne, continuing to operate throughout the 1760s. The ships were fortified, but not specially built, so there were limits to what they could cope with. On July 18th 1752, Ralph Jackson records in his diary 'the unwelcome news of Richard Liddell having lost his ship at Greenland with Three large Whales'. Presumably this sad news had come back with *The Swallow*. *The Swallow* herself eventually ran out of luck, lost in the ice in June 1766. (Barrow, T., 'The Newcastle Whaling Trade 1752-1849', *The Mariners' Mirror*, 1989 / Thornton, C. (ed.), *Bound for the Tyne*, The Company of Hostmen, 2000)

JULY 8TH

1568: On this day, John Bennet, the Master of Ordnance for Newcastle, died. He'd had something of a chequered career. Four years earlier, the Scottish authorities had questioned Thomas Peeble, who not only confessed to 'coining' (making fake coins) but also implicated John Bennet and Hugh Partridge for coining at the Great Inn, Pilgrim Street. Bennet claimed that his friend Partridge had found a way to make Scottish coins, but Bennet himself had refused to get involved, and had persuaded Partridge to stop. When a goldsmith confessed to helping Partridge make the moulds, Partridge's fate was sealed. Bennet managed to get a reference from an old patron, Lord Cecil, the Earl of Bedford, and was let off. But he soon found himself in trouble once more. John Fleming, Master Gunner of Berwick, wrote to tell Lord Cecil that Bennet wasn't looking after the gunpowder – or the funds he was in charge of – properly. Soon afterwards, Queen Elizabeth sacked him. When he died it seems that the inventory of the stores had discrepancies. It was claimed by the new Governor of Berwick that he 'sold ordnance, shot, powder, and all manner of things under his charge that any man would give him money for: and the queen must be contented with the loss, for he had died not worth a groat.' (Welford, R., *History of Newcastle and Gateshead*, 1836)

JULY 9TH

1791: On this day, anyone passing through Hanover Square in Newcastle would have witnessed a very strange scene. This was a performance put on by the celebrated quack doctor James Graham. Already barred from talking about his 'Celestial Bed' in the town, Graham developed a whole new pitch. His 'Earth Baths' (alongside his 'Elixir of Immortality') would, he claimed, cure disease, extend life, and do away with the need for food. After sceptical responses in Edinburgh and London, Graham announced in the Newcastle papers that he and 'a young woman will give one more earth-bath exhibition this day, Saturday July 9th, most positively for the last time from 12 noon to 6 o'clock in the evening in the large and commodious field at the side of Hanover Square, Newcastle in order emphatically to recommend this most natural, most safe and most radically efficacious practice to the world'. 'For the last time' was a lie he used wherever he went – indeed, he performed again a week later. His performance was remembered like this: 'The Doctor and his fair partner accordingly stripped into their first suits about 12 noon and were each interred up to the chin, their heads beautifully dressed and powdered, appearing not unlike two fine, full-grown cauliflowers. These human plants remained in this whimsical situation six hours.' One can only imagine what the crowd made of that ... (Boyes, J., 'Medicine and Dentistry in the Eighteenth Century', *Northumbrian Medicine*, Pybus Society, 1993)

JULY 10TH

1906: On this day, Newcastle was visited by King Edward VII and Queen Alexandra. Despite heavy rain threatening to ruin the occasion, the streets were decorated with bunting. Many firms declared a holiday, allowing thousands of locals into the city centre to watch the Royal procession. The itinerary involved the opening of the Armstrong College Building (later Newcastle University), the Royal Victory Infirmary (designed to cater for the poor), and the King Edward VII rail bridge across the Tyne. The bridge was financed by the North East Railway, desperate to increase their capacity across the Tyne. Building techniques were interesting. They included sending the youngest and fittest men to construct the underground pier supports, working in shifts of no more than four hours in spaces filled with compressed air. This was such taxing work that one man died from the effects. Carrying 23,000 tons of materials across the Tyne was the world's largest transport cableway, which was later used in the launch of the *Mauritania*. When Edward VII visited, his namesake bridge was not quite complete and didn't actually open for traffic until October 1st. (Manders, F. and Potts, R., *Crossing the Tyne*, Tynebridge Publishing, 2001)

JULY 11TH

1903: On this day, William Fischer was born in Benwell. He is now better known now as Russian spy Rudolf Abel. William's father, Genrich, was a Russian who had moved to England in 1901. An associate of Lenin, he spent the next twenty years encouraging the growth of communism in the Tyneside workforce. He became secretary of the Newcastle 'communist cell' whilst also smuggling weapons back home. Throughout this time, he was also bringing up his son in his own political mould. William got British citizenship when he was sixteen, which undoubtedly proved useful to him later. After the family moved away in 1921, William doesn't seem to have given his childhood home in Newcastle much further thought. Joining the Soviet Intelligence, he worked – firstly in Europe and then in America – under assumed names. In 1957, during the Cold War, he was captured by the FBI and jailed for espionage. He is best known to us now as the man America 'gave back' in 1962; he was exchanged for Tim Powers, a pilot whose U2 reconnaissance plane had been forced down in Soviet territory. (Arthey, V., *The Kremlin's Geordie Spy*, Dialogue, 2010)

JULY 12TH

1766: On this day, a party was held near Denton Colliery to celebrate reaching the coalface. This was not an unusual way to celebrate (*see* February 6th) and this one didn't have the novelty of being underground, but it did involve staggering quantities of food! The *Newcastle Journal* records: 'All the workmen with their wives, walked in procession … to a field east of the house, where several long tables were placed sufficient to contain all the company, consisting of 377 men and women, the tenants and workmen upon the estate. These tables were each furnished with a large piece of beef, mutton, or veal, to which were added twice as many fruit puddings, the size of which may be guessed at by the quantity of flour used for them and the pies, which was less than two sacks; the rest of the dinner consisted of two sheep of 144lbs each, and several hundredweight of beef. One of the sheep was roasted whole, and the other, with the beef, boiled in a large brewing vessel. Abundance of ale, strong beer, and punch was consumed. Dinner being ended, the company again returned to the great court, and being drawn up in a circle, with Mr Montagu and his lady in the centre, they toasted the royal family, the donors, the coal trade, etc., accompanied with loud huzzas, after which they concluded the evening with country dances and other diversions'. (*Newcastle Journal*)

JULY 13TH

1931: On this day, the last horse bus crossed the River Tyne. For almost fifty years, Howe and Co.'s horse bus had taken passengers across the High Level Bridge. At its height, eight horse buses worked the route. The horse bus only cost a ha'penny whereas the toll for the bus was 4*d*. Horse buses were in competition with trams from 1923, but the real crunch came when the Tyne Bridge was built, providing a more convenient route across the river for many. The final run, Newcastle to Gateshead at 10 a.m., was staffed by the longest-serving driver, Joseph McNally, and the newest recruit, conductor John Hedley. Twenty-six passengers were crowded in on the narrow seats and steep steps. McNally, who started in 1906, told the press: 'I can remember the time when things were better for us – when the crowds had to be held back by a policeman on a Saturday night. There were no trams on the route then and we did a flourishing trade. It's very sad to think of it finishing'. In fact, this was the end of an era. The horse bus had disappeared from London before the First World War, superseded by trams and trains with their cheap return fares for workmen. It declined throughout the 1920s and Howe and Co.'s High Level Bridge run was probably the last urban horse bus service in the country. The papers mourned its loss, blaming 'the modern mania for speed'. (*Gateshead Post* / www.petergould.co.uk)

July 14th

1977: On this day, Muhammed Ali – at that time the heavyweight world boxing champion and probably the world's most famous black man – took part in an exhibition match in Newcastle. Ali stayed in Tyneside, with his wife and daughter, for several days. He visited a mosque in Elswick, a Boys' Club and a special needs school, as well as getting his marriage blessed in a mosque attached to the Yemeni community of South Shields. During a television interview, he was asked about the reception he received in Newcastle. He replied that, although as a black man he was used to similar receptions in Africa, 'this was the first time in a European country I have had so much fanfare, people admiring me and coming out to meet me. This is the first time. I never saw so many people lining the streets, I mean old people, people that couldn't walk good, people that couldn't even see …' He then impersonated an old lady enthusiastically waving her cane at seeing him. Amazingly, given the size and excitement of the crowds during Ali's reception, he was actually in town at the same time as the Queen! The following day, Ali visited a Civic Centre dinner organised by the Friendship Force, a British/American organisation. Here he read a self-penned poem about friendship – even though he had only been invited on the off-chance a few days before. (Muhammad Ali interviewed by Reg Gutterage, www.youtube.com / www.hytah.com)

JULY 15TH

1854: On this day, a Commission reported 'the causes which have led to, or have aggravated, the late outbreak of Cholera in the towns of Newcastle-upon-Tyne, Gateshead and Tynemouth.' Over the course of nine weeks in 1853, 1,500 people had died of cholera in Newcastle. The report suggests that the effects of the 1853 cholera outbreak could easily have been reduced compared to previous occasions: the natural 'amphitheatre' shape of the town facilitated potentially good drainage and sanitation and the inhabitants were, generally, less impoverished than before. Instead, this was the town's worst outbreak. The Commission argued that Newcastle's Corporation could – and should – have done more. They had ignored public health regulations and the advice of the Newcastle and Gateshead Sanitary Association. Indeed, in 1851 they had put through a private bill which allowed them to ignore the Public Health Act. The worst-hit areas were the confined courts near the river, where sewerage was minimal and cramped houses between narrow chares had no real ventilation. Forty per cent of families lived in a single or shared room in a tenement. Many had no access to privies, instead using a pot they emptied into a scavenger's cart or the street. Other problems highlighted included the building of privies up against houses, thus allowing filth to seep through the walls. Notably, the military barracks (having its own sanitation facilities) had not been affected, unlike Spital Tongues just down the road. (Cholera Inquiry Commission Report, 1854)

JULY 16TH

2008: On this day, work was completed on an eighth bridge over the Tyne. This was not a permanent structure, but a short-term art installation made from bamboo, completely by hand. Australian company Bambuco spent just over three weeks building a structure over 100 metres long, 25 metres above the river, using over 20 tonnes of Chinese bamboo. It was constructed in between the Millennium Bridge and the Tyne Bridge, as part of the 2008 summer Tyne festival. This was a suspension bridge, with two towers, and ropes and bamboo struts suspended between them – rather like the archetypical jungle ravine crossing. It worked perfectly even though Bambuco had never built a bridge before! The opening ceremony was specially lit with hundreds of fire pots. Specialist musicians were brought in to play a range of instruments from around the world, all beautifully made from bamboo. Although it was only open for a few days – and no one was allowed to cross it – the bridge was claimed to be the largest bamboo bridge in the world. (*Sunday Sun*)

JULY 17TH

1784: On this day, the Newcastle magistrates met as the Quarter Sessions to hear serious, non-felonious, criminal charges. What they heard are good examples of the sorts of crimes that were more or less commonplace in Georgian Newcastle. Firstly, there was joiner Thomas White, convicted of petty larceny – the theft of goods worth less than a shilling. He was assigned hard labour in the House of Correction for one month, before being given a vagrant's pass and told to return to the place of his birth. A vagrant's pass gave any convicted person immunity from being arrested for vagrancy, provided that he was in the process of being passed back towards the parish that would have to support him if he could not support himself. In another case, a miller and a woman from South Shields were convicted of obtaining money by false pretences, fined, and imprisoned for three months each. Dorothy March was convicted of barratry and scolding – public quarrelling, arguing and causing trouble within a community. She was sent to the House of Correction until she could find someone who would pay sureties for her 'peaceable and good behaviour' over the next twelve months – perhaps a difficult task! (*Newcastle Courant*)

JULY 18TH

1735: On this day, turnkey Thomas Tate demonstrated just why you shouldn't lock a gaoler in his own gaol. He'd first been arrested on June 8th, for stealing cloth from a Newcastle shop. By July 15th, he'd figured out how to escape. With the help of some people who hid in the 'toll shop' adjoining Newgate Gaol, he and another man escaped through a hole in the wall, into the toll shop. Here his chains were broken off – his manacles were later found in a field. From there, they forced the bars of a cellar window into Tate's own house, picked the lock, and made their way to his bedroom, taking out a clothes chest. Back in the cellar, they changed clothes, and escaped back out of the window. The two men were recaptured on the 18th, near Bellingham, having gone to Tate's sweetheart's father's house. That evening they were back in the care of Newgate Gaol. Chained down, Tate taunted that the chains were pointless – and with the gaoler and two magistrates watching, proceeded to break free in fifteen minutes. After that, he was guarded. At the August assizes, Tate was sentenced to be transported for seven years. (Sykes, J., *Local Records*, Volume I, 1833)

JULY 19TH

1821: On this day, Newcastle celebrated the coronation of George IV. Thousands of people from outlying villages came into town to experience the gun salutes, flags, and bell peals and to watch a boat race from Walker Quay to Tyne Bridge. But all did not go smoothly. George IV, with his extravagant habits and estranged wife, was not generally liked, and the crowd was in a riotous mood. For many, the real highlight of the celebrations was a 12-foot-high pant (drinking fountain), newly erected in the centre of Sandhill and yielding, not water, but free wine. Predictably, this became too popular and pandemonium ensued. People rushed to fill whatever they could – even hats! One man seemingly climbed the pant while others grabbed at him and removed his clothes. Others gathered on the balconies and roofs of houses to watch the chaos. Meanwhile, an ox had been roasted at the bottom of the Flesh Market, largely for the gentry and Corporation, with only a few pieces thrown into the crowd from a stage. The crowd didn't appreciate this and stole the beast and dragged it to Sandhill. Even a passing mail coach was attacked. Eventually the people spread out in part to watch a footrace on the Town Moor, but crowds continued to hang around drinking and taking apart the temporary structures of the celebrations. The whole thing inspired artist Henry Parker to paint 'The Sandhill Wine Pant', as well as the writing of several local comic songs. (Mackenzie, E., *A Descriptive and Historical Account of the Town and County of Newcastle upon Tyne: Including the Borough of Gateshead*, 1827)

JULY 20TH

1832: On this day, 'Blind Willie', a well-known character and musician of Tyneside, died in All Saints' Poorhouse. Blind Willie was born William Purvis, son of a Newcastle waterman (not to be confused with Billy Purvis, a generation younger and a travelling piper). Blind from birth, Purvis apparently very quickly realised that music was the way to make a living. He tended not to play in the street, preferring to enter a public house and entertain the customers with singing and fiddling. Popular and always smiling, no one resented giving him a few pennies. After a while he had several regular haunts which welcomed him in, and might indulge his desire for 'a drop of Spanish', so he would walk between them, using a long stick, and apparently knowing every street and alleyway in spite of his blindness. He would always learn about new buildings, and tried to learn the name of each tenant so that he could call their name as he passed. Apparently he had something against hat-wearing, and while several people gave him one, he'd never wear it for more than a couple of days. One of his favourite songs, sometimes attributed to him, was the cheerful 'Buy broom busoms' (i.e., besom brooms) which gave plenty of leeway for adding verses about different streets and their traders, depending where you were singing. He died at the age of eighty-one, in the same poorhouse that his mother had spent her last days. She made it to 100!

JULY 21ST

1749: On this day, leading classical scholar Richard Dawes finally found it was all getting too much for him. He had taken up the post of Master of the Royal Grammar School, Newcastle, in 1738, after his outspoken manner made him unpopular at his previous post, as a fellow of Emmanuel College, Cambridge. Fellow scholar Richard Bentley claimed Dawes knew nothing of Greek except from indexes. His health was also poor, and when told he needed more exercise, he took up bell ringing, becoming an expert. It was in Newcastle that he produced his most important work, *Miscellanea Critica*, a series of essays on ancient Greek (1745). But tensions gradually rose between him and the governors – who he named 'tittle-tattle mongers' in print. One former pupil, poet John Akenside, described him in verse as 'Flushed with comic triumphs and the spoils / Of sly derision!' Always eccentric, Dawes began to display his contempt for the leading members of the Corporation in an imaginative way. Apparently he taught his scholars that 'alderman' was the correct translation for the Greek 'ass'. While you might think this would make him popular, the number of scholars apparently fell until on this day he resigned. Though just thirty-nine, he seems to have retired, spending most of the next fifteen years boating off Heworth. (Mackenzie, E., *A Descriptive and Historical Account of the Town and County of Newcastle upon Tyne: Including the Borough of Gateshead*, 1827 / Myers, A., *Myers' Literary Guide*, Carcanet Press, 1995)

JULY 22ND

1857: On this day, four men seized a golden opportunity to escape from Newcastle Prison. Blakeston Hind and George Bell were both notorious crooks, awaiting trial at the assizes for garrotting William Oley and stealing his money, near the Cattle Market. Also imprisoned was John Harris, a tailor who murdered his mistress, and William Beaumont – who, coincidentally, was also accused of a theft-with-garrotting. On this day, they found that a guard had carelessly left their cells unlocked! The four men tied bedding together to form a rope, scaled the wall of a workshop onto the outer prison wall, and lowered themselves down. Beaumont and Harris were recaptured in Carlisle, but Hind and Bell were never caught. In August the following year a much cleverer escape was attempted. Twenty-two-year-old Robert Boyd had been sentenced to six years in Carliol Square Gaol, but he had no intention of staying put! With a chisel, he prised out a metal pipe in his cell, leaving a gap 9 feet by 14 feet. He managed to squeeze through this and out onto the roof. He made his way across several buildings using bed linen, and into the stone-breaking yard. There he found a plank and two bags of teased hair. Back on the roof he used the bags to stop the row of rotating spikes on top of the wall, and the plank to get over into Carliol Square itself. No one noticed for some hours, until a policeman spotted the bed linen 'rope' hanging from the prison wall. Boyd was re-captured three weeks later. (Fordyce, T., *Local Records*, 1867)

JULY 23RD

1815: On this day, England rejoiced to the news that Napoleon had surrendered to the English ... although perhaps not as much as you'd think. In his diary, James Losh records: 'The bells rang and the cannons were fired at Newcastle for this event, but it is quite surprising what a slight effect this most singular fact has produced upon the public at large. The truth is that we are now so habituated to wonders that they have lost their power over us ...' To be fair, this wasn't the first related celebration, more like an encore. Napoleon had been forced to abdicate once before, in 1813, and on that occasion, Losh reports seeing 'fireworks and illuminations ... many houses were splendidly and some tastefully decorated with coloured lamps and transparencies.' (Hughes, E. (ed.), *The Diaries and Correspondence of James Losh, Vol. I: Diary 1811-23*, Surtees Society, 1956)

1953: On this day, the *Newcastle Chronicle* reported a new initiative by the City Council to place 250 deckchairs in strategic points at Exhibition, Heaton, and Nun's Moor Parks. For three pence, visitors could take the chairs to any part of the park they liked – while a one shilling deposit discouraged theft and vandalism. The hope was that in the following year, the scheme could be extended to Barras Bridge and Eldon Square. The same year, to celebrate the coronation, the Coronation Clock Tower was built in Exhibition Park, where it has recently been renovated. (*Newcastle Chronicle*)

JULY 24TH

1503: On this day, Princess Margaret – the thirteen-year-old daughter of Henry VII, sister of Henry VIII – travelled through Newcastle on her way to be married to thirty-year-old James VI of Scotland. John Young, one of Margaret's heralds, recorded the journey in detail. She was met with religious processions, banners and crosses on display at the end of the bridge, and children singing hymns and playing instruments. Her coach – 'richly dressed, with six fair horses, led and conveyed by three men' – might well have been the first true passenger vehicle to cross the medieval bridge. But given the state of the roads and the lack of springs in the seating, Margaret would have been glad to reach her destination! Crowds gathered to watch, and tapestries were hung in the streets. Young did note with puzzlement, however, that 'no artillery or ordnance was shot off' – this was presumably considered normal! Princess Margaret stayed the night at the Augustinian Friary. The next day happened to be the festival of St James, which, since Margaret was about to marry another James, was treated as an excuse for further celebration. There were 'dances, sports, and songs, with good cheer of hippocras [spiced wine], sucres [sweets], and other meats of many delicious manners, the entertainment lasting till midnight.' On the 26th, she and her entourage moved northward to Morpeth. (Strickland, A., *Lives of the Queens of Scotland*, 1840-1848)

JULY 25TH

1941: On this day, lightning struck Grey's Monument. It hit the statue of Earl Grey – nearly 4 metres of Portland Stone, on top of a 41-metre-high column – and knocked its head clean off. One eyewitness, who was working on the trams at the time, remembers: 'This day it was thunder and lightning. As we were passing Grey's Monument, lightning struck the head of Grey's Monument. Grey lost his head, hit our trolley (because the trams had trolleys, to make them go), knocked our trolley off, set our tram afire, threw me right the way across the tram, I ran across, afire – my old uniform was afire, it must have struck me as well. Bill tried to put his brake on, we got to the old Oxford Galleries, and the tram stopped there. I managed to get the flames out of my thing – because with it being khaki it was cotton. I got off the tram and it was pouring with rain. Where Grey's head went I don't know – it rolled down Grey Street, it must have done. I got these two ladies off, pushed them into the Oxford Galleries doorway. And Bill got a hold of me and said "Are you alright?" I stayed with them, Bill got the fire out. It didn't really set the tram alight, there was nothing burnt.' Thanks to the war, Grey didn't get a new head for over six years. Eventually Roger Hedley (son of the artist Ralph Hedley) made a suitable replacement, weighing 303kg, which was remounted on January 12th 1948. (*Beamish Museum Audio Archive*)

JULY 26TH

1756: On this day, the town centre saw a strange procession, led by a man on a mule with a white flag. Behind was an ass carrying an effigy of a man, with 'this is the villain that would not fight' written around his waist. At the Flesh Market, the effigy was 'hanged' and burned. This sort of effigy-burning was not new, but this was a new target: Admiral Byng, the commander of British forces in Minorca. Attacked by the French navy over the previous two months, a disastrous defeat eventually left the island in the hands of the French. Although it is arguable how much this was Byng's fault, he was clearly blamed by the general public. At his court-martial, the judges agreed and he was executed by firing squad in 1757 for failing to 'do his utmost' to prevent the defeat. (Mackenzie, E., *A Descriptive and Historical Account of the Town and County of Newcastle upon Tyne: Including the Borough of Gateshead*, 1827)

———◆———

1935: On this day, the Secretary of State for Air, Sir Phillip Cinliffe-Lister, officially opened Woolsington Aerodrome, soon to become Newcastle Airport. £35,000 had been enough to buy a clubhouse, hangar, workshops and garage, clustered around one end of a grass runway. The runway lights were nothing more than oil drums, which could be filled with oily rags and lit when an aircraft was coming. The first scheduled service was an eight-seat plane stopping off on the way between Croydon and Perth. (www.newcastleairport.com)

JULY 27TH

1993: On this day, controversial local politician T. Dan Smith – 'Mr Newcastle', arguably the closest Britain has ever seen to an American-style 'city boss' – died. To some, he remains a visionary who brought modern ideas to Newcastle. To others he was a corrupt charlatan. Coming from a working-class background in Wallsend, he joined the Labour Party and through energy and charm achieved a meteoric rise to power in local politics. By the mid-1960s he was leader of Newcastle City Council, and pursued a vision of 'a city free and beautiful' – a 'Brasilia of the North' to rival the best in the world. He promoted the central motorway, the Metro, and embraced modern architecture as a parallel achievement to that of Dobson and Grainger the previous century. While some of this has stood the test of time – the Scandinavian Newcastle Civic Centre, for instance – much of the concrete revolution now seems very dated, or has been demolished. Swan House and Cruddas Park flats were attempts to create 'a city in the sky' which rapidly showed their flaws. In 1973, Smith was tried for bribe-taking and corruption in planning contracts. He served six years in prison for conspiracy and corruption. After prison he worked for charities helping ex-offenders, and lived in one of his own high-rise blocks, believing in his vision until the end. (BBC North East)

JULY 28TH

1817: On this day (or possibly June 28th – the records seem confused on this), the Malings pottery at Ouseburn fired for the first time. The North Hylton Pot Works had existed in Sunderland since 1762, making use of a rich nearby seam of clay and founded by the Maling family. It initially produced brown earthenware but soon expanded into the cream and white pottery with which the name Maling later became most strongly associated. By 1788 they were using transfer printing to decorate the pots. The company transferred to the Ouseburn, Newcastle from 1815, initially making identical pots to those from North Hylton. It was a good location – coal was cheap, shipping easy. Chemical dyes were locally produced, and the clay itself was also cheap as colliers brought it up as ballast. An early set of regulations included no alcohol, except the stated allowance if you were a Fireman; no leaving your own workshop without permission; no bringing children in 'except such as are actually working there'; no 'gaming and amusements'; no cluttering up the workshops; no dogs; no 'swearing, drinking, fighting, or other disorderly behaviour'; and no damaging the Rules poster! This last one attracted the biggest fine, at five shillings. (Moore, S. and Ross, C., *Maling: The Trademark of Excellence*, Tyne and Wear Museums, 1998 / www.boltancestry.co.uk)

JULY 29TH

1700: On this day, the keelmen of Newcastle petitioned the Corporation for land on Sandgate on which to build themselves a hospital. This was a remarkable piece of organisation, but is perhaps not surprising from a group with such a distinct community within the town. They are first recorded as a fraternity as early as 1539, and in 1697 started a forward-thinking charitable fund scheme. Members paid a small fraction of their wages into it: one penny per tide, per keel. It was administered by the Hostmen's Company, who were both their employers and the trustees of the charity. The Keelman's Hospital was opened in 1701, having cost around £2,000. It provided rooms for fifty keelmen who were too sick or too old to work, or keelmen's widows. Rules included keeping the Sabbath, and not littering the corridors. It was also supposed to be a sober place, though alcohol was often smuggled in, or else the inmates just went down to the Quayside to share a few pints. However, the system of paying through wages as a matter of course broke down in 1712, and several variants were tried over the years to come – in 1788 there was even an Act of Parliament about it. (Fewster, J., *The Keelmen of Tyneside*, Boydell Press, 2011)

JULY 30TH

2002: On this day, Shieldfield nursery nurses Dawn Reed and Chris Lillie won a historic court victory. Nine years before, they had been acquitted of child abuse by the courts – but that same day, the leader of the council said he still believed abuse had taken place, and, soon after, an independent council report repeated claims linking them to a paedophile circle, in one of the largest child abuse allegations the country has seen. Government, media, and leading children's charities lined up to condemn the couple. Although there were people walking the streets of Newcastle who would gladly kill the pair, they were given no warning of the report. With *The Sun* newspaper asking readers to 'help us find these fiends!' Reed and Lillie fled the city in fear of a lynch mob. Two Acts of Parliament – the Protection of Children Act and the Youth Justice and Criminal Evidence Act – were significantly shaped by the case. Years later Reed and Lillie, supported by more sympathetic journalists, sued for libel. They argued for the self-fulfilling power of the rumour mill, selective bias in the report, and inadequacies in the examination of the children both for the trial and the inquiry. And on this day, that case was won, and the pair's reputations were restored. Evidence in child abuse cases would be dealt with a lot more carefully from this point on. (*The Guardian*)

JULY 31ST

1986: On this day, international cricketer Ian Botham began his comeback after a two-month suspension for smoking cannabis. The venue was Jesmond, at the ground used by Northumberland Cricket Club since 1887 – a tiny pitch hemmed in by Jesmond Cemetery, with room for a maximum of 4,000 spectators. Botham was given special dispensation to play (one day before his ban officially lifted) in the grandly named 'England XI *v*. Rest of the World XI' two-day festival match run by travel agents Callers-Pegasus. The event was repeated for several years, and attracted several well-known international cricketers more used to performing in much larger venues – enough to make that 'Rest of the World' label not entirely laughable. Australian fast bowler Dennis Lillee said: 'Jesmond is a postage-stamp sized ground with the Geordie atmosphere of an MCG [Melbourne Cricket Ground] crowd. Many cricket grounds are forgettable. However, in my opinion Jesmond should live forever.' While Botham's first-day performance was not stellar, on the second day he scored 96. He must have enjoyed it, too – he returned to the same match the following year. (*The Guardian* / www.newcastlecc.org.uk)

AUGUST 1ST

1963: On this day, King's College Durham officially gained its independence, becoming the University of Newcastle-upon-Tyne (and latterly Newcastle University). University education had a long history in the city. King's College was itself made up of the College of Medicine (which traced its roots back to the School of Medicine and Surgery, opened in 1834), and Armstrong College (founded by Lord Armstrong in 1871 for the teaching of physical sciences). In 1908, Durham University was formally constituted as having two divisions, one based in Newcastle, the other in Durham. In those days the Newcastle Division taught not only the fundamental disciplines in the arts and sciences but also a wide range of applied sciences which were particularly useful for the industries of the region – geology, mining, naval architecture, engineering, and agriculture. Some of these specialisms survive to this day. The two colleges merged in 1937 – and that is how it remained until tensions between the two divisions led to a formal split in 1963. (www.ncl.ac.uk)

AUGUST 2ND

1894: On this day, the board of Newcastle United made an important decision. The Club's minutes record that 'the Club's colours should be changed from red shirts and white knickers to black and white shirts (two inch stripe) and dark knickers.' The red shirts (sometimes with black) had been the usual strip of Newcastle East End since its inception in 1881. Meanwhile, Newcastle West End generally played in blue. Confusingly, there is some evidence that in the last season prior to the two uniting, they had more or less swapped, with the West in red and the East in blue and red stripes. When East End and West End combined they initially played in the East End's red strip, once even having to wear white handkerchiefs to differentiate themselves from the opposition! Rather than some combination of blue and red, the Newcastle United board went for a fresh look. History leaves no definitive reason why they chose black and white. Suggestions include: the black-and-white habit of supporter Dominican monk Father Dalmatius Houtmann; magpies nesting in the wooden stand at St James' Park; and the Duke of Newcastle, William Cavendish, whose Royalist Newcastle Whitecoats wore a very distinctive black and white uniform. Identified for so long with black and white stripes, perhaps it is worth speculating how well NUFC's modern fan base would react to a suggestion of reverting to the original colours of red and white ... (www.nufc.co.uk / www. historicalkits.co.uk / Joannou, P., *United: The First 100 Years*, Polar Publishing, 1991)

AUGUST 3RD

1910: On this day, HMS *Barfleur* had a nasty scrape. A Royal Navy battleship that had served in the Mediterranean and during the Boxer Rebellion in China, *Barfleur* was less than twenty years old when she was sent to be scrapped at Derwenthaugh, beyond the Tyne's bridges.

From the beginning it was evident that the site of this yard – opened by Hughes Bolckow Ltd in 1906 – was poorly chosen, being too far upriver. The first ship scrapped there was a Norwegian cargo ship, which ran aground on Tynemouth's Black Middens. The first warship had to be partially dismantled beforehand in order to get her into any sort of position to reach the yard. And then came HMS *Barfleur* – over 10,000 tons of metal. As she came up the River Tyne, the Swing Bridge was opened to allow her passage, and … she got stuck, jammed between the bridge's raised sides! All traffic on the Tyne was held up while workmen freed her. Understandably, Hughes Bolckow applied for a deeper water site further out to sea, but this was rejected. The following year the business moved to Cambois, on the Northumberland coast. (*Newcastle Chronicle*)

AUGUST 4TH

1845: On this day, the River Watch Committee met in the Guildhall to discuss the appointment of twenty men to form the Tyne River Police. In the morning, applications and testimonials could be made on behalf of any suitable man. They had to be of good character and between twenty-one and forty-two years old. In the afternoon, they decided who to appoint. Each man would get 18 shillings a week. At the same time, the Committee were looking to obtain four four-oared boats and two two-oared boats for the use of the force. They were also there to find a supplier for the uniforms – for each man: a coat, a waistcoat, a hat, two pairs of trousers and two pairs of shoes per year, plus a greatcoat every two years. All of this had to be ready for the start of the service on September 1st, less than a month away! Eventually the service started, and in the first few months they proved their worth. Early cases brought to court included the illegal dumping of ballast from ships (leading to a 50 shilling fine) and the theft of rope from a ship (two months in prison). The service also secured boats that had drifted away, and warned owners when they were badly moored. They put out a fire at an anchorsmith's and even acted as mediators in disputes between a captain and his drunk and violent crew, and between drunken sailors on the dockside. (*Newcastle Courant*)

AUGUST 5TH

1737: On this day, a fire broke out in the stable of Sir William Blackett, showing that fire was no respecter of class distinction. A servant accidentally set fire to some straw in the stable, by dropping a candle stub which was not quite fully snuffed out. The fire was put out before it reached the main house, but five valuable coach horses were suffocated. This is only one of several incidents which demonstrate just how vulnerable to fire the eighteenth-century town was. In fact, rarely did a year go by without serious damage to property, or death, through fire. Two years after this, a house was burned down in Pilgrim Street when a small child set fire to some wood shavings. In 1750, the heat from brewing equipment set fire to combustible goods stored in the next cellar along, separated by the thinnest of walls. Unattended rush lights and uncovered candles caused concern in homes full of cloth and yards full of straw, wood, flax – and even gunpowder. The whole town lived in fear of an accidental blaze. (Barke, M., 'Fire: An Ever-Present Menace? Newcastle 1720-1840', *Tyne and Tweed*, 2011)

AUGUST 6TH

2011: On this day, nothing happened – but it should have done. For months organisers had been putting together a two-day music festival called Ignition, due to open this day, with the intention of putting Newcastle on the map of summer festivals. It was to be held at Newcastle Racecourse and headlined by Calvin Harris, Echo and the Bunnymen, Frank Turner and many others. It had already been moved once – the original idea was to use the Newcastle Falcons rugby ground, but too many local residents had complained so it was moved to the racecourse. However, Newcastle Racecourse pulled out of Ignition with only three days to go, and the organisers were unable to arrange a suitable alternative. They tried the City Council, but for them the problem was the three-day timeframe – they could not give adequate notice to nearby residents or come up with specific plans. The racecourse, in turn, blamed their need to cancel on the failure of the organisers to provide the paperwork surrounding safety, security and first aid, and also claimed that some payments had not been made. The company went into liquidation and some angry and disappointed music fans did not receive their money back. (*Newcastle Chronicle* / www.bbc.co.uk)

AUGUST 7TH

1968: On this day, eleven-year-old Scotswood girl Mary Bell was charged with the murder of three-year-old Brian Howe. This case has burned its way into public consciousness because of the age, not only of the killer, but also the victim. Bell's upbringing, in and around the close-knit housing of working-class Scotswood, has been much discussed, but some things defy explanation. In the summer of 1968, two small boys – Howe, and four-year-old Martin Brown – were found strangled to death on waste ground. Several things, including a drawing of Brown in Bell's yearbook, had led to suspicion. When Howe was buried, according to Chief Inspector Dobson, he saw the girl laughing and rubbing her hands. At that point, he brought her in for questioning, afraid she would kill again. In her statement, Mary blamed a friend, Norma Bell (no relation), while at the same time giving too much detail herself. She was arrested, and after a nine-day trial she was found guilty of manslaughter, making her the country's youngest convicted female killer. She was institutionalised for twelve years. (Sereny, G., *The Case of Mary Bell*, Pimlico, 1995)

AUGUST 8TH

1636: On this day, at the height of the plague season, Thomas Holmes dictated his will. The scribe, Ralph Tailor, writes that, having been 'sent for', he climbed up 'upon the townes wall of Newcastle, adioining the key nere the river', and listened to the dying man's wishes through a loft window. He wrote down what he heard, then read it loudly, so that the unfortunate man could clearly acknowledge that this was correct. Two other neighbours, who also climbed up the wall to listen, added their marks to the paper. When the will was read in court, Tailor confirmed that Holmes had been 'extreame sick', and that he could not be sure, under the circumstances, whether Holmes was of perfect mind and memory. Holmes was a keelman and left his half-share in a coal boat to his cousin, 'if he live so long'. Money was distributed between his wife, daughters and other relatives. Tailor wrote many such wills over the summer of 1636. Generally he kept at a safe distance, though in at least one case he entered an infected house, listening through a wooden partition wall between the 'upper hall', with its double bed and the house's best furniture, and the 'chamber', containing several small beds and a spinning wheel. In this case he did not even see the speaker, but said he knew his voice. (Wrightson, K., *Ralph Tailor's Summer*, Yale University Press, 2011)

AUGUST 9TH

1994: On this day, a concert by Brit-pop giants Oasis went infamously wrong. This was the third time Oasis had visited the Riverside club, but five tracks in, the football-related banter between group and crowd seemed tense. There are two versions of the events that followed. According to the band, a lad climbed the stage and punched Noel Gallagher in the face. According to security staff, however, the lad simply stumbled and fell towards Noel as he climbed. Gallagher put up his guitar defensively, accidentally hitting *himself* in the face with it. Certainly he was bleeding profusely as he walked off. His brother Liam brandished his microphone stand aggressively, as the crowd chanted 'soft as sh*te'. After the band stormed off stage, Liam made a brief 'encore' by coming back on to snarl, 'No one hits our kid!' It's since been suggested that Noel was more concerned about the extremely valuable 1960s Gibson Les Paul Custom guitar. It once belonged to Pete Townshend of The Who and was on loan from Johnny Marr of The Smiths. The band left the venue hiding on the floor of a tour bus with smashed windows whilst anti-Manchester chants filled the air. The *Daily Mail* reported the incident as 'an Orgy of Violence!' whilst the whole event was broadcast live on Radio 1, doing the band's rock-'n-roll reputation (and album sales) no harm at all … (Plater, H. and Taylor, C., *Riverside*, Tonto Books, 2011)

AUGUST 10TH

1792: On this day, one man and two women were hanged at Westgate for murder. William Winter and Jane and Eleanor Clark were condemned at the assizes on the 4th, for the murder of Margaret Crozier. Crozier was an old woman who lived at Raw Pele, a tower north of Elsdon, on the Northumberland moors. Winter had built up a notorious reputation as a crook, culminating in seven years spent on a prison hulk on the Thames. Once free, he headed back home, northwards. On arrival he discovered that, while he was away, his father and brother had been hanged in Morpeth for breaking and entering. Taking up with the Clark sisters – who had also lost their father to the gallows – he immediately returned to his old thieving ways. But this burglary somehow went wrong and Crozier died. Interestingly, the man who hanged the three was not so different from them. William Gardner was convicted of sheep stealing at the same sessions, and agreed to execute the others in exchange from having his own sentence reduced to transportation to Australia. Winter is particularly remembered because, while the two women's bodies were sent to the surgeons, Winter was gibbeted. His body was displayed in a hanging metal cage near the site of the crime. A gibbet still stands on the site, though it is a replica. (www.rothbury.co.uk)

August 11th

1980: On this day, the Metro – the largest urban transport project of twentieth-century Britain – was first opened for public use. It was not the whole network as we know it today, but ran from Tynemouth to Haymarket, via Whitley Bay and South Gosforth. It took six years of building, and before that, three years of planning, lobbying and consultation, beginning with the 1971 document 'The Transport Plan for the 1980s'. Work began with a purpose-built test centre using 2.4km of track (including a tunnel) and two prototype carriages to go around it. Soon after, tunnels were dug under the streets of Newcastle. The city's boulder clay is ideal for tunnelling, though things were trickier in the sandstone-and-coal layers of Gateshead. Unfortunately, with the financial climate getting tougher, government funding was frozen, and Tyne and Wear County Council were forced to commit almost their entire capital investment into the system to get it finished. It was worth it – in its first year, more than sixty million journeys were made by Metro. The Metro system was a no-smoking area from the start, an innovation for a rail service. And it can claim other firsts – it was the first UK rail system to be designed for full wheelchair access, the first to play classical music at a station (in 1997 – apparently it really does improve atmosphere and reduce anti-social behaviour), and the first British underground system to allow mobile phone signals. (www.nexus.org.uk)

AUGUST 12TH

1758: On this day, Lady Elizabeth Montagu gave a vivid description of a visit to Newcastle. She wrote:

> It is narrow dark & dirty, some of ye streets so steep one is forced to put a drag chain on ye wheels … The streets are some of them so narrow that if ye tallow chandler ostentatiously hangs forth his candles you have a chance to sweep them into your lap as you drive by, & I do not know how it has happened that I have not yet caught a coach full of red herrings for we scrape the citty wall on which they hang in great abundance.

Elizabeth was married to Lord Edward Montagu, a man with several estates and coal mines in Northumberland. Generally she did not come with him up to the North East, but remained in Kent or London. In 1760, she was still unimpressed with the town's range of entertainment. She wrote that she was joining in to avoid giving offence, but 'diversions here are less elegant, & conversation less polite [than in London], but no one imagines retirement has any comforts'. And in 1766 she called the local miners 'little better than Savages. They are dirty, their dwellings are sordid, & their Countenances bear the marks of hard labour & total ignorance.' (Child, E., 'Elizabeth Montagu', *Huntington Library Quarterly*, 2002 / Turnbull, L., 'The Montagu Family of Denton Hall' / www.mininginstitute. org.uk)

AUGUST 13TH

1847: On or around this day, Newcastle's Industrial and Ragged School opened in Sandgate. Newcastle already had a wide array of different schools, attached to different churches and chapels, private academies, charity schools and so on, but almost all charged. None of them accepted the wild, lawless children who more or less lived on the streets. The space wasn't ideal – small and cramped, in an unhealthy corner of town – but very soon fifty boys were packing in to learn the three R's and the basics of scripture. Within a few months the charity had agreed that older boys would also spend time making matchboxes, to help pay for the school. They would have been encouraged by the pennyworth of bread they were given, amounting to two meals each day, often with cheese or milk donated by well-wishers. When the master, James Murray, died of fever the following year, it was reported that his combination of firmness and kindness had created 'a marked change for the better' in the more 'unruly elements' – a difficult task as sole teacher of fifty chaotic lads. Things changed rapidly. The following year the school occupied part of Gibson Street Chapel; a girls' school was founded, food improved and skills training increased. But it all began with a group of philanthropists, and the herculean efforts of James Murray in a damp and dark room in Sandgate. (Prahms, W., *Newcastle Industrial and Ragged School*, The History Press, 2006)

AUGUST 14TH

1786: On this day, the foundation stone was laid for All Saints' Church, in Low Pilgrim Street. This was the second church on the site. The first was built before 1286, and there are some marvellous entries in its churchwardens' book. Among other things, money was paid out to take a drunkard to the stocks, to hide the church plate in 1745 (*see* October 12th), and for the heads of two otters and a badger! But by 1785, the walls were crumbling and the steeple leaned precariously to one side. Architects concluded that it would be cheaper and easier to build a new church than repair the old one. Sadly, in the demolition, one Captain William Hedley, well-respected in the town, died when the Great West Door fell on him as he watched. The new church, with its Doric columns, high tower and spire, took ten years to build completely (although it was consecrated after three), and cost £27,000 almost all of which was raised in an assessment of the parish. It is a very unusual design, being one of only a handful in the country based on an elliptical floor plan. (Mackenzie, E., *A Descriptive and Historical Account of the Town and County of Newcastle upon Tyne: Including the Borough of Gateshead*, 1827)

AUGUST 15TH

1860: On this day, the *Newcastle Chronicle* printed an address to which men, especially 'members of volunteer rifle corps', could apply if they were interested in 'excursions to Italy and Naples'. This was a clever way to circumvent the law against recruiting for foreign armies. Garibaldi's army was fighting a revolutionary war in Italy, with a lot of support in Tyneside. The paper was run by radical Joseph Cowen, who was, behind the scenes, also engaged in smuggling arms to Garibaldi's forces. When the *Chronicle* was taken to court for breaching the law, they gleefully invited the public to come and watch the entertainment, and got clean away – claiming a victory for press freedom. (Todd, N., *The Militant Democracy*, Bewick Press, 1991)

———— • ◆ • ————

1903: On this day, novelist Jack Common, son of a rail yard worker, was born. In 1928 he moved to London, seeking work, and went on to write several important books. George Orwell called him 'the authentic voice of the ordinary working man', while Sid Chaplin claimed he was 'the nearest anybody ever got to Charlie Chaplin in print'. But his best known book returns us to the terraces and rail yards of his Heaton childhood, in a thinly veiled autobiography which vividly evokes Edwardian Tyneside, if through the lens of adult socialist perspectives. This is *Kiddar's Luck*, often seen as one of the finest working-class novels of the twentieth century. (www.bloodaxebooks.com)

AUGUST 16TH

1644: On this day, the Earl of Leven, at the head of a Scottish army, first called for the surrender of Newcastle. That spring had already seen Scots' forces pass by, with some skirmishing, at which time the Mayor also set fire to the suburbs beyond the walls. And war returned in the summer, as on July 27th, Gateshead fell, and forces began to gather. On this day, Leven summoned Newcastle to surrender, that it might 'reap the sweet fruits of peace, which other Cities under obedience of King and Parliament do quietly enjoy'. But the Mayor, Sir John Marley, was convinced of the Royalist cause, and replied that if the army really wanted to avoid bloodshed, they would go home. Meanwhile, of course, both sides were busy preparing for the siege to come, building fortifications and defensive earthworks. The defenders kept on firing, while the attackers fired back and also dug tunnels, and threw sacks full of propaganda leaflets over the walls. For over two months, the people of Newcastle lived in siege conditions, with no real hope of relief. Marley continued to be dedicated to the cause, apparently treating negotiation attempts as ways to stall for yet more time, and on October 19th again refused what were likely to be the best terms Newcastle would get. For what happened next, see October 25th. (Sadler, J. and Serdiville, R., *The Great Siege of Newcastle*, The History Press, 2011)

AUGUST 17TH

1388: On this day, English and Scots forces clashed outside the walls of Newcastle. A large Scots raiding party were on their way home, stopping off at Newcastle in the hope of easy pickings. They were to be disappointed, as the town was firmly held by Sir Henry 'Hotspur' Percy and his brother, Sir Ralph. Without siege equipment, the Earl of Douglas ordered his army to camp outside the walls. Over the next few days, skirmishes escalated, with lightning raids upon the town gates. Many of the defenders became convinced that Douglas must have more men on the way. According to chronicler Froissart (who may be colouring things a little), on this day, Douglas and Hotspur met on the field – possibly after a challenge to a duel, near Barrass Bridge. Douglas won the day, managing to capture Hotspur's pennon (a flag with his own heraldry on). He is said to have claimed that he would carry it home to his tower, at which Hotspur said, 'By God! You will never leave Northumberland alive with that.' The following day the Scots left. Hotspur charged after them without waiting for reinforcements. But the Scots had picked their ground well, and although Douglas died at Otterburn, the Scots could claim a great victory. Hotspur was captured, and never did get his pennon back. (Boardman, A., *Hotspur*, The History Press, 2003)

AUGUST 18TH

1867: On this day, eleven-year-old William Glass died from accidental burns. The previous day he had gone to visit his father at work in a tannery next to St Andrew's Church in Darn Crook. While his father's back was turned, he fell into a pit of boiling liquid. He was fished out and taken home, but he was terribly injured. A worker had been killed in a similar manner at the same tannery back in 1858. Tanneries were dangerous places, and many were still in the centre of Newcastle, where accidents were all too easy. It had only been a year since the body of George Henderson had been found in an unused, water-filled, tannery pit. The little boy had been missing for a month before he was discovered in a Newgate Street tannery, less than 100 yards from his family home. The coroner was told that children had free access to the pits, which were generally full of water. The jury considered that 'something should be done', but no case was pressed against the tannery – they hadn't done anything wrong, by the standards of the day. Tanneries, with their dangers and offensive smells, were gradually moved from the town centres. Richardsons' Elswick Leather Works moved to the outskirts after its town centre premises burnt down in 1863, and went on to become one of the biggest tanneries in the country. The streets built to house the workforce gained the nickname 'Shumac Village' – shumac, or sumac, is used in tanning leather. (*Newcastle Courant*)

AUGUST 19TH

2005: On this day, Seven Stories, the centre for children's books, was formally opened by author Jacqueline Wilson (best known for the *Tracy Beaker* series). Part of the impressive rebirth of the Ouseburn Valley as an artistic and cultural centre, Seven Stories is housed in a converted Victorian flour warehouse, which does indeed have seven storeys. The transformation took five years, and cost £4.5 million, with much of the original interior left intact and blending with more modern architectural features. The actual process had begun several years before that, with a long campaign of fund-raising and voluntary work by people with a vision to provide a focal point for children's literature. The idea was quite new – and even at the time of writing it is the only gallery dedicated to children's literature in Britain, and one of only a handful in the world. It also houses internationally significant archives relating to childrens' authors. These include the papers of Newcastle-born David Almond, patron of Seven Stories and the award-winning author of *Skellig*, and North Shields-born Robert Westall, some of whose most enduring works are based in war-torn Tyneside. Enid Blyton and Philip Pullman are also represented. (www.sevenstories.org.uk)

AUGUST 20TH

1384: On this day, a miracle occurred – at least according to monk Thomas Walsingham, who was alive at the time. He claimed that two Newcastle sailors were in the process of cutting a piece of wood, to mend their boat. But 'when one of them struck the piece of timber with his axe, he was amazed to see blood spurting copiously from the wound, as though it were an animal'. Understandably, the sailor was confused as to what this meant, until he remembered that it was St Oswin's Day. Hence he should not have been working, and he vowed never to do manual labour on that day again. But his friend was of a more sceptical turn of mind, and was determined to finish the job that day. So he began to hack at the wood, trying different angles on it, though each axe blow caused more and more blood to flow. When the sailor realised that no matter which way he cut into the wood, the result was the same, he too repented his action, and swore never again to work on St Oswin's Day. St Oswin was the patron of Tynemouth Abbey, and his bones are interred there. When word of this miracle reached the abbey, the monks there agreed to take the wood and place it in with St Oswin's body. (Walsingham, T., *Chronica Maiora*, Boydell Press, 2009)

AUGUST 21ST

1999: On this day, the Mayfair Ballroom on Newgate Street closed its doors for the last time. It had opened as a ballroom and concert hall in 1961, with room in the main hall for 1,500 people, and a small stage on one of the long sides. In the early days it had a resident band, Jimmy Bence and his orchestra, for dance nights. For most of its run, the Mayfair was one of the go-to stages in the North East both for well-known bands, particularly from the rock scene, and for up-and-coming groups. As well as Nirvana (October 23rd), and Led Zeppelin (October 4th) other household names including U2, The Who, Queen, Pink Floyd, Kylie Minogue and The Police came to the Mayfair early in their careers, often as support for others acts. It didn't change much over the years, though the 1970s saw a revolving stage allowing each band to set up and then begin immediately. From start to finish, the balcony allowed people to throw missiles on bands they didn't like! At the time of closure, it laid claim to being the longest-running rock club in Europe, lasting nearly forty years in the same venue. The closing night was one of these rock nights, and around 5,000 people crammed into the venue (and also took away with them more or less everything that was not nailed down!) (www.newcastlestuff.com)

AUGUST 22ND

1820: On this day, an inquest was held into the death of Ann Armstrong, a servant at the Fighting Cocks Inn in the Bigg Market. In the nineteenth century, the ideal complexion was thought to be pale and blemish-free, and lots of treatments were on the market to help achieve this. Ann took a dose of 'brimstone in milk' and was violently sick. A few hours later, she was found dead. A post-mortem found the lungs were full of blood due to a ruptured blood vessel, probably caused by the violence of her vomiting. The inquest concluded that something she had eaten was responsible, though they could not be certain what. The name of the inn, the Fighting Cocks, is a reminder that, for many years, cock fighting was a commonplace leisure activity, and several cockpits were situated in and around the Bigg Market. In 1736, antiquarian Henry Bourne said it was, 'A favourite sport of the colliers, the clamorous wants of their families solicit them to go to work in vain, when a match is heard of'. But it gradually became less popular as sentiments regarding animal cruelty changed, and was banned in 1835. Nonetheless, rumours persist that in 1874, the police closed a cockpit in Gallowgate, probably the last active cockpit in the North East.

AUGUST 23TH

1791: On this day, a trial at the Guildhall was interrupted when a piece of the ceiling fell down. The court had gathered to try T. Dunbar with a shipping offence, which you wouldn't think was that exciting, but courtrooms always drew a big crowd. One of them had clambered up into the beams, between the roof and the ceiling, lost his footing, and slipped – leaving his whole lower body dangling through a hole in the ceiling. The missing piece of ceiling fell onto the green oval table in front of the judge. The panic was understandable, especially given that a recent fire in the next door St Thomas' Chapel had weakened the roof structure. So the entire crowd and participants rushed out. Apparently no one suffered serious injury, though there was some hilarity, as the *Courant* put it, at the 'temporary losses of hats, wigs, caps, shoes, cloaks, shawls etc.' Apparently this wasn't the first time that people suffered from their attempt to get a ringside view of a trial. In 1785, two boys climbed into a window of the Moot Hall to watch a legacy dispute and, perhaps falling asleep on the narrow window ledge, fell to the ground. One broke his leg, and the other was killed. (Redfern, B., *The Shadow of the Gallows*, Tynebridge Publishing, 2003)

AUGUST 24TH

1493: On this day, Robert Green of South Shields came to Durham in a panic, and claimed sanctuary. He said that, while walking in the Close, Newcastle, Robert Nicholson of Winlaton and his friends attacked him. In self-defence, Green hit Nicholson on the chest twice 'with a Scots-axe', which killed him instantly (which is not surprising, as a 'Scots-axe' was probably a Lochaber axe, which is a kind of halberd, with a long cutting edge and a hook attached to a 6-foot long pole). These were dangerous times, but it has never been explained what Green was doing walking around the streets of Newcastle with a Scots-axe. He made his way to Durham Cathedral and touched the door knocker, a large bronze in the shape of a monstrous lion head, claiming the liberty of St Cuthbert. He would be allowed to stay within the cathedral for up to thirty-seven days. This would give time to try to arrange his affairs, make peace with God, or try to come to a compromise with any accusers. At the end of this time, he would have had to either go to the authorities for execution, or leave the country on the first boat out from Hartlepool, never to return. A steady stream of such men came to Durham in the fifteenth and sixteenth centuries, usually accused of murder and often from Tyneside. Unfortunately, we do not know what happened in Robert Green's case. (Hutchinson, W., *The History and Antiquities of the County Palatine of Durham*, 1794)

AUGUST 25TH

1830: On this day, a rather unusual performer arrived in town – a Siamese elephant called Miss D'Jeck. Miss D'Jeck was actually quite famous, and had starred in a play. When she performed in Edinburgh, *The Caledonian Review* called her 'talented and colossal', 'stupendous', 'triumphant' and 'the wonder of the age'. Miss D'Jeck was supposed to travel by sea from Edinburgh to Newcastle, but high seas, and the elephant's aversion to carriages, forced them to make the whole journey on foot. It took four days to walk 120 miles from Edinburgh, the elephant following her keeper without the need for a tether. Thousands of people gathered in Barrass Bridge to watch Miss D'Jeck's entry into the town and she performed that very night (they had to enlarge the Theatre Royal stage door specially). Most of the crowd would not have known Miss D'Jeck's dark secret. The previous day, near Morpeth, one of her regular attendants, the Italian Baptiste Bernard, had died. Apparently the two had been at odds since the man, drunk, had stabbed her with a pitchfork three years before. On the 22nd, finding themselves alone, she grabbed him around the waist with her trunk and squeezed so hard that his ribs were broken. He died two days later. After finishing her Newcastle engagement, the triumphant Miss D'Jeck boarded a ship for London. (Sykes, J., *Local Records*, 1833)

AUGUST 26TH

1945: On this day, Newcastle staged a massive victory parade in celebration of the end of the Second World War. Victory in Europe was declared in May, while Japan surrendered in early August. A few weeks later, everything was in place for what was thought to be the biggest parade the city had ever seen. Represented were every branch of the British and Allied military services. Several unusual military vehicles took part, as did several bands, and two squadrons of fighter planes flew over in formation. Decorated war heroes rubbed shoulders with the military police, veterans of the Boer War and First World War, the Fire Service, and many more. Women's contribution was well represented, with Wrens, nurses, land girls and others; and hundreds of children participated, including the Boys' Brigade, the Girl Guides, and the British Junior Red Cross. Included in the naval personnel were the crew of HMS *Newcastle*, built in the Tyne in 1937 and widely known as the 'Knock 'Em Down Newcastle' for her part in the Battle of Britain. In beautiful weather, the parade walked from around Fenham Barracks along Barrack Road and Blackett Street before heading north to Haymarket, finishing at the South African War Memorial. It is estimated that up to 100,000 people turned out to watch. (*Sunday Sun / Evening Chronicle*)

AUGUST 27TH

1826: On this day, a drunken joiner stood up in the middle of Sunday service at St Nicholas Church, Newcastle, and shouted out, 'Bell for ever!', in support of a Parliamentary candidate. His trial was exceptionally swift (one suspects some magistrates were probably witnesses) and the man was placed in the stocks in the churchyard for two hours that afternoon, in punishment. This is all slightly odd given that the election was long over. Colliery owner Bell was a Tory, one of the two MPs for Northumberland, first voted in in February 1826 following an unexpected death, and then narrowly being returned as Northumberland's second choice in a bitterly fought contest in June. While he didn't last 'forever', he did pretty well – he took the new seat 'Northumberland South' in 1832 despite a smear campaign, and kept the position for twenty years. 1826 was a good year for political strangeness in Newcastle. At the time, the Bullman family were building Bullman Village, a cluster of houses in Gosforth, specifically to create housing for people who would vote the way they wanted. Each house had just enough land to qualify the owner for a vote … the area had so few voters that every new one made a difference! (www.historyofparliamentonline)

AUGUST 28TH

1640: On this day was fought the Battle of Newburn Ford, the only battle of the Second Bishop's War. The Scottish leaders declared they were not against the king, only against those who were misleading him. This was largely to do with religion, and bitterness stemming from an attempt to impose Anglicanism on the Scots. Around 4,000 English troops had been sent to cover the ford at Newburn, and bar passage to the Scots army, all 20-25,000 of them. They withdrew to the south side of the Tyne, and hastily built defensive structures, but they were not well positioned. They were also ill-equipped, and often reluctant, conscripts. The Scots, much better prepared and motivated, were able to take higher and less open ground on the northern side, in and around Newburn village. From here, they began a bombardment. The tide ebbed, the ford became passable, and the Scots army crossed the river to finish off the now demoralised English. Around 250 soldiers were killed, but most surrendered. (As a side note, this was one of the last times that bows and arrows were used in battle on British soil.) Two days later, Newcastle was surrendered to the Scots. Charles I tried to get Parliament to raise more taxes to fight the Scots army, but failed. In the end he more or less had to buy the town back – and the Civil War drew one step closer. (Melia, S., *The Battle of Newburn Ford*, Tyne Riverside Country Park, 2004)

AUGUST 29TH

1851: On this day, surgeons became thieves in a daring, if somewhat surreal, raid. At this time, the medical school building was being demolished to make way for a railway line, and a new building was being built at Rye Hill. But in 1851 a complex argument led to the school dividing, with one half moving out, while the other half remained. The latter had a problem – they had to work in the gardener's house, and build a temporary structure for preparing dissection specimens. Things became heated between the groups, with impassioned letters appearing in the *Lancet*. But the biggest point of contention was the museum of medical specimens, without which neither the College of Surgeons or the Apothecaries Society would recognise the school. So there was only one thing for it – the Rye Hill group broke into the Nun Street storage room, stole most of the museum, and hid it in an Eldon Lane stable. One of those involved was Dr Glover, who had actually donated many of the items in the first place. The whole thing was sufficiently well publicised to inspire poet John Cargill to write a satirical 'border ballad'; 'The Knichts of St John and the Cross, or the Raid o' the auld Musee'. In the end, complex circumstances caused the two groups to reform a few years later (with the gardener's house group keeping the upper hand). (Dale, G., 'Newcastle's Medical Schools', Medicine in Northumbria, Pybus Society, 1993)

AUGUST 30TH

1368: On this day, chaplain 'Sir' Robert Merlay found himself in trouble – for building work in the churchyard. Over the previous 150 years, the old St Nicholas Church had twice suffered fire damage, and in 1359 a programme of repair and extension work was begun, as a project of the Bishop and Prior of Carlisle. This was quite extensive, including heightening the walls to let more light in, and work was still going on nine years later. It appears the locals had had the temerity to begin a replacement for the choir area of the church, intending to pull the old one down, without getting permission from Carlisle (or at least, that's what the men who were sent to investigate thought was going on). They found Merlay in the churchyard, 'chipping and working on a certain stone'. Merlay refused to stop, or to say who was in charge of the work, despite being shown the Bishop's seal. The commission then took Merlay to two town burgesses and demanded that they do something, telling them 'that they should not proceed further in building the new work, or in demolishing the ancient choir, to the prejudice and damage of his said masters'. They placed a new procurator in charge of the building work and went home, hoping that it wouldn't happen again. (Welford, R., *History of Newcastle and Gateshead*, 1836)

AUGUST 31ST

1853: On this day, a man died of cholera in St Andrew's parish. Cholera was rife in Hamburg and the Baltic at this point, and there were many ships coming in. The first deaths had been a few days earlier, in Bill Quay, on the south bank of the Tyne; while we can't be entirely sure, it seems likely that this death was the first cholera victim in Newcastle that year. It was the first indication of what was to become a major outbreak, lasting until late October and killing over 1,500 people. This was much more severe than previous outbreaks, which claimed 300 lives in 1832, and 400 in 1848. At its worst, in mid-September, more than 100 people were dying each day. The pattern of death has been closely mapped, and you can clearly see the clusters around individual tenement blocks. The worst impact was in St Nicholas' parish, where the death rate was around one in forty-five. For example, thirty-nine people died in Pudding Chare and a single alleyway off it. In October, the Mayor asked people to observe high standards of cleanliness, and open their windows to ventilate the rooms during the day – but this was often virtually impossible to achieve. More generally, the advice was to avoid 'strong opening medicine', treat loose bowels immediately, keep clean and warm, and avoid getting damp, drunk, or eating stale fish, unripe fruit or raw vegetables.

SEPTEMBER 1ST

1939: On this day, the Second World War began when Germany invaded Poland. Closer to home, the first effects of war hit hard and fast. Plans to evacuate local children had been drawn up in mid-August, and full-scale rehearsals took place with children gathering in school yards with gas masks in hand and identification labels tied to their clothing. But today, it began in earnest, as around a fifth of the area's children – around 30,000 – were evacuated. This was only 71 per cent of those eligible; probably because some parents did not want to see their children go. They were sent right across the north, many to Cumbria, Teesdale, and North Yorkshire. Peg, from Paradise, Benwell, remembers that day: 'My mum was crying and saying "you'll be all right", and the police was saying, "You'll only be away a couple of days and you'll be home". And the vicar came, and he took me, and I thought, "ee, I'll have to be a good girl all the time!" – I remember that distinctly. But when he took me he was taking me for the people I stayed with, because they couldn't come. And I remember thinking "ee thank goodness for that".' Around a third of children went back home within the first few weeks, as the area was not instantly bombed, but Peg did not return home for years. (*Beamish Museum Oral Archive* / www.genuki.org.uk)

September 2nd

1813: On this day, a steam engine began to pull coal wagons in Newcastle. This was not the first steam engine to haul coal – that was in Cornwall in 1804 – but it was a big step forward in the commercial use of rail transport. Coxlodge wagonway had been built over the previous five years as a way to transport coal to the River Tyne. The owner then converted the track using special toothed rails – the 'rack rail' system – and bought a steam locomotive, the *Lord Willington*, patented by John Blenkinsop, a Tynesider working in Middleton Colliery, near Leeds. Its central cog wheel allowed it to pull several wagons (a total weight of over 70 tons) at nearly 3mph. *Lord Willington* was soon joined by two other locally-built engines. But the steam-powered wagonway lasted less than two years. Samuel Smiles, in his book *Lives of the Engineers: George and Robert Stephenson* (1975), called it 'very unsteady and costly; besides, it pulled the rails to pieces, the entire strain being upon the rack-rail on one side of the road. The boiler, having shortly blown up, there was an end of that engine, and the colliery owners did not feel encouraged to try any farther experiment.' However, some claimed the scheme had been scuppered, with the connivance of the pit's new agent, who had an interest in a horse-drawn wagonway from Fawdon which was being inconvenienced by the locomotive. (suscram.weebly.com)

SEPTEMBER 3RD

1892: On this day, Newcastle East End played its first game of football at St James' Park. Newcastle West End had had a poor season, and was finding it impossible to survive financially – shareholders had lost too much money to continue. In this climate, a deal was made allowing the East End team the use of the St James' Park pitch, which was more central than their old Heaton ground. West End would cease to exist, but their members had the chance to join their old rivals. After a few months of consolidation, Newcastle East End began at St James' Park by paying £80 to attract Glasgow Celtic down to Newcastle for a pre-season friendly. They were hoping for a big crowd, and in the event almost 7,000 – very few of whom would have been women, despite ladies being allowed in for free – turned out. The local press called it 'the greatest event known in the local history of the game', despite the visitors being half an hour late to arrive. Celtic won 1-0, but only due to a hotly contested goal, which the referee later said should not have been allowed. With receipts of £147, a small profit had been made and Newcastle East End had staked a claim as a serious contender. (Joannou, P., *United: The First 100 Years*, Polar Print Group, 2000)

SEPTEMBER 4TH

1645: On this day, the House of Commons debated, and decided to send a substantial quantity of weaponry to Newcastle. The town at this point was in the hands of the Scots, who held it on behalf of Parliament (rather than the King, whose fortunes in the Civil War were at a low ebb at this point) and the weaponry was presumably to ensure it stayed that way. They resolved to send 500 muskets and twenty barrels of gunpowder, with enough money for another twenty barrels – all to be delivered to the Mayor, John Blakiston. ('House of Commons Journal Volume 4: 4 September 1645', *Journal of the House of Commons: Volume 4: 1644-1646*, 1802)

———— • ◆ • ————

1838: On this day, Gateshead pipe maker Thomas Cowley walked to the middle of the Tyne Bridge and jumped into the river, where he quickly drowned. While many of those who have jumped into the Tyne over the years have been intent on suicide, Cowley was instead acting on a bet. Perhaps he underestimated the cold, or the strong underwater currents. His death didn't stop others from similar antics: just over twelve years later, a man named Williamson, a worker at the important foundry of Hawks and Crawshay, also jumped into the Tyne, this time from the new High Level Bridge, before swimming to safety. It was put about that he had done it on a wager, for a quart of ale. (Fordyce, T., *Local Records*, 1867)

SEPTEMBER 5TH

1864: On this day, a rowing match on the Tyne was spoiled by the north-eastern weather. Tyneside and World Sculling Champion Robert Chambers was competing with Robert Cooper. The match was set over three and a half miles, from the High Level Bridge to the Scotswood Bridge, and at stake was £400. Chambers was champion – but Cooper was the only person to have previously beaten him, and it was predicted to be a close race. Local factories closed at midday and workmen gathered on every vantage point to place bets – so thick was the crowd that the police could hardly get past. There were even people clinging to the girders of the High Level Bridge. Nineteen packed steamers had turned out on to the water. But the wind was rising, and soon the normally calm Tyne looked more like a rough sea than a river. The two boats smashed into each other, and then Chambers, pulling ahead, clashed with a keelboat that had lost its moorings. He was taking on water, and the match had to be stopped. Amid much argument, the match was rearranged for the following day, with each man in a new boat. In spite of his previous soaking, Chambers went on to show better form in the continued rough water, and won the match comfortably. (*Newcastle Courant*)

SEPTEMBER 6TH

1825: On this day, the Literary and Philosophical Society was celebrating the opening of its new purpose-built premises. Having spent time in several other buildings, in 1822 they finally bought land of their own. The building of the new Lit & Phil (as it became known) was more expensive than first hoped, but made good time. However, the society lost money in a decision to produce their own oil gas to light the building. They found out about a cheaper supply of gas from the Gas Company just too late to cancel the experiment. The building opened in August, and had its first meeting on this day. This was an address by William Turner on the history of the Lit & Phil itself, and the way it had gradually developed from a discussion group to also incorporate a library and a museum. At the same meeting, William Hutton donated 1,200 geological specimens, and other historical and scientific collections soon followed. A few months later they hired two full-time servants to tend to the building – scrubbing the floors, tending the fires, cleaning the windows, polishing the brass, and so on. They also had to spend two days a week making gas! This quickly proved inadequate and the Society had to go back to the Gas Company and take the higher rates then quoted. (Watson, R.S., *The History of the Literary and Philosophical Society of Newcastle upon Tyne*, Walter Scott Ltd, 1897)

SEPTEMBER 7TH

1789: On this day, a meeting was held in Newcastle in celebration of the French Revolution, which had begun a couple of months previously and was still in full swing. At the time, for many of the more radically minded, the revolution was seen as a wonderful thing, overturning a repressive regime; radicals and conservatives debated the issue, and what England could learn from it. So, a small group of Radicals and Whigs arranged to meet in the Turk's Head pub, where they discussed sending a petition to the Mayor asking him, in turn, to call an official meeting to attest 'the sympathy of Englishmen with the cause of the liberty of France'. This second meeting was on the 7th. Here they agreed that, 'This meeting views with joy and admiration, the virtuous, brave and just Struggle of the French People, in Defence of their Rights and Liberties, against the aggressions of a despotic and tyrannical Government'. More incredibly, they stated that the French deserved the gratitude of all Europe, 'and this country in particular ... for their Courage displayed during the conflict ... the unparalleled Calmness, Forbearance and Moderation evinced'. Presumably word of the guillotine had not yet reached them! (Cadogan, P., *Early Radical Newcastle*, Sagittarius P, 1975)

SEPTEMBER 8TH

1814: On this day, reformer and author Thomas Spence died. He had moved to London in 1787, but spent his first thirty-seven years in Newcastle, attempting to win favour for his unusual ideas. A schoolmaster from a very large Quayside family, as a young man Spence joined the Philosophical Society, a group dedicated to debating moral and social philosophy. Aged twenty-four, he presented a paper on the 'Rights of Man' – which he viewed as liberty, air, the light and heat of the sun, and most importantly, the right of property in land. Where it got radical was in the demand for action. He wanted the people of each parish to gather and claim the land for their own, as a corporation, run by an elected parish council, the sole form of government. It would rent the land to its own, everyone getting a plot, and this would be the only taxation. The Society might have tolerated this had it remained within their lecture theatre (although they later claimed indignation that he had only joined to push his dangerous ideals). Then Spence began selling a related pamphlet in public, much as his mother sold stockings from a market stall. This, for the Society, was going too far, and they unanimously expelled him. (Ashraf, P., *The Life and Times of Thomas Spence, Newcastle upon Tyne*, Frank Graham, 1983 / Beal, J., *English Pronunciation in the Eighteenth Century*, Oxford University Press, 2002)

SEPTEMBER 9TH

1874: Figures published in the *Newcastle Courant*, and calculated by Medical Officer Henry Armstrong for the week ending on this day, are a stark reminder of how tough things were in Victorian times. The population of Newcastle may have grown slightly – there were 103 births, and only eighty-two deaths – but those eighty-two deaths still equate to a rate of 31.6 deaths per 1,000 inhabitants (the modern figure is more like one third of that). Thirty-two of those that died were under one year old, and another fifteen under the age of five. That means 57 per cent of those who died were under the age of five. At the other end of the scale, eleven people had made it past sixty, and two had reached eighty. Among the diseases responsible, scarlet fever took five victims, whooping cough two, and diarrhoea eight. For the latter, obviously a greater problem in the summer heat, Armstrong not unreasonably recommends care with food and drink, like tainted fish, and milk that is even slightly sour – as well as the avoidance of raw vegetables and unripe fruit. The biggest killers were heart and lung problems which together took twelve victims. Two people died 'by violence', and inquests were held on another six (which found causes of 'neglect, apoplexy, heart disease, epilepsy, burns, and wilful murder'). (*Newcastle Courant*)

September 10th

1575: On this day, the guilds of coopers, turners, rope-makers and pulley-makers announced that 'no Scotsman born, or any other alien, was to set up shop or be employed in these trades in Newcastle under a 40 shilling fine'. There were a lot of Scotsmen in Newcastle – with plague and other diseases, immigration was necessary to keep the population up – and most of them ended up as keelmen and labourers. In Tyneside, 'Scot' remained a term of insult, and the archetypal Scotsman the butt of jokes well into the eighteenth century. (www.freemenofnewcastle.org)

———◆———

1999: On this day, the computer game 'Driver' was released for the PC, a couple of months after its Playstation release. It was made by Newcastle company Reflections Interactive, and revolved around a series of challenges undertaken in a car, pioneering the freedom to explore many of the streets of a virtual city. In many ways this was a direct ancestor of the better-known Grand Theft Auto. As a nod to its origins, a section of Newcastle was modelled and played through the end credits. With the right software, this can be 'unlocked' and driven around. Reflections Interactive is now Ubisoft Reflections, a subsidiary of major games developer Ubisoft. It is still based in Newcastle, and still specialises in racing games. (http://uk.gamespot.com/driver)

SEPTEMBER 11TH

1991: On this day, and the following day, the streets of Scotswood and Elswick were aflame as rioting hit Newcastle. The chaos had begun in Meadowell, North Shields, on the evening of the 9th, in response to the deaths of two young car thieves on the 8th. Believing that the deaths were caused by an over-aggressive police pursuit, the youth of Meadowell were fired up into burning and looting. This spilled into Benwell on the 10th, before intensifying for the next two nights. This was the tail end of the Thatcherite era, and life was grim in the West End. Unemployment had quadrupled over the previous five years, with massive job losses in the Vickers factories. The West End had the worst health and mortality rates in Newcastle, which was itself the poorest, sickest city in England. On this night, around thirty fires were lit across the district, stretching the resources of fire-fighters. When they went to a blaze at the derelict pub, The Dodds Arms, they were met with hundreds of youths throwing stones, bricks and petrol bombs; they had to return with police in riot gear. A solicitor's office, a school and a housing office were set alight, and Armstrong Road blocked with burning cars. The motive was more frustration and alienation than any coherent vision or protest, and a wave of protests in other poverty-stricken estates followed. (*The Guardian* / Reed, D., 'The Meadowell Riots of 1991', *North East History*, 2011)

September 12th

1823: On this day, the glassmakers undertook one of their spectacular processions through the streets of Newcastle and Gateshead. There were several glass-houses along the banks of the Tyne and the Wear, which combined forces to display their produce in procession. While several guilds did this sort of thing, the glassmakers procession must have been particularly fine. As well as the usual music and flags, every man's clothing was decorated with glass ornaments – the best, most beautiful examples of their art, which shone in the rays of sunshine on a gorgeous late summer day. Mackenzie described the 'glittering column' as possessing a 'richness and grandeur of appearance that defy description'. An extra dimension came from the sound of a glass bugle, played to sound the halts, and its 'rich and sweet tone' – and the finale was a salute from a 'fort mounted with glass cannon'. Large crowds turned out to watch and admire the spectacle. Interestingly, Mackenzie contrasted the procession with that of 1789. He called the earlier display a 'ludicrous and boyish show (intended to ridicule the silly exhibition of the cordwainers)', and complements the glassmakers on their improved taste! (Mackenzie, E., *A Descriptive and Historical Account of the Town and County of Newcastle upon Tyne: Including the Borough of Gateshead*, 1827)

SEPTEMBER 13TH

1917: On this day, broadcaster and journalist Nancy Spain was born in Jesmond. Spain grew up a tomboy with a love of literature (playing St George to her elder sister's damsel in distress and father's 'dragon'). At eighteen, she was reporting on women's sports for the *Newcastle Journal* as well as playing in several teams herself. She also fell in love – with team-mate Winifred Sergeant, with whom she had a relationship for several years. At nineteen, she had her first of several radio roles, in BBC Newcastle's *The Lang Pack*. The producer told her, 'As an amateur actress, you were a remarkably good professional screamer'. Serving with the WRNS during the Second World War widened Spain's horizons, and she moved to London, writing a well-received book about her wartime experiences, a biography of her great-aunt Isabella Beeton, and some quirky detective fiction. In the 1950s and '60s she was a regular columnist for the *Daily Express* (during which time she was twice sued by Evelyn Waugh), *Good Housekeeping*, and *The News of the World*. At the same time, she was living openly as a lesbian – at one stage with the editor of *She* magazine – and socialising with the likes of Noel Coward and Marlene Dietrich. Her death, with her partner in an aeroplane crash on the way to the Grand National, was a fitting capstone to an eccentric life. (Collis, R., *A Trouser-Wearing Character*, Continuum International, 1999)

September 14th

1782: On this day, a novel use for the roofless and crumbling Castle Keep was proposed. The *Newcastle Courant* carried this advert: 'A Wind-mill in the centre of the town of Newcastle. To be Let, the old Castle, in the Castle Garth, upon which, with the greatest convenience and advantage, may be erected a Wind-mill, for the purpose of grinding corn, and bolting flour, or making oil, &c. There is an exceeding good spring of water within the Castle; which renders it a very eligible situation for a Brewery, or any Manufactory that requires a constant supply of water. The proprietor, upon proper terms, will be at a considerable part of the expense. Inquire of Mr. Fryer, in Westgate Street, Newcastle.' Certainly it wasn't functioning terribly well as a jail. It was only used during assize week, to store prisoners from across the county, but that was bad enough. Five years later, philanthropist John Howard visited as part of his tour of prisons. He describes conditions as 'a dirty damp dungeon … having no roof, in wet seasons the water is some inches deep. The felons are chained to rings in the wall'. On Assize Sunday, the public could pay sixpence to peer at the prisoners. The advert apparently had no takers, so the keep remained an untenanted shell except when its prison was needed. Around it the Garth became packed with shops, tenements, rag-markets and taverns. (Boyle, J., *Vestiges of Newcastle and Gateshead*, Andrew Reid, 1890)

September 15th

1746: On this day, twenty-three-year-old soldier Alexander Anthony was taken out onto the Town Moor and executed by firing squad. His crime was to turn his coat and enlist with the French army. He had been wounded at the Battle of Fontenoy the previous year (this had been a French victory against the British and Dutch, oddly over something directly claimed by neither – the succession in Austria). Taken prisoner by the French, Anthony somehow escaped and went to join the Scots army in the 1745 rebellion. Taken prisoner again at Culloden, he managed to re-join the British army that held him. It is unclear whether he actually directly supported the French cause, although he certainly was a Roman Catholic. (Sykes, J., *Local Records, Volume I*, 1833)

———◆———

1966: On this day, the North East Labour History Society was formed, when four members of the Society for the Study of Labour History met at Rutherford College and formed an *ad hoc* committee aiming to draft a constitution and get things up and running locally. Things were formalised later in the year, and the first programmed meeting was held in early 1967. The North East was the first English region to form its own labour history group, and is still going strong today. (www.nelh.net)

September 16th

1825: On this day, at half past ten in the evening, staff at the coach office of The Turf Head, Collingwood Street, were left a travelling trunk, with instructions to send it on to Edinburgh in the morning. Unfortunately it was accidentally left in the south-going pile, so it missed the Saturday service north, and there was no north-bound Sunday service. On Monday, 'a most nauseous smell was felt from a liquid oozing therefrom'. When the trunk was opened, on magistrate's orders, it was found to contain the remains of a fair-haired woman of about nineteen, without marks of violence. She was swiftly buried. This wasn't an isolated incident. Demand for corpses for dissection – for research, but also for education – was growing far faster than legal supply could cope with. The biggest demand came from Edinburgh, so anywhere near a road to Edinburgh was fair game for bodysnatchers trading in corpses. It's not clear whether The Turf Head's staff were particularly vigilant or just unlucky, but they found two more corpses – a man, and an elderly woman – in January 1826. Another, a man over 6 foot tall, was found in a coach from Leeds the same month. The trade did not go away until the Anatomy Act of 1832 – and that brought its own problems (*see* December 19th). (Sykes, J., *Local Records, Volume II,* 1833)

SEPTEMBER 17TH

Over the course of this month, each year, term starts for students at Newcastle and Northumbria Universities (the latter being Newcastle Polytechnic before September 1992). Many famous people have been within their number – some are mentioned elsewhere in this book. Those who are not include several creative figures. Scott Henshall, the youngest designer to show at London fashion week, studied fashion at Northumbria from 1994. Then there is Stephen Appleby, one of the country's foremost political cartoonists, and Jonathan Ive, the designer of the iPod and iMac, who studied Design for Industry from 1986. The former Poly has also educated sportsmen, including world-class middle distance athlete Steve Cram (1980), international rugby player Scott Hastings, Olympic gold-medal winning cyclist Victoria Pendleton (1999), and Stephen Miller, who has won numerous medals in paralympic throwing events, and has held a world record for club throwing since 1997. Newcastle University's alumni include journalist and war reporter Kate Adie (Scandinavian Studies), Richard Adams, the founder of Traidcraft (Business Administration), and Princess Eugenie (English Literature and Art History). Bands and singers with a Newcastle higher education include Sting, Bryan Ferry, members of Maximo Park, the Lighthouse Family, and Prefab Sprout. Politician Mo Mowlam also taught politics at Newcastle University, from 1979 to 1983; a former colleague describes her as 'taking the department by storm ... a breath of fresh air'. (www.ncl.ac.uk / www.northumbria.ac.uk)

September 18th

1773: On this day, poet John Cunningham died in his Union Street lodgings. Cunningham was born and brought up in Dublin, but travelled a lot as a young man and often used Newcastle as his base of operations. As he grew older, he settled in the town and called it home. He was a pastoral poet, in spite of the urban setting, and had had a major success with his play *Love in a Mist*, written at just seventeen. Cunningham was also clearly something of a character. When artist-engraver Thomas Bewick carefully overtook him on the street, in order to sketch a quick pen-portrait, he ended up with an image of an old man clutching a herring in a handkerchief. Locally, Cunningham's biggest hit was perhaps the poem 'Newcastle Beer', in which he praises what antiquarian R. Charleton called 'the local nectar' in fulsome terms. This was also set to music, the better to enjoy it in the pubs. The poem ends:

> Your spirits it raises,
> It cures your diseases -
> There's freedom and health in our Newcastle beer.

John Cunningham is buried in St John's churchyard. (Myers, A., *Myers' Literary Guide*, Carcanet Press, 1995)

SEPTEMBER 19TH

1786: On this day, an early ballooning demonstration went tragically wrong. Ballooning was still new and exciting – the first ever balloon flight had only taken place in 1783. The first English flight was the following year, undertaken by Italian showman Vincent Lunardi, with a cat, a dog, and a pigeon. After this Lunardi seems to have toured around the country, eventually coming to the North. His balloon would have been oiled silk filled with hydrogen, created by a volatile reaction of sulphuric acid and iron filings. At his Newcastle demonstration, Lunardi tested the chemistry, causing a loud expulsion of gas. Some of the men holding the ropes panicked, thinking the balloon was on fire. This wouldn't have been a problem, but because only one side was attached, the balloon developed a tear. In the chaos, the balloon broke free of its remaining ropes, but one man, Ralph Heron – son of the under-sheriff of Northumberland – still had a rope coiled around his hand and arm. He was carried up into the air, before his weight tore the section of balloon to which his rope was attached. He fell into a nearby garden, and died a few hours later. This probably makes Ralph Heron the first ever casualty of air travel. (Mackenzie, E., *A Descriptive and Historical Account of the Town and County of Newcastle upon Tyne: Including the Borough of Gateshead*, 1827 / Stuart, S. and Potts. W., *Richard Gillow and Vincent Lunardi*, Contrebis, 1999)

SEPTEMBER 20TH

1745: On this day, the inhabitants of Newcastle were preparing for an invasion of Scottish soldiers supporting the claim to the throne of Charles Stewart, Bonnie Prince Charlie. John Wesley had arrived in town two days earlier, and wrote in his diary that on the 19th, the Mayor had gathered together all householders and asked them to swear to defend the town, either in person or by sending a substitute. 813 men signed up. Wesley records that today, 'The Mayor ordered the townsmen to be under arms, and to mount guard in their turns, over and above the guard of soldiers, a few companies of whom had been drawn into the town. Now, also, Pilgrim-Street Gate was ordered to be walled up.' The next day, with news of a defeat, the Pandon and Sally-Port gates were also walled up. And on the 22nd, 'the walls were mounted with cannon, and all things prepared for sustaining an assault. Meantime our poor neighbours, on either hand, were busy in removing their goods. And most of the best houses in our street were left without either furniture or inhabitants. More and more of the Gentry every hour rode southward as fast as they could.' Wesley also reports a huge congregation for Sunday service at St Andrew's: 'The sermon Mr. Ellison preached was strong and weighty, which he could scarce conclude for tears.' (*The Diary of John Wesley*)

SEPTEMBER 21ST

1892: On this day, a golf course was opened on the Town Moor. This was to be the course for the 'Newcastle United Workmen's Golf Club', formed in Lockhart's Cocoa Rooms, Clayton Street, a couple of months earlier with the intention of making golf accessible to all. At some point in 1892 they also took a fascinating building as a clubhouse. This was the Chimney Mills windmill, in Spital Tongues, only decommissioned a few months previously, and still with sails. Built in 1782 and working for over 100 years, Chimney Mill was the first five-sailed smock mill in Britain (a smock mill is wooden, rather than stone-built, and usually hexagonal). It was designed by John Smeaton, a master civil engineer who also designed the third Eddystone Lighthouse. Though the sails were removed in the 1930s and weatherboarding now replaces its top cap, Chimney Mill still stands. Other nearby golfers apparently didn't appreciate sharing the moor with such an egalitarian group, and went off to form Northumberland Golf Club in 1898. Both clubs survive to this day, though the mill is no longer used for golf. (www.newcastleunitedgolfclub.co.uk / www.english-heritage.org.uk)

SEPTEMBER 22ND

1752: On this day was executed a man who became something of a local legend. Ewan McDonald was a Scottish soldier billeted at the Black Bull Inn, in the Bigg Market. According to his confession, he was provoked until he lost his temper (the last straw being insults against Scotland), and lashed out. Killing someone with a knife was deemed murder, and Ewan McDonald was hanged, despite a last-minute attempt to make a break for it from the scaffold. Usually that would be the end of the tale, but here things get interesting. The *Newcastle Courant* for October 14th gives a conventional account of a public dissection, with exhibition of the body parts, but antiquarian Sykes then said that, on this day, when the body was first taken from the scaffold to the barber surgeons' hall, the surgeons left the room and returned to find MacDonald was sitting upright. The surgeon, 'not wishing to be disappointed of the dissection, seized a wooden mallet with which he deprived him of life'. In 1887, the hapless criminal gained the nickname 'half-hanged'. (Redfern, B., *The Shadow of the Gallows*, Tynebridge Publishing, 2003)

September 23rd

1717: On this day, the Holy Jesus Hospital began to run under new regulations. Built on the site of the old Augustinian Friary, the hospital had been in existence since 1681. Run by a charity, the Holy Jesus Hospital was more a hospice and old people's home than a modern hospital. There were thirty-six inmates – male and female, known as brothers and sisters – and six women, drawn from widows and daughters of freemen of the town, aged between thirty and fifty, to care for them and ensure that they kept their rooms and passages 'sweet and clean'. Every Christmas, each inmate was given a purple gown – and no wonder they needed one every year, since they had to wear them to divine service every Wednesday, Friday, Sunday and lecture day. The inmates were given £1 per three months from the town's funds, and a share of the donations placed in the charity box outside – but they were banned from begging. There was a curfew – 10 p.m. in summer, and 8 p.m. in winter. Any sort of immoral behaviour – being of 'ill fame, namely a drunkard, swearer or disorderly person' – would lead to ejection. They would also be removed if they were to 'marry, take inmates, or otherwise misbehave'! (*Tyne and Wear Archives*)

September 24th

1958: On this day, the Northern Sinfonia – the first permanent chamber orchestra in Britain – played its first concert. The key mover behind the development of the Northern Sinfonia was Michael Hall. Aware that the withdrawal of Liverpool Orchestra from the region left Newcastle's classical music scene looking distinctly bare, with no professional orchestra within 130 miles, Hall decided to solve the problem himself, by putting together a chamber orchestra. It helped that he'd been working with the amateur Tyneside Chamber Orchestra over the previous two years. He borrowed £1,000 from his father and began raising funds and interest, lobbying councillors and MPs, trying to get different local authorities to work together to support the proposition (an idea which, he recalls, seemed somewhat radical at the time). Initially the meetings were in a temporary space within the Quaker Meeting House, and the performers were freelance, gathered from local players, former members of the Yorkshire Symphony Orchestra, and freelancers brought in from Liverpool, Manchester and London. Many of them received more in travel expenses than in fees, and concerts were scheduled on Wednesdays to take advantage of cheap rail fares. The *Northern Echo* reported that the orchestra 'astonished the audience with the high quality of their playing' on the first night at City Hall. The Sinfonia went from strength to strength, and recently moved to the Sage, Gateshead. (Griffiths, B., *Northern Sinfonia*, Northumbria University Press, 2004)

SEPTEMBER 25TH

1701: On this day, coal owner John Fenwick of Rock was hanged. Unusually, this took place within the town walls. This was because Fenwick was a member of a large family of Northumberland Fenwicks, and the authorities were afraid that they, or his mining workforce, might try to stage a rescue. A second reason was that the hanging took place on the exact same spot as the crime. Fenwick's crime was an unusual one. He had apparently entered the Black Horse Inn, Newgate Street, singing a song which was derogatory to a rival family, the Forsters of Bamburgh. Presumably he knew that Fernando Forster, a Northumberland MP, was having dinner there (this being the best inn in town). They quarrelled – probably aided by drink – and Fenwick challenged Forster to a duel, which Forster apparently accepted. According to one version of events, they fought and Forster lost – and deaths within a duel were murder in the eyes of the law. A less likely story is that Fenwick stabbed Forster in the back as he left the inn. Unfortunately for Fenwick, this was assize week, and the jury had gathered in the Black Horse Inn for a relaxing evening meal. Hence his crime was committed in full view of the people who tried him when he was caught a few days later! (Bath, J., *Violence and Violent Crime in the North East*, PhD, Newcastle University, 2000)

September 26th

1748: On this day, Cuthbert – later Lord – Collingwood, was born. Newcastle Quayside would have been a constantly shifting scene of sailors with tales from around the world, attractive to a small boy living just up the hill, on Side. After a few years Collingwood moved with his family to Morpeth, but still attended Newcastle's Royal Grammar School. Indeed, George III noticed his good English, and even understood the reason for it – Collingwood, like Lord Eldon, 'was one of Moises' boys'. In 1761, Collingwood volunteered for the navy as a low-ranking midshipman on board the *Shannon*, a twenty-eight-gun frigate commanded by a family friend, with his father paying £30 for his introduction to the harsh life of the navy. Collingwood rose steadily through the ranks, along the way meeting and befriending Horatio Nelson. By the time of Trafalgar, Nelson was given command and Collingwood was his second – and after Nelson's death, Collingwood took over in the heat of battle. That's how a Geordie came to be given command of the British Fleet. He retained links to the North East, promoting other Tynesiders to prominent naval positions and planting oak forests in the Cheviots to provide wood for the naval vessels of the future. (Adams, M., *Collingwood: Northumberland's Heart of Oak*, Tynebridge Publishing, 2005)

SEPTEMBER 27TH

1847: On this day, William Maclachlan – better known as Cuddy Willy – died. Although he has been called one of the great Victorian eccentrics of Newcastle, there is nothing romantic or charming about his tale. A beggar and a drunk (who tended to pawn any decent clothing he was given for drinking money), he spent his days wandering from pub to pub singing and playing a rough 'violin' – a piece of wood with a couple of strings attached. Eventually he drank himself to death, when a pub offered him as much brandy as he wanted, presumably for reasons of cruel amusement rather than kindness. The same year, with a certain inevitability, Cuddy Willy's story was itself turned into a song, by Joshua Bagnall. 'Cuddy Willy's Deeth' waxes lyrical about how 'silly' Maclachlan was, how much he drank, how he would eat almost anything, and how often he would end up in jail for smashing windows. All in all, Cuddy Willy reminds us not to be overly sentimental about the Victorian town, its beggars, or those who treated them as entertainment. (Colls, R., *The Colliers Rant: Song and Culture in the Industrial Village*, Croom Helm Rowman and Littlefield, 1977)

SEPTEMBER 28TH

1849: On this day, the Royal family visited Newcastle … sort of. They were on their way back from a holiday in Scotland on the Royal Train, and travelled – very slowly and in the pouring rain – through the town. Thousands of people lined the route; triumphal arches were made for the train to pass under, flags and flowers placed on every available surface. Queen Victoria and her family nodded and waved from the windows, while the crowd craned for a glimpse. In the centre of the High Level Bridge, a platform had been erected with dignitaries from Newcastle and Gateshead alike. The Royal Train stopped for ten minutes to take in the view, and listen to addresses from the two Mayors, before it set off again. This is thought to be the first visit of a Queen of England to Newcastle since 1461, when Margaret of Anjou, wife of King Henry VI, fled the Battle of Towton. But does it really count, since Victoria never set foot off the train? Either way, it is often thought of as the official opening of the High Level Bridge, which certainly didn't have another one. Allegedly, many years later, Victoria developed a reputation for closing the blinds of her railway carriage whenever she passed through Newcastle, not because she thought it ugly, but because she thought it contained a lot of Republicans. (www.gateshead-history.com / Todd, N., *The Militant Democracy*, Bewick Press, 1991)

SEPTEMBER 29TH

1763: On this day, the Newcastle Lamp and Watch Act was passed. This stated that up to fifty able-bodied men would be paid to 'watch within the walls' between September 29th and March 25th, and whenever else required. Their job was to 'prevent all Mischiefs happening by Fires, as all Murders, Burglaries, Robberies, and other Outrages and Disorders', with power to arrest 'Nightwalkers, Malefactors and suspected Persons who shall be found wandering and misbehaving themselves.' They were to take these people to a jail tower on the middle of the old Tyne Bridge until they could be seen by a magistrate. All this was administered by forty-eight commissioners and paid for by a special levy on land rent. The commissioners also regulated chairmen (who carried sedan chairs), hackney coachmen, cartmen, common porters and watermen. The other half of the Act involved lighting the town with oil lamps; again, their exact number, position and timing was left in the hands of the commissioners. Anyone convicted of 'wilfully damaging the posts, irons or other furniture thereof' would be fined £10 per lamp 'broken, taken away, thrown down, extinguished, or otherwise wilfully damaged'. If, on the other hand, they did it accidentally, they would have three days to pay costs for whatever damage was done. The lamps were put up and lit for the first time on October 1st. The area covered was not extended beyond the walls until 1812. (*Tyne and Wear Archives*)

SEPTEMBER 30TH

1761: On this day, the last accounts for the first Lying-In Hospital were produced. By this point, they had discharged around 3,500 women (while the home birth charity had dealt with three times as many), and only twenty-two had died in hospital. This figure – around six deaths per 1,000 live births – did not improve until the 1930s. The accounts from this date show that the books were being balanced at a little over £250 for the year. £108 went on 'housekeeping', and £20 on building rent. When it came to wages, the matron did well – £30 compared to £13 13s for all the servants' wages put together. £14 went on medicine, and £3 on registering those children baptised within the hospital. Over £21 went on 'advertising, printing, stamps, stationery articles, and insurance of furniture in the Newcastle Fire Office'. Most of this money came from big donations and subscriptions – only 17 shillings was left in the poor box. The building was abandoned when a new purpose-built Lying-In hospital was built in New Bridge Street. The land was donated by the Corporation, and John Dobson gave his services as an architect for free. The hospital was opened on October 4th, and still stands. (Mackenzie, E., *A Descriptive and Historical Account of the Town and County of Newcastle upon Tyne: Including the Borough of Gateshead*, 1827)

OCTOBER 1ST

1832: On this day, a training school in surgery was opened in Bells Court. James Miller remembered, 'The lectures were delivered in a large room fitted up as a lecture room which had adjoining it a small retiring room for the lecturers – the room was crowded with medical men and their pupils'. Another student was John Snow. Best known for his London investigations into cholera, Snow first met the disease in the pit villages of Tyneside. These two men, and a handful of others, took lectures in chemistry, surgery, anatomy and physiology, alongside infirmary training. The first man dissected at Bells Court was J. Morgan, a Groat Market cutler. He was deformed, and sold his own body to the surgeons for £10, saying that, as he had made his money by the medical profession, he would let them have his body to assist the school. (*Medicine in Northumbria*, The Pybus Society, 1993)

———— •◆• ————

2009: On this day, Catherine Douglas and Peter Rawlinson of Newcastle University were awarded the Ig Nobel Prize for Veterinary Medicine, for demonstrating that cows who have names give more milk than those which do not. This was not the first Ig Nobel Prize ('for achievements that first make people LAUGH then make them THINK') to go to Newcastle. Five years previously, a Newcastle team won the Peace prize for 'electrically monitoring the activity of a brain cell in a locust while that locust was watching selected highlights from the movie *Star Wars*' – the point being to monitor responses to moving objects. (improbable.com)

OCTOBER 2ND

1648: On this day, the newly elected Mayor, Thomas Bonner, received a nasty shock at the hands of his citizens. As he was walking towards his home with other Corporation men, apprentice Edmond Marshall threw a stone at him. The group got indoors, and in the darkness people threw stones at the windows and knocked over lit torches. That was nothing compared to events twelve years later. On this day in 1660, Bonner was lying seriously injured following an incident the previous night. When he passed the staff of Mayoral office to the next incumbent, Bonner was (according to Ambrose Barnes) 'so pushed and bruised ... that he was carried out in his chair half dead, such was the violence of the faction'. The possible reasons are complicated, ranging from anger against local political corruption and nepotism, to anti-commonwealth sentiment or protest against developments along the Tyne. Bonner died twelve days later. (Bath, J., *Violence and Violent Crime in the North East*, PhD, Newcastle University, 2000)

———◆·◆———

1952: On this day, John Dewhirst, the only Englishman to die on the Killing Fields of Cambodia, was born in Jesmond. While on a backpacking holiday, teacher Dewhirst was kidnapped with two friends (a Canadian and a New Zealander), when their motorised junk, the Foxy Lady, drifted into Cambodian waters. They were taken to a prison camp and tortured by Pol Pot's executioner, Comrade Duch, until they signed confessions admitting to being CIA agents, and were executed. (*The Observer*)

OCTOBER 3RD

2002: On this day, the Environment Agency announced that the Tyne was the best salmon river in England and Wales. Salmon swim out to sea and back inland again every year, so they can only thrive if the river is unpolluted all the way up. Salmon fishing on the Tyne goes back a very long way. On June 12th 1755, more than 2,400 salmon were caught by a single net fishery, just above Newcastle Bridge. And in 1759, the river's largest ever individual fish was recorded, weighing in at 54lb. In Victorian times, over 100,000 might be taken in a single year. But numbers were starting to decline. The river was being dredged, disturbing habitats, and huge fishing nets at the river mouth took their toll on fish stocks. As the first flushing toilets were brought in, thousands of gallons of untreated sewage poured into the river. This added to the products of expanding industries – the riverside was crowded with tanneries, alkali works, soap works, breweries, gas works, and abattoirs, and oxygen levels plummeted. By the 1930s, what few fish were caught tasted tarry! In the 1950s, the Tyne salmon was almost extinct. But in the 1970s, several large industrial complexes along the river were closed down, and the massive Tyneside Sewage Treatment System came online. The salmon started to come back, supported by a restocking programme. (*The Independent / Environment Agency report on the Tyne Hatchery*)

OCTOBER 4TH

1968: On this night, legendary rock group Led Zeppelin played their first English gig – in the Newcastle Mayfair. Technically, the group on stage were billed as the New Yardbirds (featuring Jimmy Page). The Yardbirds had split up in July, but guitarist Jimmy Page got permission to put together a new line-up, and use the name to fulfil contract obligations in Scandinavia. To all intents and purposes, this was Led Zeppelin taking to the stage for the first time, with Page joined by singer Robert Plant, bassist John Paul Jones and drummer John Bonham. Returning to this country, the New Yardbirds stayed together, and now they had new material. Fans knew they were getting something special, and many sneaked in through the exit doors. Norman Kemp, the manager of the Mayfair, had been standing with the bouncers and as various interlopers made their way in, he tapped them on the collarbone with his pipe before ejecting them. They could later be identified by a yellow stain on their shirts! The tour was a modest success (though a reviewer of a London gig a couple of months later said, 'Generally there appears to be a need for Led Zeppelin to cut down on volume a bit'!) From here, the stage was set for success in America and then a triumphant return to Britain (and indeed, in 1971, to the Mayfair). (*Evening Chronicle* / www.newyardbirds.co.uk)

OCTOBER 5TH

1767: On this day, young Thomas Bewick had his first day at work. Four days previously, he had travelled with his father into Newcastle, and to the Cock Inn, where engraver Ralph Beilby was waiting. There was apparently some disagreement about the terms of the apprenticeship – Bewick later wondered if Beilby had heard some bad report, having been something of a wild youth – but when his local vicar came out in praise of his good nature, Beilby accepted the deal. Ralph Beilby at this point had a small, specialised silver engraving business, and was branching out into seal carving, and copperplate printing. The latter was particularly appealing since the major local competition, Thomas Jameson, had recently been disgraced when he was tried for cashing some of the £5 notes he had been licensed to print for Newcastle Old Bank! Bewick's workload was varied from the start. Within the order book for Bewick's first week were orders for a regimental seal, tankards and soup spoons, a punch ladle and a teapot, writing on dog collars, whips, and nameplates; and even a £20 note. Fittingly, a year later – having moved into wood carving, which was later to become his stock in trade – Bewick made the bar bill for the Cock Inn, where he had signed his papers. (Uglow, J., *Nature's Engraver*, Faber and Faber, 2007)

OCTOBER 6TH

1854: On this day, the warehouses, shops and houses packed along the Quaysides of Newcastle and Gateshead alike were devastated by fire. Beginning in a Gateshead warehouse in the early hours, it soon spread into other warehouses filled with a lethal mix of noxious, flammable and explosive chemicals and sharp objects. It would be hard to create a more dangerous combination, and although fire precautions had been taken, they were not up to the task. Spectators had gathered on the High Level Bridge and the Newcastle quay to watch the explosions of purple flames and streams of molten lead and liquid sulphur. But then came a massive explosion, big enough to be heard 20 miles away, which killed or injured almost the entire fire brigade of Tyneside. It also sent large quantities of stone and flaming material into the timber structures on the northern shore. Dilapidated tenement blocks 'fell like houses made of cards' into the growing flames, as scores of people were injured. The fire blazed on, visible 50 miles away, and did not die down until well into the morning of the 7th. Half of the Quayside's buildings were completely destroyed, and many more severely damaged. Around 200 families were made homeless, several hundred people were injured, and about fifty died. (Rewcastle, J., *A Record of the Great Fire of Newcastle and Gateshead*, 1855 / *The Illustrated London News*)

OCTOBER 7TH

1876: On this day, politician and journalist William Adams launched the Dicky Bird Society within the *Newcastle Weekly Chronicle*. His pseudonym – Uncle Toby – came from a character in *Tristram Shandy* so well-disposed towards animals that he even helped flies. The aim was to create a group of children united in a love of wildlife, especially birds. At the time children would commonly steal nests or eggs; in contrast, members would pledge 'to be kind to all living things, to protect them to the utmost of my power, to feed the birds in the winter time, and never to take or destroy a nest.' They would put nest boxes and food out and campaigned against egg theft, feathers in millinery, and live bird target shooting. They had a distinguishing mark, the yellow ribbon, and a weekly column in the newspaper. There were also competitions, often for essay writing. Boys who excelled themselves were titled 'captain', while girls were 'companions'.

The Dicky Bird Society spread quickly, praised by the children themselves. Adams even received letters from workhouse children who saved their crumbs for the birds. Though Adams died in 1906, Uncle Toby went on – in 1938 the society had nearly 500,000 members. It had branches right across the world, and spawned copycat organisations in many other newspapers. It must have made a massive contribution towards changing attitudes on the environment. (Milton, F., *Taking the Pledge: A Study of Children's Nature Conservation Movements in Britain 1870-1914* / www.eh-resources.org (2005))

OCTOBER 8TH

1752: On this day, Newcastle Infirmary opened the doors of its permanent home for the first time, with a service, procession, and formal examination of new patients. It was the seventh infirmary in the country, providing up to two months of hospital care for ninety patients. As well as beds, the Infirmary boasted a chapel and an operating theatre. Soon after it was built, Wesley praised the Newcastle Infirmary building as 'finely situated on top of a hill … the best ordered of any place of the kind I have seen in England'. All this was paid for by subscription. The infirmary ran on the 'letter' system, which was to dominate hospital care of the next century. It would help those poor who could provide a letter of recommendation – and these letters were handed out to donors, churches and other 'suitable' people. In theory this meant that a certain amount of vetting could go on in advance – but this did not necessarily mean patients came with high behavioural standards. The patients' drunk and disorderly habits drove the regime to 'name and shame' the wrongdoers in all the wards. Patients had very little power to affect their circumstances – when in 1754 they complained about the poor quality of their meat and drink, they were rewarded by being put on toast and water for a week! More than five times more money was spent on food than on medicine.

OCTOBER 9TH

1715: On this day, an infantry battalion arrived in Newcastle, aiming to keep the town out of Jacobite hands. The authorities were worried that Newcastle was not sufficiently pro-Royalist. The celebrations for the coronation of George I the previous year had seen counter-demonstrations, the keelmen were notorious for strikes and disorder, and there were suspicions that Sir William Blackett, a Newcastle Tory MP, would help the rebellion given a suitable opportunity – he had the manpower (his workers) and the weapons, and must have known the enemy leader (Thomas Forster, a Tory MP for Northumberland) well. How true this was we'll never know, but one Jacobite did later claim that an Alderman of the town intended to open the gates. But perhaps the Sheriff was right that the people were 'better inclined than thought of'. When the crunch came, Jacobite feeling in the town seems to have stayed at a low-level murmur. Still, by the 9th, all the gates except the Pandon Gate were walled up with stone and lime. On this day the Sheriff raised a posse of men, quickly bolstered by a battalion of infantry who had marched up from York. The following day, £100 was paid out for improving defences, and Blackett protested his loyalty. More troops arrived over the next fortnight, until Forster gave up waiting in Hexham (within striking distance of Newcastle) and moved north into the borders. (Oates, J., 'Responses in Newcastle upon Tyne to the Jacobite Rebellions of 1715 and 1745', *Archaeologia Aeliana*, 2003)

OCTOBER 10TH

1928: On this day, the Tyne Bridge was officially opened. Newcastle and Gateshead Town Councils had for decades been considering building a high level road bridge, especially as it became clear that the North East Railways were continuing to draw profits from a toll on the High Level Bridge long after they had recouped their costs. But though various committees met over the years, no one was willing to put their money behind the proposals. In the 1920s, as traffic increased and the government put money into schemes for the unemployed, the idea became more appealing than ever. Dorman, Long and Co. of Middlesbrough eventually won the contract. They had recently finished a design for Sydney Harbour Bridge, and utilised much of the same design over here (so while the Tyne Bridge was finished first, because it was much smaller, it wasn't started first). The whole thing (including buying land) cost around £1,200,000, of which the government paid 60 per cent. The granite towers were intended as five-storey warehouses, but in the end the internal floors were not built, leaving massive empty spaces (apart from lifts). The bridge was opened by George V with much celebration and the novelty of a camera crew for British Movietone News. (Manders, F. and Potts, R., *Crossing the Tyne*, Tynebridge Publishing, 2001)

OCTOBER 11TH

1819: On this day, tens of thousands of people gathered together on Town Moor. The catalyst was the Peterloo Massacre, in which unarmed demonstrators in Manchester had been hacked down by soldiers, but additionally drew on local tensions that had already been bubbling away. Tyneside at the time had its share of radical thinkers, reformers and strikers, and desire for a reform of Parliament was growing here and across the country. After Peterloo, things deteriorated further. Plans were set in motion for a massive demonstration bringing together all the different organised groups as well as the massed labour force of Tyneside. The organisers flooded the area with leaflets, detailing the planned marches. Thirty thousand marchers followed different routes before walking together from Haymarket to the racecourse area on the Town Moor, many carrying banners relating to Peterloo, local politics, the treatment of ex-soldiers, the voting system, and so on. Once at the moor there were speeches. It is very difficult to judge how many people were there, but something in the region of 40-50,000 is quite possible, even though that would have made a ghost town of Tyneside. (Charleton, J., '1819: Waterloo, Peterloo and Newcastle Town Moor,' *North East History*, 2008)

OCTOBER 12TH

1745: On this day, defences against Scottish invasion were much bolstered. Following the general preparations made in town (*see* September 20th), by the 25th, 600 of the Northumberland militia had come into the town. These volunteers were well equipped; many were Northumbrian gentry. One group are recorded as wearing fetching red and pink rosettes. Wesley records hearing that one of the volunteers was a spy. When this was discovered, the man cut his own throat, but a surgeon saved his life so that he could be questioned about the disposition of the rebel forces. On this day, the town also had to find space for 600 Dutchmen, the regiment of General de la Roque. With the weapons they brought with them, the total number of cannon on the hastily repaired walls reached 200. Over the following fortnight more and more English forces poured into town, until it had almost doubled in size, with 15,000 stationed troops. This combined force of volunteers, militia, English and Dutch forces was probably what convinced the rebel army to enter England on the other side of the Pennines. (Oates, J., 'Responses in Newcastle upon Tyne to the Jacobite Rebellions of 1715 and 1745', *Archaeologia Aeliana*, 2003)

OCTOBER 13TH

1915: On this day, Ruth Dodds wrote in her diary a description of her first day at the Armstrong munitions factory, Elswick, as one of the many women newly pushed into arms manufacture by the trials of the First World War. She was keen to point out that, although the 2,000 women on the factory floor hardly ever saw the sun at this time of year, they were still full of smiles and 'little girlish jokes'. Even older women with 'the dinner and the washing always on their minds' had not forgotten how to smile. Some parts of the job might have helped – some 'very young and gigglesome girls' were packed in tight over baths of methylated spirits, although one passed out from the fumes and 'abstainers became very tipsy and gay'! Young women worked huge machines, or sat at benches, each with their own small and precise task – 'filling, polishing, burnishing and fitting together'. Dodds was shown how to work 'indexing machines for time fuses', and told about the arduous twelve-hour nightshifts, 'where the artificial lights are always on & the rushing of the machinery never stops'. She was also told of a time the previous year, when the buzzer went and the girls waited for hours in the dark and cold 'expecting Zeppelin bombs any minute'. (Dodds, R., *A Pilgrimage of Grace*, Bewick Press, 1996)

OCTOBER 14TH

1914: On this day, the War Office officially sanctioned the creation of the Tyneside Irish and Tyneside Scottish Brigades. As early as September, a group of prominent local Irishmen had written to the newspapers suggesting the formation of a regiment of local Irish, much as other areas were raising 'pals' battalions. It was a similar story for the Scots. Originally the War Office rejected the idea of these units, but the interest was clearly there, and the army was being forced to expand rapidly. On this day, Lord Haldane decided to allow it, and recruiting meetings began. One problem was that the units had no obvious military leaders with previous experience – anyone with experience who volunteered was soon pressed into training the others. There were parades in Eldon Square and drill on the Town Moor. By November 4th the Tyneside Irish had over 5,000 recruits, enough for a brigade. They, and the Tyneside Scottish, were stationed in the thick of battle when the push we now know as the Battle of the Somme began. On the first day, July 1st 1916, each brigade lost around 2,000 men – amongst the highest casualties of any unit. (www.tyneside-scottish.co.uk)

OCTOBER 15TH

1901: On this day, Heinrich Fischer – an ethnic German who had lived in Russia and been punished for revolutionary activity there – arrived in Newcastle for the first time. His son was to go on to notoriety (*see* July 11th). But Fischer's first impressions of Newcastle are also interesting, and not a little damning: 'Right in Newcastle station, as you leave the train, you are surrounded by a crowd of ragged boys. They are so dirty that you wonder what has happened to England's famous personal hygiene. With trousers torn, shirts sticking out behind and barefoot. We never came across so many of them as on Tyneside. Is there another place in Europe with so many poor children running around the streets? Wherever you look, there are little ones selling newspapers, matches, picture postcards, advertisements etc. You immediately feel something is not right here'. As for the streets: 'Everything was blackened so that you could not tell what material a building was made of. The houses were low, and while districts had the same style of architecture, I was often astonished that people could manage to find their own homes … The streets were narrow and dirty'. He and his wife took lodgings at no. 46 Armstrong Road, Benwell, a district dominated by three nearby collieries and the massive shipyards of Armstrong Whitworth in Elswick. (Slatter, J., 'Observations and Reminiscences of a Petersburg Worker', *North East History Journal*, 1988)

OCTOBER 16TH

1888: On this day, St George's Church in Osborne Road, Jesmond, was consecrated by the first Bishop of Newcastle, Ernest Roland Wilberforce. It was planned by Somerset Pennefather, vicar of the nearby Clayton Memorial Church, and his friend, the shipbuilder Charles Mitchell. While it was being built, locals had to make do with an iron structure, a temporary church which had served the same purpose at Cullercoats four years earlier. Mitchell had agreed to pay for the land and building provided he had a free hand in design – and he soon hired his friend, Thomas Spence, who designed an exceptional Arts and Crafts style building. The exterior is relatively plain, early-Gothic with touches of Art Nouveau. The most remarkable exterior feature is probably the distinctive campanile – a detached bell tower – which is inspired by the tower of St Mark's Cathedral in Venice. Inside, most surfaces are covered in a harmonious array of intricate decoration, with Ravenna-inspired mosaics and carved marble alongside painted glass, glazed tiles, Pre-Raphaelite wall paintings and delicate woodwork and metalwork. George Bernard Shaw remarked: 'Wherever Mr Spence's artist's hand has passed over the interior surface, the church is beautiful … ' The windows also feature a Clog Calendar – an interpretation of a medieval method to help people keep track of the feasts and fasts of the year. Each week is represented by a lozenge decorated with now-obscure symbols representing different saints. *(The Open Churches Trust* / www.stgeorgesjesmond.org.uk)

OCTOBER 17TH

1831: On this day, the Northern Political Union organised a massive rally on Town Moor in support of Earl Grey and the Great Reform Bill. The group had been formally established four months earlier, and their desire to improve conditions soon took on a political aspect, as the electoral system always meant a government reflecting the bosses' views. When news reached Newcastle that the Reform Bill had been thrown out by the House of Lords, plans for today's rally were immediately begun. A procession marched to the Town Moor from Westgate Road, and, walking four abreast, took fifty minutes – complete with a dozen bands and thirty flags – to pass. Eighty thousand people – from various points on the spectrum of Liberal and reformist and radical politics – gathered on the moor, under a banner declaring for 'the King, Grey, and Liberty'. Here they listened to speeches by the great and good of the left. One man stated the hopes of all those present when he said that under Grey, 'The great and manifold abuses of the laws will shortly disappear under his reforming sway; justice will be rendered cheap and of speedy attainment; and the instruction of the people in useful knowledge will be universally extended'. A variant of the Reform Bill was passed the following year. (Cadogan, P., *Early Radical Newcastle*, Sagittarius Press, 1975)

OCTOBER 18TH

1833: On this day, fourteen-year old William Wilkinson, fresh from a technical education at Dr Bruce's Academy, started his apprenticeship. For seven years he worked for Robert Robson, a plasterer in Clayton Street, for three shillings in the first year, four in the second, and so on. But over time his skills widened, and he set his mind to improving the fireproofing of buildings. His invention, patented in 1854, was a way to embed strips of iron into a type of concrete based on broken coke, sand and Portland cement, and to construct concrete slab floors including iron rods or second-hand wire ropes. While Wilkinson was not the first to try to combine metal mesh or wire into a cement or mortar, his patent was a crucial step forward, making the best use of the iron to take the strain of the structure. This, effectively, was reinforced concrete, although at the time it was called 'ferroconcrete'. The new technique was much in demand, and some of the first reinforced concrete buildings in the world were built in Newcastle. Additionally, Wilkinson was keen to demonstrate the material's versatility. To that end, in 1865 he built a concrete servants' cottage at the concrete works, which lasted almost 100 years before its demolition. (Brown, J., 'W.B. Wilkinson and his place in the history of reinforced concrete', *Transactions of the Newcomen Society*, 1966)

OCTOBER 19TH

1344: On this day, merchant John Denton died in prison. At this time there was great rivalry between the trade guilds and the craft guilds. John Denton was elected as Mayor in 1341, but another candidate, Richard of Acton, had the support of the craft guilds, who independently elected him. This led to riots, severe enough to draw the attention of King Edward III, who fined the town 500 marks 'for transgressions and excesses' and placed it under direct control of his own men. To win back the right to self-government, a new procedure for electing a Mayor was created, and Denton and Acton were fined. A few years later, most of the power was in the hands of Denton's enemies, and he was dragged to court and accused of treasonously feeding the Scots army in 1341. Denton did not reply, perhaps knowing a kangaroo court when he saw one – if he was found guilty, his family would get nothing, but if he died without pleading, they would inherit. He was returned to gaol, where he died – probably starved to death, though crushing with rocks was a legal penalty for those who refused to plead. The King ordered an investigation. Over thirty men were accused, probably on the basis of their involvement in the trial, and several were hunted down – some were executed. The King, citing 'notorious contempts and disobedience newly committed by the Mayor and community of Newcastle', took control for a year again … ! (www.the-orb.net)

OCTOBER 20TH

1880: On this day, Joseph Swan demonstrated how far his researches into electric lighting had come, when he lit the lecture room of Newcastle Literary and Philosophical Society. He had lectured on the subject to the same group twice before, over the previous couple of years, demonstrating a prototype electric bulb which only lasted a few minutes. But this was something new, which he titled 'progress in electric lighting'. Turning down the seventy gas lamps, he replaced them with twenty steady electric bulbs, making the lecture room the first ever public room to be fully lit by electric light. His bulbs were becoming so reliable that he was able later that year to light his own home in Gateshead, and that of his friend William Armstrong (Cragside near Rothbury) by the same method. The Cragside bulb was the first to be made commercially, from 1881, in a factory in Benwell by the Swan Electric Light Company. This company joined forces with Thomas Edison, who had been independently developing light bulbs in America, and went from strength to strength. Swan continued his association with the Lit & Phil, becoming president from 1911 until his death three years later. (www.litandphil.org.uk)

OCTOBER 21ST

1724: On this day, a fire in a merchant's house on Side killed several people. For no readily apparent reason the owner, Joseph Partis, had stockpiled gunpowder in his garret room, under the eaves of the house. This didn't seem to alarm people, until at seven in the evening it caught fire, blowing up a large part of the house. In the chaos and smoke, families were separated and for an hour panic prevailed. For one thing, it looked as if nearby houses, and even the church, might catch light. Twelve people died, and around 100 injured, one of whom was blasted onto the leaded windows of the church. The Mayor and Aldermen got personally stuck in to save neighbouring houses, and some were even injured. The town surgeon alone could not cope with the mass of casualties, and all the town's surgeons were brought in. The Mayor paid £50 to those who had gone above and beyond in risking their lives to extinguish the fire, preventing it from becoming a major conflagration in Newcastle's narrow streets. Strangely, a second fire occurred on the same premises on August 28th 1799, although no one could work out how it started. Gunpowder at this time was stored next door, and an intrepid group scaled the warehouse to remove the powder before it helped history to repeat itself further. (Sykes, J., *Local Records*, 1833 / *Newcastle Courant*)

OCTOBER 22ND

1835: On this day, the official opening ceremony for the Grainger Market was held. As part of the building of Graingertown, the old Butcher and Vegetable Markets had been bought, and demolished. Grainger had hundreds of men working on the replacement, and they worked at speed. The plan was extremely ambitious, the largest and finest indoor market in the country (and perhaps, it was argued at the time, in Europe). It covered 2 acres, boasting fourteen entrances, 243 shops (divided between the Butcher Market and the Vegetable (or 'green') Market), and two huge ornamental fountains (with basins containing 3,000 gallons of water). The whole thing was covered by a complex timber roof, and lit with gas lamps as well as hundreds of vertical windows, a partial glass ceiling, and fifty skylights. To celebrate the opening of the market, 2,000 men, seated at rows of tables stretching nearly the length of the market, enjoyed a grand dinner. Women could only watch from a gallery! When the market opened for business, two days later, the quantity and quality on offer was thought unsurpassed. To add to this, as the shops vied for custom they made beautiful displays, including sculptures made from fruit and vegetables. By evening, the whole market was so packed that it was barely possible to move. One speech at the opening ceremony summed up Grainger's achievement: 'Under the magic hand of Grainger a City of Palaces had suddenly sprung up.' (Ayris, I., *A City of Palaces*, Tynebridge Publishing, 1997)

OCTOBER 23RD

1989: This day saw a landmark gig at the Riverside – the first British (and indeed European) date for legendary grunge band Nirvana. The tour was a double headliner with Tad, a scene heavyweight (pun intended – he weighed 20 stone). There were fewer than fifty people in the audience. Most of Nirvana's set came from their first album, Bleach, but it also included Polly, later to feature on their multi-million selling Nevermind. Apparently Kurt Cobain had his back to the audience for most of the gig, but he did interact with his new-found English fans – one of them remembers, 'We had a brief conversation – basically he was impressed that I was looking even scruffier than he was ... Nirvana's set was a blinder'. In fact, it was a typical Riverside gig – dark, hot, sweaty, and featuring a carpet you could stick to. Tad tried to stage-dive, but found everyone moved out the way at the last moment, allowing him to fall straight to the floor! Nirvana weren't the only group to play in the Riverside early in their career. Other groups who visited as complete unknowns include the Manic Street Preachers, Wet Wet Wet (tickets for 50p!), and Blur. (Plater, H. and Taylor, C., *Riverside*, Tonto Books, 2011)

OCTOBER 24TH

1860: On this day, at a meeting at the Mayor's house, a committee was formed to work alongside the Society Promoting the Employment of Women, aiming to introduce women to 'such occupations as are suitable to their powers'. The committee's aims were modest – not turning 'factory girls into clerks, nor cooks and housemaids into physicians and lawyers' but rather allowing women not raising children to enter a wider variety of jobs requiring skill, within factory and domestic settings. Early steps included putting ten women through a three-month bookkeeping course. While some did well, others were hindered by a lack of knowledge of arithmetic, and by 'the angular handwriting now commonly taught in girls' schools'. The committee next made a register for governesses, but soon worked out that there were far more women wanting the job than employers providing it. They commented on the poor training given to servant girls – many wanted to be servants, but no one wanted to show them the ropes. The committee also surveyed the major local employers of women to find out about working conditions. They concluded that 'many hundreds of women and girls are employed in the lower and dirtier departments of the factories on the Tyne, at field work, even in brick yards'. Wages were between 4s and 12s for a week of ten-hour shifts. (*Newcastle Courant*)

OCTOBER 25TH

1644: On this day, word reached Parliament of the breaking of the long siege of Newcastle by their Scottish allies. They announced that this was a 'great blessing', ordering all ministers in London to give public thanks on their behalf within the next Sunday service. Not only did this news mean a return to a safe coal supply, it signalled the collapse of the war in the north. For the people of Newcastle, however, the results were more mixed. The battle itself had been fierce, from the opening bombardment, through the storming of the broken walls with ramps and hooks, to a desperate last stand in the Cloth Market. Casualties were probably in the hundreds. Inevitably there were incidents of looting by the Scottish, especially as strong gales forced the soldiers to shelter within the walls – though it is noted that pickings actually worth stealing were slim! Still, some probably favoured Parliament, or at least were happy to see the end of a siege which must have left them permanently hungry and afraid of death from random bombardment. But their town had been left in ruins. There were holes in the walls, all the churches had suffered damage, the bridge needed major repair, there were virtually no houses left outside the walls and many inside had suffered from bombardment or fire. And the Scots army remained in town until February 1647! (Sadler, J. and Serdiville, R., *The Great Siege of Newcastle, 1644*, The History Press, 2011)

OCTOBER 26TH

1947: On this day, the *Newcastle Chronicle* revealed a scandal reaching from Tyneside deep into wartime Germany. While Tyneside suffered its share of wartime bombing, given the concentration of industry along the river bank it is surprising that things were not worse. They easily could have been, if Jean Jacques Serre had had his way. Serre was a French consul stationed in Newcastle, who in late 1940 – soon after the British Government revoked his consulship – went to Grand Admiral Raeder, head of the German navy, and described the most promising targets in Tyneside. Raeder wrote to Hitler on March 18th 1941: 'When at the German Embassy in Paris, Jacques Serre expressed his surprise that Newcastle has not yet been attacked, because the Vickers-Armstrong shipyards there contain an aircraft carrier (to be completed in five to six months), two battleships (to be completed in five to six months), one light cruiser, six or seven destroyers and three or four submarines under construction ... When he left the Tyne he said not a single bomb had hit Vickers-Armstrong's large ammunition plant in Newcastle, which employed 20,000 workers ... He also pointed out the importance of the three large Tyne bridges linking Scotland and England.' Tyneside did suffer several serious raids in the weeks and months following Raeder's letter, although we do not know if there is any connection between the two. (*Newcastle Chronicle*)

OCTOBER 27TH

1899: On this day, William Sadler Junior dived into the Tyne to save a man in distress. At the time he manned a ferry across the Tyne between Paradise, Benwell, and the Delta steelworks, Raines. This simple rowing boat was extremely busy and essential to daily life for many local workers. Near Benwell, the tide was running strongly and the water around 12-foot deep when J.T. Errington accidentally fell in. He was seen by Sadler, who was a member of a family well known in the area not only for the ferry but also as landlords of the Boathouse pub, Scotswood, and owners of a boat builder's yard in Dunston. When Sadler saw what was happening, he dived into the swirling waters, fully clothed, and pulled Errington to safety. He was later awarded a bronze medal by the Royal Humane Society, an honour given to those who place their own lives in great risk to save, or attempt to save, another. (Life Saving Awards Research Society / www.webwanderers.org)

1978: On this day, the first title from local poetry publisher Bloodaxe Books was launched, with the poet Ken Smith reading from his work, *Tristan Crazy*, at Morden Tower. Bloodaxe Books has been publishing a wide range of poetry ever since, from new authors to award-winning figures, and is now one of the country's leading poetry publishers. (www. bloodaxebooks.com)

OCTOBER 28TH

1935: On this day, one Mr Combe, along with several other local notables, visited Newcastle's Carliol Square jail – then just eleven years old – for a rather odd purpose. He had been lecturing in town on the subject of phrenology – the assessment of character using measurement of the features and skull – and particularly wanted to demonstrate to his audience that because of variations in brain shape, the skulls of the virtuous and the criminally inclined were different. For instance, Combe noted that 'P.S.', aged twenty, had large areas associated with secretiveness and acquisitiveness, and undersized conscientiousness and 'lower animal' areas – and guessed that he was a swindler or thief; the attendant surgeon to the jail confirmed that he was indeed a thief and trickster. (Barrett, A. and Harrison, C., *Punishment in England: A Sourcebook*, Routledge, 1998)

1941: On this day, Brian Robson Rankin – better known as iconic guitarist Hank Marvin – was born. Brought up in Newcastle, Marvin was interested in music from an early age, playing the banjo and – after hearing Buddy Holly – the guitar. At Rutherford Grammar School he met fellow-Geordie Bruce Welch, and they formed the Riverside Skiffle Group. At sixteen, the pair moved to London, where a chance encounter with Cliff Richard's manager (who was actually looking for a different guitarist) got them a place in backing band The Drifters (which soon afterwards became The Shadows). Solo work and other collaborations followed.

OCTOBER 29TH

1789: On this day, a building described as a circus or amphitheatre, designed by David Stephenson, was opened on the Forth. At this point a 'circus' was more or less purely an equestrian event, and this one was run by Mr Jones and Mr Parker, equestrians from London. The lane alongside – which was also where Thomas Bewick lived – was renamed 'Circus Lane'. Bewick was apparently a fan, and often drew images of what went on there, especially trick horsemanship. He also drew an early newspaper advert for the circus, promoting 'a Grand Display of TRAMPOLINE TRICKS over Men, Horses, etc., by Mr Parker. Likewise his astounding SOMERSET over a Garter Ten feet High'. Other attractions included a lot of dancing – ballet, tambourine dance, and rope dancing by 'the celebrated Mr Spinicuta'. The building also served as a riding school, and this function gradually dominated over the pantomimes and displays of horsemanship. Some displays were quite odd, like the 1799 panorama of the British fleet off the coast of the Isle of Wight, cleverly painted so that, while actually 120 feet long, 'appears to the spectator to be several miles in length'. Sykes says the building had a 'very curious roof', but doesn't go into detail. (Sykes, J., *Local Records*, Volume I, 1833 / Uglow, J., *Nature's Engraver*, Faber and Faber, 2007)

OCTOBER 30TH

1994: On this day, the *Turbinia* – once the fastest ship in the world – arrived at the Discovery Museum. Her journey from her previous home in Exhibition Park – where she had previously been on display before undergoing years of restoration work – was a sedate pull by tractor and trailer at 5mph. Apparently at one point she went through a red light, though goodness knows what the police made of the resulting traffic camera images. The *Turbinia*'s new gallery was later altered to allow viewing from three storeys. The *Turbinia* is impressive in many ways. She was the world's first steam-turbine-powered vessel, with a top speed of 34.5 knots (almost 40mph). Charles Parsons, the designer, had apprenticed at Armstrong Works, then worked in Leeds and Gateshead before setting up Parsons and Co. in Heaton. Throughout this time he was inventing new turbo engines and generators, leading to *Turbinia*'s construction in 1894 (the unusual pointed bow once punched a hole in the side of another ship!) The *Turbinia* was also included within the celebrations for Queen Victoria's Diamond Jubilee. Other turbine-driven ships followed over the next ten years, from warships to ocean-going liners like the *Mauretania* (also built in Wallsend). (Smith, K., *Turbinia: The Story of Charles Parsons and his Ocean Greyhound*, Tynebridge Publishing, 2009)

OCTOBER 31ST

2006: On this day, newspapers reported that scientists at Newcastle University had made a major breakthrough in 'artificial' organ development. They had made a 'mini liver' (a flat shape about the size of a penny piece in normal conditions, or a 3D shape if grown in zero-g) with functioning cells. It was made using stem cells, which are capable of developing into a range of different tissue types depending on stimulus by nutrients and other chemicals. In the short term, liver tissue like this is being used to test new drugs. The aim, however, is to build on this research to create an artificial liver to which patients could be 'hooked up' (much as a dialysis machine functions in place of a kidney) while their own liver healed, or ultimately even to grow liver tissue which could be transplanted. This discovery was described as a 'Eureka moment' – while previous scientists had made individual liver cells, the new technique worked faster and created sizeable pieces of tissue. It was also important in using umbilical cord cells, bypassing the controversy surrounding the use of embryonic cells. One day, umbilical stem cells could be regularly collected to provide a 'bank' for the future. (*Daily Mail*)

NOVEMBER 1ST

1883: On this day, the Newcastle Cathedral Nursing and Loan Society (CNS) was founded. The nineteenth-century district nursing movement was often run by charitable groups associated with churches. The CNS was one such group, boasting the Bishop and vicar as patron and president. It aimed to ensure that each parish had a nurse – an 'educated Lady of Hospital training ... to nurse the Sick Poor in their own homes'. They also wanted to provide 'a Collection of Necessaries and Comforts' to lend out, and run an 'invalid kitchen' providing food for the sick poor. A few years later they expanded into convalescent homes. Nurses would go to the poorest districts of town to feed and wash patients, lay their fires, teach basic nursing care, lend clothing, and help with access to the Dispensary. The CNS cared about the soul as well as the body – even in the early days, with just two nurses at work, they were confident that 'many have been led, by the influence of our nurses, to higher ideals. The moral and physical effect of such work is needed more than ever at this present time.' On the other hand, the society made clear that most of the poor were deserving of sympathy (and donations) and indeed had many virtues, like patience, obedience, hopefulness and gratitude. (Gould, E.M., 'Gender and class as reflected in the beginning of district nursing in Newcastle & Northumberland', *North East History*, 2007)

NOVEMBER 2ND

1822: On this day, a new weapon was brought into play in the bitter wrangles between the keelmen and coal owners. The keelman's strike, or 'long stop', had begun in October, and things were growing tenser as the weeks passed. As London began to run short of coal, the coal owners turned to the armed forces, and HMS *Swan* was anchored off the Quayside with her guns pointed at the shore. There were arrests, and a reading of the Riot Act. Meanwhile, engineers were converting Thomas Hedley's steam engine, used to pull heavy chauldron wagons of coal around at Wylam Colliery, to marine use. Officially the *Thomas and Jeremiah*, it was very quickly known as the *Tom and Jerry*. But there were no smiles on the faces of the keelmen when, on this day, it took to the river pulling behind it barges full of coal. The conversion wasn't perfect, so it kept stopping, allowing the keelmen to wade out to tip the barges, and throw stones and mud at the operators. Only 50 tons of coal made it out that day, compared to a usual 2,250 tons. What ended the strike a month later was probably simply hunger. But *Tom and Jerry* hurt morale, and signalled the march of technology over muscle power. Ultimately, the keelmen's role continued to decline. (Sadler, J. and Serdiville, R., *The Little Book of Newcastle*, The History Press, 2011 / www. sunnisidelocalhistorysociety.co.uk)

NOVEMBER 3RD

1832: On this day, the Corporation attempted to start up a police force modelled on that created in London by Sir Robert Peel three years earlier. The town already had the watchmen, but this was something new, 'a body of the new police in Newcastle, and a few of them have this week appeared in the streets, in a blue uniform.' Unfortunately the public wasn't yet ready for police, and less than a year later the service was withdrawn. People didn't want to pay for it, and they didn't want to risk encouraging a military-style power, crushing individual freedoms. Three years later, councillor and reformist Thomas Doubleday was able to argue that Newcastle was a town 'remarkable for its good behaviour' which did not need to import an 'Austrian-like' police system. (Latimer, J., *Local Records*, 1857)

———— • ◆ • ————

1930: Around this date, city councillors were preparing to debate the proposal for a swimming pool for Jesmond. In November's council meeting, Mr Wallace argued that 'a number of Councillors lived in Jesmond, and they could testify that Jesmond did not need baths'. Another compared travelling from Jesmond to Scotswood as 'going from Heaven to Hell', but others said that the locals were enthusiastic, and besides, swimming was good for fitness as well as saving lives. The pool was eventually built, opening in 1938. The locals remain enthusiastic, keeping the place running even after the council decided to close it in 1991. (www.jesmondcommunityleisure.co.uk)

NOVEMBER 4TH

1646: On this day, the Common Council of Newcastle instituted the town's first street lighting. They ordered 'lanthorns to be hung out in every ward in Newcastle. A common lanthorn to be provided for each ward. The lanthorns to be lighted at 6 o'clock and to burn until the captain goes.' There were twenty-four wards, one for each of the towers of the town wall. These twenty-four lanterns cannot have done much good, especially since they were made with sides not of glass but of thinly sliced horn. This was during the period when King Charles, captured in May, was being held prisoner in Newcastle (this is because he chose to surrender to the Scots army, rather than directly to the Parliamentarians). He stayed in Anderson House – the largest, finest house in town – until February 1647. He may even have seen the street lights – we know he was let out to play 'goff' (presumably early golf). He also occupied himself trying to gain support among the Scots, playing chess, trying to escape, and attending services at St Nicholas Church. He was certainly kept warm, for also on this day it was agreed that coals for the king were to come from Sir Thomas Riddle's pit in Gateshead, with the Corporation paying half the cost. (*Tyne and Wear Archive*)

November 5th

1907: On this day, James Alexander 'Alec' Burns was born in the West End, son of a Scotswood Road shipyard worker. Showing early promise as an athlete, he first competed for the Boys' Club of the Fenkle Street YMCA at the age of twelve. Burns competed for Britain in the Olympics of 1932 and 1936. The 1932 Olympics was held in Los Angeles, in the midst of the Great Depression. Burns crossed the Atlantic in style on the *Empress of Britain* ocean liner, and visited the mansions of several Hollywood stars. His accommodation was in the first ever purpose-built Olympic village (for men only; the women remained in hotel accommodation). He competed in the 5,000 metres, coming seventh in the final. The 1936 Berlin Olympics, of course, was notorious as a showcase of Nazi power which was thwarted by the likes of black sprinter Jessie Owens, but which also saw the first live television broadcast of Olympic events. Here Burns came fifth in the 10,000-metre final, setting a new British record. He says he and Jesse Owens 'often sat together in the dining room drinking gallons of Horlicks'. He also won bronze in the 3-mile race at the 1934 Empire Games, and silver in the International Cross-Country Championships. He still holds the English national record for 4 miles, as this was abandoned as a running distance shortly afterwards. He lived in the West End all his life. (*Evening Chronicle*)

NOVEMBER 6TH

2009: On this day, the Queen visited Newcastle. As you would expect, it was a packed trip, beginning with a school opening in Washington, followed by a 'walkabout' in Northumberland Street. She then went to the City Library, and was the first person to sign its visitors' book. The City Library replaced another on the same spot, and is in the Charles Avison Building, named after the eighteenth-century composer. The library opened properly to the public the following day. Unusually, it features a limited twenty-four-hour lending service via a vending machine in the outside wall. Next for the Queen was the official opening of the new Great North Museum. Housed inside the old Hancock Museum building – itself opened by the Queen's great-great-grandmother, Queen Victoria – the Great North Museum includes all the collections of the Hancock (natural history and ethnography) as well as the collections of the Museum of Antiquities (local history and archaeology) and the Shefton Museum (ancient Greece). Highlights include a large scale model of Hadrian's Wall, a planetarium, a life-sized Tyrannosaurus Rex model skeleton, live reptiles and Egyptian mummies, as well as all-new displays of local and global wildlife, and finds from the region through the ages.

NOVEMBER 7TH

1866: On this day, printer Robert Ward went to the magistrates and asked that they grant a summons against the notorious Davenport Brothers for obtaining money on false pretences. The Davenport Brothers, Americans who had already taken London by storm, had held their show on two days the previous week. These featured a mixture of escapology and séance – they went, bound, into sealed cabinets from which musical instruments seemed to play themselves. The local newspapers were pointed in describing the shows as 'absurd and childish', mere conjuring tricks dressed up in the trappings of spiritualism. Still, the Lecture Room was packed with over 200 people, though whether they all expected real magic is unclear. Robert Ward argued that the customer had not seen the show of genuine spiritual activity which they had paid for. But the magistrates did not agree, saying that while they were sure the show was indeed a deception, 'If people will pay their money for being gulled in such a manner, the magistrates cannot help it', and that anyone who paid a guinea to see 'such nonsense' was 'a great fool'. *Punch* commented on the case, saying that while the wording of the Witchcraft Act did not currently quite cover the case, a slight adjustment to include claiming dealing with Spirits was a good idea, to protect sillier minds from those happy to use this method to pick their pockets. (*Newcastle Courant / Punch*)

NOVEMBER 8TH

1989: On this day, the first episode of BBC North's *Byker Grove* was aired. Created by Adele Rose, *Byker Grove* ran for seventeen years and started many entertainment careers, including those of Donna Air, Jill Halfpenny, and several actors in *Emmerdale*. Most notably, Anthony McPartlin and Declan Donnelly had chart success as their characters PJ and Duncan, and subsequently forged presenting careers as Ant and Dec. Although set in Byker, the series was filmed in Benwell. Benwell Towers (an attractive Dobson-designed 1831 manor house) was creatively turned into the sets of Byker Grove's youth club, as well as the programme's production offices and other facilities. Ironically, the 'rival' club, for the kids of the fictitious 'Denwell', was filmed in the home of the real Raby Street Youth Club in Byker. The pilot episode featured an after-school club for eight to eleven year olds. It was picked up by the BBC for its children's programming, but with a difference – the age focus shifted to twelve to sixteen, making this one of the few programmes on CBBC aimed squarely at teenagers. Controversial subjects like drugs and teenage pregnancy were tackled, and several characters died or were maimed (PJ, for instance, was blinded in a paint-balling accident). *Byker Grove* notably showed the first homosexual kiss in British children's drama, when, in 1995, two male characters got close in the back of a cinema. (www.imdb.com)

NOVEMBER 9TH

1828: On this day, during afternoon service at All Saints' Church, smoke gradually started to build up within the building. As the sermon progressed, the smoke grew so thick that many people began to leave, coughing. Eventually the preacher, Reverend Shute, took the hint, cut the sermon short and went to investigate the source of the problem. The church was heated with a stove and, upon investigation, it was found that the upright flue 'had been filled with soot, and this having ignited, had heated the iron flue red hot, and as this passed near one of the main timbers of the roof, and separated from it only by lime, the beam had caught fire, and the flames had communicated to some of the rafters which it supported'. Fire engines came but it took until 6.30 p.m. to put out the blaze – and even then, it was fortunate that a fireman was still present at half past ten when a flicker of flame re-emerged. A 'fire engine' at this time was usually a cart, wheeled into position, with a leather hose and a pump mechanism which allowed several men working together to get some degree of water pressure going, using water from a fixed point or a bucket chain. The verdict was that if the fire had gone on for another half an hour, the whole building would have been reduced to ruins. (Sykes, J., *Local Records*, 1833)

NOVEMBER 10TH

1760: On this day, the first child was born in a Newcastle maternity hospital – a house in Rosemary Lane aiming to help 'poor, married women or widows pregnant at the time of their husband's death'. The building was founded on October 1st, but obviously it took a while to get everything sorted out – they hadn't even got the staff roster confirmed, as the appointments were not approved until November 26th, and the official opening was December 3rd. In 1761, a charity was also set up which paid for an experienced midwife to go to the homes of women in labour – it consisted of twenty 'lady visitors', fifteen midwives, two physicians and two surgeons. The facilities were, however, open to abuse – in 1850 the minute books of the Lying-In Hospital urged that 'in consequence of several frauds' the visiting ladies must check that the recipient of the letter really was a suitable case (a woman who was genuinely of good character, married and of a fixed residence 'except her husband be a soldier or a sailor'). Still, the hospital did provide a valuable service (*see* September 30th). (Tacchi, D., *Childbirth in Newcastle upon Tyne 1760-1990*, Bewick Press, 1994)

NOVEMBER 11TH

1918: On this day, the First World War finally came to an end. Ruth Dodds was in Newcastle for the celebrations. She wrote: 'All the buzzas began to go, & the sun shone & and there was such a noise & wonder. So we all shook hands and declared a holiday … there was such a crowd before the Town Hall all the time, & the bells ding-donging away, so that if the Lord Mayor had made a speech no one could have heard him possibly … Then we all three had coffee at Tilleys, which I don't think I've done since the War. The orchestra played God Save the King & we all stood up … Then we walked about in the streets … such crowds, & little flags, & big flags on all the shops & buildings & crowds of children marching with flags & tins & guys but I suppose they are Kaisers now. And there was no traffic except now & then a big car or motor dray loaded with munitions girls or wounded soldiers; & the NER [North Eastern Railway] men were letting the little dirty children ride in swarms in empty rolleys. The tramway men & girls came marching down the street singing. Here & there were soldiers giving away scraps of paper ribbon red white & blue for favours … I went into St John's to give thanks … And this is my last War Journal.' [*sic*] (Dodds, R., *A Pilgrimage of Grace*, Bewick Press, 1996)

NOVEMBER 12TH

1844: On this day, midget General Tom Thumb – real name, Charles Sherwood Stratton – was part way through a packed four-day visit to the Music Hall, Newcastle. Stratton was actually only five years old, but was presented to the audience as thirteen, to make his tiny frame even more impressive. Even for a five year old, he was indeed very small at only 25 inches tall, and weighing just 15lb. In fact he had grown normally until he was six months old – and then stopped. He only began to grow again – very slowly – at the age of nine, at the same time as his second tour of Britain, and even then only ever reached 3 feet 4 inches. His manager was the famous showman and freak show organiser, P.T. Barnum. Barnum had discovered Stratton as a toddler, and taught him to sing, dance, and do comedy routines and impressions (he apparently did an excellent Napoleon). Adding to the spectacle, before the performance Tom Thumb was driven around the streets in a tiny ornate chariot. He first toured his native America, and the following year took the show to Europe. Ironically, when in America he was presented as English, but to the English he was presented as very much a Yankee. Stratton was one of the aristocracy of the freak show – he became rich, married another dwarf, and was even able to bail out Barnum when he fell into difficulties. He died at the age of forty-five. (history1800s.about.com)

November 13th

1967: On this day, Newcastle University granted Martin Luther King an honorary doctorate, the only one he received during his lifetime. Remarkably, King came to Newcastle in person, in a one-day trip to Britain. This was a busy time for him, as he was supporting Carl Stokes in his successful campaign to become the first black Mayor of Cleveland, Ohio. King was only in Newcastle for eight hours – and was lucky to make it at all. Apparently King's organisation, the Southern Christian Leadership Conference, weren't really sure where Newcastle was – his secretary asked whether they should get a plane from London to Newcastle, or go by taxi! More seriously, King had only got out of jail weeks before and was suffering from a virus. The degree was given by the Duke of Northumberland, the University's Chancellor. In his acceptance speech, King said: 'Words are certainly inadequate for me to express my deep and genuine appreciation to the University of Newcastle for honouring me in such a significant way ... In honouring me today, you not only honour me but you honour the hundreds and thousands of people with whom I have worked and with whom I have been associated in the struggle for racial justice'. It was less than five months before he was shot. Newcastle University flew its flag at half-mast that day. (Ward, B., 'To Honour a King', *Arches*, 2007)

NOVEMBER 14TH

1554: On this day, the Merchant Adventurers Company described the behaviour of apprentices: 'What dicing, carding and mumming! what tippling, dancing and brasing of harlots! what jagged hose lined with silk, and cut shoes! what use of gitterns [musical instruments] by night! what wearing of beards! what daggers is by them worn crosswise overthwart their backs!' [*sic*] In 1603, a bye-law forbade Newcastle apprentices from wearing a huge range of specific luxury garments, from velvet girdles and hats to cork shoes and ruffled bands. Those who ignored this would be put in a new short-term prison built in the West Gate. And in 1649, as well as (again) trying to stop the wearing of a wide variety of fancy clothes, the guilds even tried to control haircuts, decreeing that every apprentice 'cut his hair from the crown of his head, keep his forehead bare, his locks, if any, shall not reach below the lap of his ear, and the same length to be observed behind'. Nine apprentices who broke this order were literally given pudding bowl haircuts in open court, a dish being placed on their head then the hair cut around. They were placed in prison for their stubbornness, and after eleven days on bread and weak beer petitioned for their release, promising to conform to the regulation in future. (Mackenzie, E., *A Descriptive and Historical Account of the Town and County of Newcastle upon Tyne: Including the Borough of Gateshead*, 1827)

November 15th

1831: On this day, Isambard Kingdom Brunel arrived in Newcastle. He had already come to the area once before – he unsuccessfully applied for the post of engineer on the Newcastle to Carlisle line, England's first coast-to-coast railway, in January 1830. Nearly two years later, he applied to work on designing the Monkwearmouth Docks in Sunderland. He arrived at 4.40 a.m., spent a few hours sleeping at the Queen's Head, and then spent the day with the Dock Committee, 'smoking etc'. He said that they were 'shrewd clever fellows – but a rum set'. He stayed in the area until December 2nd, and as ever turned his enquiring mind to what he saw around him. He made detailed sketches of Scotswood Suspension Bridge, and then travelled to Stockton to look at the railway bridge over the Tees. Apparently he wasn't impressed – he worked out that the weight of two coal wagons deflected the floor of the bridge by 12 inches. Unsurprisingly, it was replaced with a cast-iron bridge in 1844. But he had little luck locally – his plan for the Monkwearmouth Docks was rejected, as was his design for Newcastle's High Level Bridge. (www.sclews.me.uk)

November 16th

1771: On this morning, it started to rain heavily across the region – and it kept on raining. Residents going to bed on this Saturday night would have had no idea what awaited them the next morning – though those living near to the river cannot have slept easy. In the event, by midnight the river was 12 feet higher than the highest of tides. As the water rose, boats were pulled from their moorings – some ended up on the Quayside itself, while many others were smashed or swept out to sea – and timber and other goods lost to the water. Soon, 'all the cellars, warehouses, shops and lower apartments of dwelling houses, from the west end of the Close, to near Ouseburn, were totally underwater'. And shortly after midnight, the Tyne Bridge – standing since around 1250 – gave up the struggle. The middle arch and two other arches, along with seven shops (with houses above), were simply swept away, along with six people. Pieces of one house were later found 8 miles downstream, empty but for a cat and dog, alive but bedraggled! Another family were left stranded between two fallen arches for six hours, until they were rescued in a bold scheme involving narrow timbers laid from pier to pier and breaking through the side of the house. (Garrett, W., *An account of the Great Foods of 1771 and 1815*, 1818)

November 17th

2008: On this day, the Bridge Folk Club celebrated its fiftieth anniversary. It is difficult to say exactly when it started, but it is certainly one of the oldest folk clubs in the country. Its real claim to fame is that – bar a six-month refurbishment – it has always met in the same venue, The Bridge Hotel at the end of the High Level Bridge. It started life as Newcastle Folk Song and Ballad, founded by Louis Killen and Johnny Handle, but went on to spawn a well-loved local group, the High Level Ranters. Eric Burdon of The Animals has said that he first heard 'the House of the Rising Sun', later their greatest hit, sung by Handle in The Bridge. The club can also indirectly claim to have started the band The Dubliners. Luke Kelly was working in Newcastle as a builder's labourer when he dropped in to The Bridge for a drink, and heard folk singers for the first time. That inspired him to go home and form The Dubliners (though it's hard to believe he'd not encountered folk singers in Ireland!). (www.bridgefolkclub.co.uk)

NOVEMBER 18TH

1834: On this day, local dignitaries were privileged to watch the lighting of a part of Mosley Street with gas lamps. The occasion was a grand dinner held at the Assembly Rooms by the friends of 'Radical Jack' – John Lampton, the 1st Earl of Durham. It was a politically turbulent time, as the Tory Duke of Wellington had returned to office only two days before. The Earl of Durham was a Whig, and so a big statement of Whig support – complete with addresses from 'the working men of Newcastle' – was logical. But what drew the crowds were the gas jets set up in front of the Assembly Rooms, each engraved with the words 'Durham' and 'Reform'. This was the first gas illumination in the North, and perhaps the whole country. From this start, gas lighting was rapidly taken up across the region over the next few years – Hexham was first lit two months later, Houghton le Spring and Barnard Castle the month after that. When in July 1835 a new clock was placed in the tower of St Thomas' Church, the dials were illuminated with gas. (Latimer, J., *Local Records*, 1857)

November 19th

1705: On this day, rules were formalised for the St John's Charity School, newly opened to educate thirty-four poor children in St John's parish. The master was to be young, healthy, and a practicing member of the Church of England. His home would be above the single large schoolroom. In summer the school day was eight hours long (with a two-hour lunch break); in winter, six hours. Each child would stay at the school until he or she could read well, say the Catechism by heart, and do practical arithmetic. Then they would be off, with a leaving present of two books – devotional text *The Whole Duty of Mankind*, and a combined *Bible and Book of Common Prayer*. Money was set aside to place two boys per year in apprenticeship either at sea or as shipbuilders, or two girls to 'some honest service'. One of the trustees was at the same time involved in a small school which would develop into a charity school for All Saints. Funded by the Allan family, this would evolve into Dame Allan's school. The rules were to be identical to those of St John's. Forty poor boys learned to read and write, 'and so much of vulgar arithmetic as to fit and qualify them for mechanic trades', and twenty poor girls learned 'to read and knit and sew plain work' from a mistress, and how to write from the schoolmaster. (Smith, E., *Dame Allan's Schools*, Dame Allan's Schools, 2005)

November 20th

2000: On this day, the Millennium Bridge was brought down the Tyne. It was the second low-level bridge across the River Tyne in Tyneside, and the only one for pedestrians and cyclists only. Six designers followed a complex brief intended to link communities while providing no further impediment to river traffic – and there was one clear winner. Fabricated in sections in Bolton, the bridge was put together and painted in Wallsend. When the time came, it took all the power of the Asian Hercules II – one of the largest cranes in the world, with a deck the size of a football pitch – to bring the span of the bridge upriver and into position. Its final placing had to be accurate to less than 2mm. Yet at 126 metres long, it had to be brought up the river sideways, as it is wider than the Tyne in places. Approximately 100 million people worldwide watched the journey on television, and thousands watched in person from the river banks. It was another seven months before the Millennium Bridge was ready to tilt for the first time; the public could step on it in September 2001, and it was not officially opened until April 2002. Its pivoting structure is a world-first in bridge design, and it has won several prestigious awards and been praised for its elegance and efficiency. (www.gateshead.gov.uk)

NOVEMBER 21ST

1817: On this day, a public meeting was held, and committee formed, for the establishment of a Newcastle Savings Bank. While there were around eighty saving banks around the country at this point, until 1817 they were not allowed to pay interest – unlike their Scottish cousins – which inevitably limited their appeal. But following a scheme which allowed savings banks to connect their funds with the Bank of England, the stage was set for a rush of new banks (by late 1818, there were over 450 of them across the country). Social reformers in Newcastle saw an opportunity, petitioned the Mayor, and got the meeting arranged. While not everyone on the committee was a social reformer, more than half of them were in some way involved, whether with the anti-slavery movement, a charity school, or similar. The group worked fast, and by January 10th the bank was open from 11 a.m. to 1 p.m. during the day, and 8 p.m. to 9 p.m. in the evening. And clearly it fulfilled a need. On its first day, it took £300 from seventy depositors. By October, it had more than £15,000, and within eight years, £200,000. Newcastle Savings Bank began in the Merchant's Court, though it soon moved to the Tyne Bank and then the Royal Arcade (*see* December 6th). (Harbottle, S., *The Reverend William Turner*, Maney & Son, 1997 / Mackenzie, E., *A Descriptive and Historical Account of the Town and County of Newcastle upon Tyne: Including the Borough of Gateshead*, 1827)

NOVEMBER 22ND

1844: On this day, the Newcastle papers indignantly reported an attack on one of their own. The *Newcastle Journal* had been around since 1832, and was an avowedly Tory publication in a time of intense political rivalry. Two months after first publication, half a dozen men came into the office and beat the proprietor, John Hernaman, with sticks. In 1844, Hernaman was in trouble again when Addison Potter, the eldest son of the Mayor, accosted him over an article about Potter Senior, a former brewer who had previously been considered ineligible for election. When Hernaman refused to tell him who had written it, Potter began to use a riding crop on his shoulders and legs. Fortunately at this point some passers-by intervened. The *Journal*, of course, was extremely negative in its reporting of the event, while the *Courant* trod a more complex line. It condemned the breach of the peace, but noted the unjustness of journalistic attack on private and family matters, and said it is 'difficult to decide' how far such libels justify summary punishment. The London papers, however, said that Hernaman had only been 'performing the duty which the public have the right to expect of him'. Potter was sent to prison for two months (the judge was a prominent Tory), but many well-wishers went to visit him in prison and if anything his status was improved – thirty years later he became Mayor himself. (*Newcastle Courant* / www.tomorrows-history.com)

NOVEMBER 23RD

1861: On this day, Bainbridges – then a drapers shop – first closed at six o'clock, in support of the 'great and glorious' national Early Closing Movement. They continued to close this early throughout the winter months for many years. This was a popular move – in 1867 the employees even organised a meeting to thank the Bainbridges for it. The Bainbridges' stated aim was to avoid the 'bad atmosphere' caused by hours in gas-lit rooms. Also, 'when a man worked ten hours a day, the last three in a hot workroom, he had no energy, mental or physical.' Over-long hours caused the 'dissipation' of second-rate drapers, who were too 'fagged out' after work to improve themselves through books, but instead turned to drink and the music hall. It was also better for the customer to close earlier; 'If people would shop by gas light, they must expect to get indifferent goods', since they couldn't see what they were buying. Hours were certainly long elsewhere. One Newcastle shop assistant recalled that in 1859, he had worked fifteen hours each day. Three of his nine fellow shop lads had left within six years – the others had all died before they were thirty-five, 'gradually worn down by the grinding weariness of their long hours.' The campaign was successful. By the time of the Early Closing Bill, in 1888, Sir John Lubbock could argue that 'Newcastle-upon-Tyne was an early closing town.' (*Newcastle Courant / Parliamentary Debates*)

NOVEMBER 24TH

1931: On this day, the famous Bostock and Wombwell's menagerie entertained the public for the last time. For many years the premier travelling menagerie, they had visited Newcastle several times over the previous hundred years, performing at the Town Moor Hoppings, Jesmond Park, and at the Haymarket (which had been an important fair site prior to the foundation of the Hoppings). Bostock and Wombwell's show included, at different times, two midgets (both female, one clean-chinned, one bearded), snake dancers, lions and tigers, camels and giraffes – even penguins and (they claimed in 1880) the world's only domesticated zebras. At this point they were also calling themselves the largest travelling zoological collection in the world, with almost 600 animals. But during the First World War, menageries went into decline. The final show, after 127 years on the road, was in the Old Sheep Market, Newcastle. It is said that the two elephants – Rosie and Dixie – walked the 240 kilometres from Hull, probably pulling a wagon. Once the show was over, they walked down Northumberland Street, and gave their last farewells from outside Fenwick's store. Most of the animals retired to zoos, and while a few smaller shows stayed on the road, this was the swan song of the large-scale travelling menagerie. (*National Fairground Archive*)

NOVEMBER 25TH

1835: On this day, three convicts – Rogers, Sterritt and the appropriately named Legget – made a dramatic attempt at escape. As they were returning from the day room to their cell in Carliol Square Jail, Legget grabbed a long brush and smacked Smith, the turnkey, around the head with it. They were captured and clapped in irons before they got out, but they had had it all worked out – in their room was found bedding converted into a rope 40 feet long. Others had things planned out even better. A similar attempt had taken place in 1800, when three prisoners – Outerside, Lowe and Graham – managed to wrench a bar from their cell's chimney and squeeze themselves up to the roof. They made a rope from their clothes, and tied it to a sundial and climbed down. There was a fourth man, John Sill … but he was rather fatter than his fellows. It's a good thing that he was the last to climb, because he got jammed fast in the chimney and was stuck there till the jailers freed him! Outerside was recaptured later, but the other two got away. (Sykes, J., *Local Records*, 1833)

1886: On this day, John Fenning allegedly killed prostitute Elizabeth Tait. In court, his mother-in-law told of the threats he had made towards his estranged wife, earlier on the 26th, after a court decided he must pay her 5 shillings a week in maintenance. According to labourer William Baker, Fenning 'showed me a white-handled razor ... and said that he meant to cut his wife's throat with it.' Soon afterwards a policeman talked to Fenning in Dean Street and he continued to complain, and to threaten murder. Shortly before midnight he was seen on Low Bridge Stairs with Elizabeth Tait; a few minutes later, she apparently tried to bring him into a house, but the other occupant would not let her in. And then ... she was murdered, by a single strong cut across her neck, probably with a razor. By ten past midnight, Fenning had been identified as present, though there was also a mysterious man in a grey coat, whose presence seems to have thrown massive confusion onto the trial proceedings. The judge noted that the evidence was contradictory and formed 'the worst got up case of murder' he had ever seen. But despite Fenning's bloodstained cuffs, the jury took just thirty-four minutes to acquit him. John Fenning has since found a place in Jack the Ripper folklore – Jack operated two years later, and also killed prostitutes in the open street, one of them with a razor to the neck. (*Newcastle Courant*)

NOVEMBER 27TH

1688: On this day – or at least within a couple of days of it – Newcastle declared for Prince William of Orange. The Glorious Revolution of 1688-9 is often forgotten because there was very little bloodshed – but there were still two armies moving around the country, each supporting a different claimant for the throne. Parliament had been worried that James II was a Catholic and too connected to France. So they invited Dutch Protestant William of Orange, who was married to Mary, James II's daughter, to take the throne. In Newcastle, anti-Catholic feeling was whipped up by the arrival of Lord Lumley, come in William's name. They took it out on a huge bronze statue of James II riding a horse, which had only two months earlier cost the Corporation £1,700. As antiquarian Henry Bourne, writing fifty years later, tells it: 'A few soldiers, as drunk with loyalty as with liquor, assisted by the busy, hot-headed geniuses of Sandgate, being provided with ropes for the purpose, pulled it down, and threw it in the river.' Perhaps it was never fully constructed at all, but was just lying nearby. It took over six years for someone to fish it back out again. Much of the metal was then given to All Saints' Church, and recast as church bells, while one leg (presumably of the horse) went to do the same job at St Andrew's. (Sykes, J., *Local Records*, Volume I, 1833)

NOVEMBER 28TH

2002: On this day, the *Evening Chronicle* reported on a dramatic rescue in the Tyne two days previously. Stephen Cairns had been larking around on the Swing Bridge, when his hand slipped and he fell into the icy, fast-flowing waters below. His friend Anthony Wakefield, a soldier, immediately dived in to rescue him, and tried to hold him above the water, even when Cairns fell unconscious. Within minutes, a helicopter had arrived, and, hovering above, used a blast of air to blow the men to the bank, where they were helped out. Cairns had actually 'died' during the ordeal, but was revived by doctors. Both men needed treatment for hypothermia. (*Evening Chronicle*)

———•◆•———

2005: On this day, the *Evening Chronicle* reported a practical joke played by staff at Tesco on one of their customers. Margaret Cooper had written to the Jesmond branch of Tesco querying their removal of her favourite brand of cooking chocolate. Someone within the store must have had their own ideas about customer service, as the letter she received back was far from what you would expect. It accuses Cooper of having 'astonishingly bad taste in chocolate' and suggests she try Sainsbury's instead, 'since their food is especially bland'. It was signed by S. Upton – the name of the real store manager. Tesco, of course, distanced themselves from the letter and said they would take better care to secure the comments box in future … (*Evening Chronicle*)

NOVEMBER 29TH

1941: On this day, Joe Wilson, one of the great singers of the Geordie music hall tradition, was born in Stowell Street. At just seventeen, he published his first book of songs (though he later disowned this sentimental work). At twenty-one he started his own publishing business, opening with 'Wor Geordy's Account o' the Greet Boat Race atwixt Chambers an' Green' (*see* September 5th). At twenty-three he started performing professionally. Wherever he performed, he sold copies of his home-produced books, for a halfpenny each. In 1871, after marrying, he tried settling down as a publican on New Bridge Street, but apparently the life didn't suit him – he remarked that, 'If aw drink with iv'rybody that asks us, aw's a drunken beast; if aw dinnet, aw's a surly beast'. After a year he took the pledge and went back on tour, his new repertoire including many songs about the evils of alcohol. Since he avoided pubs, he was one of the first entertainers to promote the newly created Working Men's Clubs. Wilson tended to write about ordinary working-class Tynesiders, setting his affectionate portraits in the privies, pawnshops and streets of the town. His most famous song is perhaps 'Keep your Feet Still Geordie Hinny'; other songs included 'The Gallowgate Lad', 'The Row upon the Stairs', and 'Come Geordie ha'd the Bairn'. But he fell prey to tuberculosis and died in Railway Street, Newcastle, aged just thirty-three. (www.jesmondoldcemetery.co.uk)

NOVEMBER 30TH

1969: On this day, a Christmas decoration led to the worst fire ever seen in the city centre. Callers Furniture Store, in Northumberland Street, prided itself on its Christmas display. In 1969 the theme was Dickensian, complete with fake snow. On its opening day, dozens of children had gathered to watch. Then smoke began to rise from the head of one of the moving figures. The fire quickly spread, helped by electric fans intended to turn paper windmills, and by the presence of papier-mâché, cloth and cotton wool, and flammable polystyrene grains as 'snow'. Soon the whole of the ground floor was in flames, and as firemen went to work, one of them, Harry Louvre, was seriously burned. He later received an Expression of Commendation from the Queen. The blaze crossed the narrow alley behind the building, and set ablaze a nightclub and two shops. The fire brigade brought in more engines, but were hampered by the Christmas decorations across the street, which got in the way of the hydraulic platforms. It took eighty-eight officers nearly five hours to calm the blaze sufficiently to enter the basement – where they found a fire so intense that water seemed to have no effect. It took a further five hours, and 1.2 million gallons of high expansion foam, to finally defeat the flames. Amazingly, there were only three injuries reported, although over £2 million-worth of damage had been done. (March, G., *Flames across the Tyne*, Pererson & Son, 1974)

DECEMBER 1ST

1350: On this day, Edward III granted the people of Newcastle the right to dig coal and stone from various lands just beyond the town walls, on 'the common ground of the town … called the Castlefield and the Frith'. More importantly, they could also keep the profit, taking coal 'as often and in such way as may seem to you to be expedient'. This was in response to a petition, and cost 20 shillings. There has long been some confusion about this date, probably because in 1655 Ralph Gardner claimed that it was Henri III, in 1238, who first gave this grant – but no original documentation survives, and Gardner is the earliest reference we have. The 1350 document, however, still exists (and doesn't reference anything earlier). Certainly coal was already being shipped out from Newcastle in the thirteenth century. In 1235, there is reference to a French merchant who was captured by Englishmen, and said that he was nothing to do with the wars – he had just taken a cargo of wheat to Newcastle, and was returning with a cargo of coal. But whichever date is correct, this charter confirmed Newcastle as the world's first coal port. ('Coal in the North', www.rapper.org.uk)

DECEMBER 2ND

1941: On this day, South Shields fireman Lawrence 'Larry' Barclay Young was awarded the George Cross at Buckingham Palace. His lifesaving bravery took place on May 31st, on Black Tarset Street, Newcastle. The street had seen heavy bombing, and the landscape was full of craters and rubble. Seven-year-old Irene Page had been playing among the debris when she fell into a crater (or more accurately, a camouflet or underground chamber caused by an explosion) and disappeared, falling around 10 feet. The first to the scene was a Boy Scout, who, though only eleven, tried to rescue the girl, tying a rope to himself and dropping down into the hole. Unfortunately, noxious fumes had built up, and both children soon passed out, probably from carbon monoxide poisoning. Two firemen who happened to be passing nearby swiftly entered the crater themselves – and also succumbed. At this point the Fire Brigade was sent for and two firemen, Leading Fireman Bruce and Fireman Young, made their way into the crater – also with no protective equipment. Bruce fell unconscious, but Young was made of sterner stuff. He passed his superior out, and proceeded to recover all four of the others, one by one. Sad to say, they had all spent too long down there, and were dead. Young received the George Cross; Bruce was awarded a posthumous commendation, as did another of the victims, Auxiliary Fireman Wanless. (www.ne-diary.bpears.org.uk)

DECEMBER 3RD

2010: On this day, the *Evening Chronicle* revealed a secret operation undertaken by Newcastle City Council a few days earlier. The city's Christmas celebrations had started as usual, with the erection and lighting of a Nordmann Fir outside the Civic Centre. This tree was a gift from the people of Bergen, the latest in a succession of more than sixty such trees which celebrate the relationship between the twinned cities. It is sometimes felled by the Mayor of Bergen, who is often present in Newcastle to turn on the lights. Another symbol of the same relationship was the granting of the Honorary Freedom of Newcastle to King Harald V of Norway, when he visited in 2008 during the Ruby Anniversary of the opening of the Civic Centre by his father, Harald IV. The tradition also commemorates the Tynesiders who helped Norwegians during the Second World War. However, the 2010 tree was found to have a crack in the trunk, which – it was feared – might send it crashing down in high winds. So later the same night, council workers quietly replaced the Nordmann Fir with a Sitka Spruce from Kielder Forest. They also transferred the decorations, Norwegian white lights which represented peace and goodwill. Officials insisted that the symbolism remained unchanged. (*Evening Chronicle*)

DECEMBER 4TH

1926: On this day, a boxing tournament was held inside the Hippodrome, a former skating rink on Northumberland Road. Notably, it was promoted by Tommy Burns. Despite being only 5 feet 7 inches tall, Canadian Tommy Burns had held the world heavyweight championship title for two years and eleven challenge fights before he lost in 1908 and retired. He dabbled in promoting matches and hunting for champions, before investing in property, including the Forth Hotel in Pink Lane. Perhaps this was because he had just met local actress Dorothea Hall, around twenty years his junior. Some accounts say they married. He certainly settled locally and for five years he managed the Forth – and allegedly kept a ring on the first floor for illegal bare-knuckle matches. It is interesting to speculate whether he ever met Jack Palmer, one of those he beat to keep the heavyweight title, who lived only a mile away. Burns was still keen to promote local talent, hence going out on a limb to provide an alternative to the established St James Hall bouts (in fact he was only the second person to try this in twenty years). Topping the bill was a contest for the Northern lightweight title, the contenders coming from Hazelrigg and Middlesbrough. This was Burns' only promotion in Newcastle – months later, he and Hall moved to America, where she appeared on Broadway, and he ran a speakeasy. He later lost his fortune in the Wall Street crash. (blog.boxinghistory.org.uk)

DECEMBER 5TH

1827: On this day, Lambert's Leap claimed its first (human) victim, surgeon's apprentice John Nicholson. The spot was named after physician's son Cuthbert Lambert. In 1759, Lambert was riding over the bridge across the deep ravine of Sandyford Burn. His horse took fright and leapt the 3½ foot wall, falling 36 feet. Lambert was fine, but the mare, which took the brunt of his weight, died instantly – its skin was preserved by the family. Twelve years later, the horse of a servant of Sir John Delaval charged straight down the road, and over the bridge wall. This time the man lost his seat, but landed between rocks which protected him from the falling horse. He was able to ride home, though not on the same horse, which had to be shot. Then we come to 1827, and another young medical man riding a panicked horse. The two horses even leapt at exactly the same spot – the 1827 horse knocked from the wall a carved commemorative stone from 1759. But Nicholson was so badly bruised and battered by the fall that he died eight hours later. His horse, conversely, was apparently in such good nick that a passer-by rode it into town to fetch medical assistance! The ravine was not filled until the late nineteenth century, and the stone which was carved as a replacement to the one that fell with Nicholson is still visible. (Sykes, J., *Local Records*, Volume II, 1833)

DECEMBER 6TH

1838: On this day, fire engines were called to the Savings Bank in Royal Arcade. In a blazing room was found Joseph Millie, assistant clerk, his skull smashed with a poker and his pockets filled with paper and coals. Across the room was Archibald Bolam, bleeding and semi-conscious. He explained that he had entered the bank at night to find Millie on the carpet. He walked forward, thinking Millie had fallen asleep, but was then struck by a man with a blackened face. After the inquest, Bolam was accused of murder. His housekeeper's story was so confused that she was briefly imprisoned as an accessory after the fact. Bolam's case had to be postponed to bring in jurors who didn't already know the case. He was found guilty, but then, surprisingly, the judge argued in favour of a reduction to manslaughter – and got his way. Bolam was transported to Australia. (Latimer, J., *Local Records*, 1857)

1851: On this day, William Glover accidentally killed himself on his own security measures. He lived in an upstairs room of a tenement flat in Northumberland Court, and believed someone was coming in and stealing things. So he set up a loaded horse pistol opposite the door, attaching the trigger to the door so that it would go off if you walked in, concealing a string that could be pulled to disengage the mechanism. Amazingly, one day he simply forgot ... and blew his own head off. (Sykes, J., *Local Records*, 1833)

DECEMBER 7TH

1666: On this day, the Mayor of Newcastle had a decision to make. Times were even harder than usual down in Sandgate – England was at war with Holland, the Tyne was blockaded and the Hostmen of Newcastle had ordered the pits to stop work, because coal stocks were backing up. The keelmen were hungry, angry and idle – a dangerous time to introduce a new tax. In late November, the collectors began their work, only to be driven out with thrown stones, twice. The third time, Mayor John Marley decided to get involved. He saw the aggression for himself, then came back with the Aldermen of the town in tow. He tried persuasion, arguing that the tax was small, and would only be taken from those who could pay. But the Sandgate crowd argued that 'they had not bread to eat, that hundreds of them had lived for weeks upon oatmeal and cudbush boiled in water, and therefore, had no money for taxes'. (Cudbush may be the plant cudweed, usually eaten by cattle.) In a rare triumph of compassion over tax collection, the Mayor ordered that taxes should only be taken from those who were willing to pay! (Fewster, J., *The Keelmen of Tyneside*, Boydell Press, 2011 / Welford, R., 'Newcastle Householders in 1665', *Archaeologia Aeliana*, 1911)

DECEMBER 8TH

1742: On this day, John Wesley signed for two pieces of land, so that he could build a Meeting Room. He had first come to Newcastle a few months earlier, and wrote: 'So much drunkenness, cursing, and swearing, (even from the mouths of little children) do I never remember to have seen and heard before, in so small a compass of time.' He clearly had his work cut out. At 7 a.m. on Sunday May 30th, he stood in Sandgate and began his performance of song and sermon. Numbers around him steadily grew, until 'I suppose there might be twelve or fifteen hundred, before I had done preaching … Observing the people, when I had done, to stand gaping and staring upon me, with the most profound astonishment, I told them, "If you desire to know who I am, my name is John Wesley. At five in the evening, with God's help, I design to preach here again." At five, the hill on which I designed to preach was covered, from the top to the bottom.' Wesley went on to build his meeting house, and returned to the area around fifty times over the next fifty years, and became very attached to Grace Murray, the nurse at the Newcastle Orphan House, which he also founded. However, a series of about-faces and miscommunications, and the intervention of John's brother Charles, found her married to one of Wesley's preachers. (www.visionofbritain.org.uk / Dobré, B., *John Wesley*, Duckworth, 1933)

DECEMBER 9TH

1892: On this day, Newcastle United formally came into being, when around 250 football enthusiasts gathered for an open meeting at Bath Hall Lane. Names proposed included Newcastle City, Newcastle Rangers, and Newcastle Football Club – but the voting was almost unanimous for Newcastle United, since the new team brought together the old clubs of the East and West End. As the *Newcastle Journal* said, 'The club certainly deserves better support than it is at present receiving, and if a change in name will have the effect of bringing up the public, by all means let us have it'. And while the next match only attracted 2,500, the team's first FA Cup match with the new name attracted a much more respectable 8,000. The Football Association agreed to deal with the new club after only a few weeks (though not before confusion occurred when the team tried to buy a Dundee player and were told the transfer could not be accepted by the FA because they had never heard of the club). Oddly, Newcastle United Football Club Ltd only came into being in 1895. (Joannou, P., *United: The First 100 Years*, Polar Print Group, 2000)

DECEMBER 10TH

1979: On this day, the first issue of *Viz* magazine went on sale. Its creator, Chris Donald (along with his brother and a friend), drew it out on a card table in his bedroom in his parents' house in Jesmond. Donald had 150 copies printed by Tyneside Free Press, and picked them up in a single cardboard box on the 7th, soon discovering that four of the twelve pages were bound in the wrong way around. This and other early editions were sold by the writers walking from pub to pub, or standing outside gigs. Then a couple of record shops took it on, as did Kard Bar. The manager of Kard Bar also donated a load of old teenage pop posters, which the writers idiosyncratically cut up, giving a quarter-poster away with each magazine. Staff at HMV began to stock *Viz* by the till, hiding it if anyone from head office came in. *Viz* was in the spirit of the punk fanzines of the era, but also parodied tabloid newspapers, with its in-your-face mock adverts, and comics like *The Beano* and *The Dandy*. Donald said: 'Being a provincial magazine helped enormously. It gave us our whole identity ... *Viz* took six years to become commercially viable. Newcastle was an ideal place to nurture it.' By 1989, *Viz*'s circulation peaked at over 1.2 million; it was the country's third most popular magazine, with characters like Sid the Sexist and the Fat Slags entering popular culture. (*The Independent*)

DECEMBER 11TH

1860: On this day, a new cattle market was opened, immediately to the west of the Infirmary, on Knox's Field. While the *Newcastle Courant* claimed that this was a quiet occasion, 'unmarked by some of those demonstrations which often distinguish less important occurrences', it tripled the number of cows coming in to market in Newcastle each week, to 3,000. That must have made a real difference to the appearance of the streets. It was certainly a big undertaking, with a huge wall surmounted by iron railings, numerous gates and alleyways, and forty sturdy pens for bulls. That morning, the church bells were rung from the small hours of the morning, and throughout the day – even though, the *Courant* says, many people didn't know why! The only people unhappy about the cattle market were those stuck in the Newcastle Infirmary. When the Infirmary had first been built, the setting was virtually rural. But then the railway was built nearby, and the goods yards had spread out. Now thousands of cows were housed right next door, one day a week – as were the dogs of the drovers, which apparently barked right through the night. (*Newcastle Courant*)

DECEMBER 12TH

1984: On this day, all four members of pop group Bucks Fizz were taken to the Royal Victoria Infirmary following a road accident. The band had played a sell-out gig at the City Hall, given 'hundreds of autographs', and were on their way back to their hotel when, somewhere in the middle of roadworks on the Great North Road, their tour bus collided head-on with an articulated lorry. Fourteen people were injured, including every member of the group. Three band members had back and neck injuries – Cheryl Baker had broken three vertebrae. The fourth member, Mike Nolan, had suffered severe head trauma – later this day he fell into a coma and was rushed to the General Hospital for emergency surgery. Waking from the coma a few days later, he recuperated over a period of several months, but has suffered significant health problems related to the crash ever since. Baker and Nolan later became involved in the foundation of Headfirst, a charity funding research into head injuries. On this same day in 1999, three members of the band, including Nolan, played again at the City Hall to mark the anniversary of the crash. (www.bbc.co.uk)

DECEMBER 13TH

1990: On this day, 'Fog on the Tyne Revisited', a musical collaboration between two Newcastle icons, was sitting at number 23 in the charts. Lindisfarne, a long-lived Newcastle folk-rock band, first wrote 'Fog on the Tyne' in 1971, and named a chart-topping album after it; it became something of a local anthem. It was brought to a new generation, though, when Lindisfarne released a new version with lyrics written and sung by Newcastle United's Paul Gascoigne. Released in late November, there were hopes for a Christmas hit. But Gascoigne's high press profile was beginning to turn the corner from adoration to something much less pleasant. Massive press coverage was generated; perhaps too much – the backlash was inevitable, as some magazines, pressured to include the song but dismissive of its content, pulled no punches with their reviews. This may be part of why chart success did not follow, as 'Fog on the Tyne' peaked at number 2 in its second week and then dropped steadily away. Opinions vary, but it seems likely that the critical response to his musical career was a factor in the gradual downward spiral of Gazza's career. (obscuremusicandfootball.com)

DECEMBER 14TH

1816: On this day, the Grand Duke Nicholas of Russia came to visit Newcastle. He had come to England with his elder brother, Tsar Alexander I, but the twenty-year-old Nicholas soon broke free from the Royal party to explore the country for himself. He travelled up to Tyneside, apparently determined to see a coal mine being worked. In Newcastle he visited the Royal Jubilee School (it being a Saturday, they had to round up all the boys specially), and was introduced to engraver Thomas Bewick. He also ventured to Wallsend Colliery, at the time considered one of the best in the country. The story goes that, after an above-ground tour, he changed into a deputy-overman's outfit, and was told to climb onto a large iron hook, which he would cling to as the rope was lowered down into the pit. This was actually considered to be safer than the alternatives. Nicholas, it is said, looked down into the pit and said in French 'Ah! My God! It is the mouth of hell! None but a madman would venture into it!' – quickly changing back into his military garb and heading away. Two years later his younger brother Michael also visited Tyneside, stopping off at Heaton Colliery and the Low Glasshouse. He also went to the Royal Jubilee School, to which the boys were again specifically recalled, having broken up for harvest holiday the day before! (northeasthistorytour. blogspot.co.uk / Sykes, J., *Local Records*, Volume II, 1833)

DECEMBER 15TH

1892: On this day was published a damning expose of the conditions within Newcastle's leadworks. Tyneside had relatively few industrial jobs available to women, but there was always the heavy, dangerous and unskilled work offered by the lead industry. Women stoked furnaces and handled lead 'cakes' and pots of strong acid, often working barehanded and even barefooted. Most developed a range of symptoms associated with lead poisoning as white lead attacked the skin, lungs or digestive system, sometimes killing slowly, sometimes fast. They earned up to 12 shillings a week if they kept working fast, but men would get double that. In 1883 women were given 'muzzles' – primitive respirators – but these did little to keep the poisonous dust at bay. The *Daily Chronicle* reported this work was often a last resort for the wives of drunks, widows struggling to feed children, or 'the girl whose character does not stand scrutiny'. The writer argued that women were more susceptible to ill health because of the particular tasks they were doing, while others argued that it was down to women being weaker to start with, or due to their lives of vice and alcohol. Some of the women who had lasted longest (speaking to an inquiry into the death of one lead worker) actually agreed with this viewpoint. Women were banned from working in leadworks in 1898, but often struggled to find alternative employment. (Long, J., *Conversations in Cold Rooms*, Boydell and Brewer, 1999)

DECEMBER 16TH

1964: On this day, popular sitcom *The Likely Lads* was first broadcast. Written by Dick Clement and Newcastle-born Ian La Frenais, the backdrop city was never specified but it is generally assumed to be Newcastle. In reality it was filmed in London, apparently due to a shortage of actors in the North East at that time. The two lead characters are Geordies, but their actors were from Yorkshire and Sunderland. Still, the sitcom (and its successor, the early 1970s *Whatever Happened to the Likely Lads?*) was well received – at its height *The Likely Lads* had twenty-seven million viewers. It can still be read as a social commentary of Tyneside at the time, revolving around the tensions between classes, and the interests, work and leisure of a couple of 'likely lads'. *The Likely Lads* proved a springboard for Clement and La Frenais, who have since been involved in many successful projects. Those with a local connection include *Auf Wiedersehen, Pet* (which follows a group of construction workers, including three Geordies, as they work abroad) and *Spender* (a detective drama set in Newcastle). *Spender* was filmed in Tyneside, a sign of the improving fortunes of the region's television industry.

DECEMBER 17TH

1867: On this day, eight people were killed on Town Moor. Earlier that day, the police discovered nine tins of nitro-glycerine, meant for blasting in mines, in a cellar in the White Swan Yard. The Town Clerk ordered it removed from the town or else destroyed. The railway company refused to carry it, so it was decided that it would be tipped into the earth on the Town Moor, at a point where the Spital Tongues colliery had subsided. The Sheriff and Town Surveyor accompanied the canisters out to the moor, where they were joined by a curious crowd. On arrival the corks were removed and all of the canisters emptied into the ground. Sub-Inspector Wallace stayed behind to pile soil over the site, while the others moved away to bury the canisters. Perhaps they were more complacent in handling the empty canisters than they had been with full ones, maybe they even started smoking, but something went badly wrong, and Wallace could only watch in horror as a massive explosion shook the site. He ran to ground zero to find that some of those present had literally been blown to pieces. The blast had been so great that Mr Walpole, a local surgeon out for a walk, came upon a foot around 300 yards from the centre, and rushed to see what he could do. The four survivors were taken to the Infirmary, but all died within the next few days. (Fordyce, T., *Local Records*, 1876)

DECEMBER 18TH

1938: On this day, Bryan Chandler was born in Heaton. He grew up in Newcastle and started work as a turner in a shipyard. He learned to play the guitar and bass, called himself 'Chas' Chandler and started playing in bands. In 1962 he met fellow-Geordie Eric Burdon, and the pair formed The Animals. For two years they dominated the Newcastle music scene, frequently playing at the Club A Go Go (then one of only two clubs in the country with a full gambling licence) and fuelling speculation that Newcastle could develop its own sound to rival that appearing in Liverpool at the same time. The obvious move was to London, where a string of hits followed. But the pressures of touring, and an unfavourable contract, drove them to split. Chandler had a second career, though, as a manager. He invited Jimi Hendrix – then merely Jimmy James – to London after hearing him play. Risking most of his money to launch Hendrix, he helped transform him into an icon while also managing his business and producing his hits. In 1979, Chandler retired back to Tyneside and got involved helping young bands on the local scene and backing the development of the Newcastle Arena. He died in 1996. (*The Independent*)

DECEMBER 19TH

1840: On this day, an Irish family and the town's barber surgeons nearly came to blows over the handling of a corpse. An elderly Irish woman, Sophia Quin, had died in the workhouse. Under the Anatomy Act of 1832, if she was not claimed by family within forty-eight hours, she was fair game for dissection (the aim being to discourage trade in bodysnatching – digging up corpses – for medical education). But three hours after she had been placed in a leaden trough to be 'heated preparatory to injection', a group turned up for the body. Rosanna Rox said that Quin was her mother. She had gone to the Mayor for support, and received it – he turned up in person, vehemently arguing with the surgeons. When they argued that the body was legally obtained he replied, 'I don't care for that, it shan't be done here! You'll be taking live ones next!' It turned out that only forty-four hours, not forty-eight, had passed. Rox explained why it had taken so long to claim the body – apparently some friends even followed the body, believing it was going to the burial ground, not to the Surgeons' Hall. The surgeons continued to argue that they had believed their actions legal. The surgeons' servants – a porter and two house carpenters – were fined £20 each for bearing the body away, and the lecturers had to pay £109 in costs and fines. (*Provincial Medical and Surgical Journal / The Lancet*)

DECEMBER 20TH

1299: On this day, Pandon – then called Pampeden – was incorporated into Newcastle by the Royal Charter of Edward I. This cluster of houses was near the river, east of Pandon Burn. For many years it was thought to have been the site of a Saxon palace, though this is disputed. Certainly by the thirteenth century it had something of a quay wall, though this may have been very short-lived, and as many as twenty taxpayers. The Pandon Burn was particularly troublesome, subject to tidal influence as well as flooding from heavy rain. It often flooded part of Pandon as far up as the bottom of Manor Chare. In the mid-fourteenth century it flooded badly enough to destroy 140 houses and kill almost as many people. But the incorporation of Pandon was important to Newcastle as the town wall was being built at the time, and a route around Pandon was much preferred (the alternative, and original plan had the wall going through the castle itself). The wall on this stretch may even have included some remnants of the old Roman wall. (Mackenzie, E., *A Descriptive and Historical Account of the Town and County of Newcastle upon Tyne: Including the Borough of Gateshead*, 1827)

DECEMBER 21ST

1832: On this day, 'Captain Stewart' arrived in Newcastle and provided good entertainment. Calling himself the Wandering Piper, he paraded to and fro playing the bagpipes. The story he told in his own 'Tour of the Wandering Piper Through Part of Scotland and Ireland, Written by Himself' is that he and a friend had disagreed about which countries were most hospitable, and entered into a staggering bet – to spend five years travelling, one as a fiddler in Europe, the other as a piper in Britain and America, establishing which would be given most along his way. Since Stewart didn't actually need the money, in each town he entered, he was also giving money away to charities, which might have encouraged people to pay up – by Newcastle, according to his own account book, he'd given away £700. And he didn't stop. In July 1834, American magazine *Niles' Register* recorded that the same man had been in America for just over a year and had given over $7,000 in small sums to charities. On another occasion, it called him 'a full-blooded Scotsman, of eccentric habits – but his heart is in the right place'. (Latimer, J., *Local Records*, 1857 / *Chambers' Edinburgh Journal* / *Niles' Register*)

DECEMBER 22ND

1965: On this day, influential poet Basil Bunting gave the first reading of his epic work, *Briggflatts*, at Morden Tower, which was already known as a beacon for contemporary poetry. He wrote the poem in his sixties, and it incorporates many of the themes of his life. Born in 1900, son of a Scotswood doctor attached to the Montague Colliery, he lived in Newcastle until he was twelve. As a teenager he also developed a love of poetry and began to write. He caused a minor stir in 1918 when he stood before a tribunal as a conscientious objector, refusing to take even non-combatant service – he was held prisoner in the guardroom of Fenham Barracks, and later served 112 days in Wormwood Scrubs. His later life took him all around the country, but he never forgot his Tyneside roots, and his poems have more than a touch of local accent about them. In the 1950s, he worked for the *Newcastle Daily Journal*, though he disparagingly recorded that 'provincial journalists are not capable of any thought of any sort at all'. `he continued to write poetry, and by 1965 was ready to unveil what was to become his most famous piece, a somewhat autobiographical musing on a lifetime's journey, a few months before it was published. Basil Bunting once said that *Briggflatts* was the only autobiography he needed. (Caddel, R. and Flowers, A., *Basil Bunting: A Northern Life*, Tynebridge Publishing, 1999)

DECEMBER 23RD

1905: On this day, arguably the first beauty contest in the country was held – at the Olympia Theatre in Northumberland Road. Open to girls over the age of sixteen, it was called the Blonde and Brunette Beauty Show, and the prize was a gold bangle and bracelet. (*Evening Chronicle*)

———◆·———

1919: On this day, tragedy struck the city as fire gutted Cross House. Cross House was a wedge-shaped seven-storey office block on Westgate Road, built in 1911. The basement was used by Famous Laskey Film Services for storing volatile celluloid film – which on this day spontaneously caught fire. With the flames spreading quickly and shooting up the lift shaft, many office workers were trapped on the higher floors. Fire-fighting efforts were hampered by the thick and noxious smoke pouring from the burning celluloid. Tragically, the firemen's ladders were not quite long enough to reach the top floor. Some jumped to their deaths to avoid the flames, while others were exhorted to wait while blankets were brought to cushion their fall. Several firemen also entered the building through windows and gained recognition for their acts of bravery in rescuing those trapped in the building. Nonetheless, eleven people lost their lives that day. As a direct result of the tragedy, the Celluloid and Cinematograph Film Act was brought in to control the storage of celluloid. The façade of Cross House still stands, but the interior has been completely refitted. (March, G., *Flames Across the Tyne*, Peterson, 1974)

DECEMBER 24TH

1924: On this day, W.E. Johns, the creator of *Boy's Own* hero Biggles, arrived in Newcastle to begin employment as a recruiting officer for the Royal Air Force. He had served with distinction on various fronts during the First World War, ending up a bomber pilot in the newly-formed RAF. After the war he was given work in the Inspectorate of Recruiting, in London. Here he actually turned down the application of John Hume Ross – Lawrence of Arabia – but was forced to take him on by his bosses. Johns was then posted to Newcastle. His wife, Maude Johns, was ill, and their marriage had broken down. Although he continued to send money to Maude and their son, the woman who followed him to Newcastle was his mistress, who called herself Doris Johns. Apparently, on his first night in Newcastle – in a disused nursing home in Ellison Place – Johns' bed collapsed and he could hear rats scurrying around in the dark. After that he got lodgings in Whitley Bay, travelling to Newcastle each day for a year. At this point he had only written one book, but the North East is touched on in some of his later writing. (www.wejohns.com)

DECEMBER 25TH

1862: On this day, Dante Gabriel Rossetti finished work on his painting of Mrs Leathart. He had known the Leatharts for some years – we know they bought the painting 'Found' from him in 1859. Rossetti apparently disliked Newcastle, though he enjoyed visiting Hexham and did come up to stay on several occasions. He was friends with reformer Robert Spence Watson and artist William Bell Scott, with whom he stayed several times. The friendship began when Rossetti read some of Scott's poems, liked them, and wrote to him to say so. This 1862 visit is also notable for producing one of the best known photographs of Rossetti. Bell Scott's studio (probably used by Rossetti on this occasion) still stands, at the rear of St Thomas Crescent.

———— • ◆ • ————

In Edwardian times, children's experience of Christmas Day was quite different from our own. For instance, a Newcastle woman named Mary recalled: 'My mother used to make lovely "mistletoes" with the two hoops from butter barrels. She used to cover them with newspapers to give them a bit of thickness. Then she used to fold the tissue paper and cut it, and wind it around, so it was all fluffy and nice. And you used to put one through the other, crossways, and then put all the decorations on, the sugar mice and sugar watches and those sort of things.' (*Beamish Museum Audio Archive*)

DECEMBER 26TH

1292: On this day, King John of Scotland met King Edward I of England in the Castle Keep. John had been king for less than a month, having been crowned on November 30th. At that stage in the wars between England and Scotland, England had the upper hand, and it was expected that John would also make a formal submission to Edward. He probably hoped that this would only be a short-term arrangement, but the ceremony, nonetheless, had to be done with full pomp. And it soon became clear that for Edward, this was just part of a long-term plan to turn Scotland into another corner of England. He forced John to accept an English chancellor, who began to alter Scottish taxes and customs. John even had to alter the wording on the Royal Seal of Scotland, while Edward heard anyone who had complaints about their treatment at John's courts. All in all, this day in Newcastle was the start of a period of humiliation for the Scots. In 1296, when the Scots nobles finally did rebel they were crushed at the Battle of Dunbar. John was made to beg for forgiveness, but he was then publicly stripped of his throne. It was from this low point that Sir William Wallace ('Braveheart') began his doomed campaigns. He was eventually executed, and his right arm displayed on the old Tyne Bridge. (Sadler, J., *Border Fury*, Longman, 2005)

DECEMBER 27TH

1900: In the early hours of this day, William, Lord Armstrong, engineer, industrialist and inventor, died. Born in Pleasant Row, Shieldfield, in 1810, Armstrong's career touches on most of the great achievements and milestones of Victorian Newcastle. Even as a child he was fascinated by how things worked, but engineering was not considered a reputable profession. His father pushed him into law, and he worked as a solicitor, but he kept tinkering in his spare time. In his late thirties, the success of his new hydraulic cranes encouraged him to set up his own company, based in Elswick. Then, in 1854, he designed a new gun, which became known as the Armstrong gun, selling first to the government during the Crimean War, and later to others (including, for instance, both armies engaged in the American Civil War). In 1859 he was knighted and effectively became gun-maker to the British army, as well as expanding his market to governments from Russia to Peru. Armstrong Works continued to grow, expanding into the production of battleships, Gatling guns and bridges (including, in 1876, the Swing Bridge, to allow ships access to the works). At its height the company employed over 25,000 men. Armstrong was also an advocate of hydroelectric power, and donated Jesmond Dene to the people of Newcastle. (Dougan, D., *The Great Gun-maker, Lord Armstrong*, Sandhill Press, 1992)

DECEMBER 28TH

1750: On this day a letter was written by one B.K. which, when it was published in the *Courant* the following week, directly inspired the building of Newcastle Infirmary. It argued that there was a growing need for a hospital for the town, to deal with a growing population and the spread of industries and industrial accidents. B.K. reminded readers of a recent incident on the steep slope of Side, when the wheel chain broke on a wagon. It careered down the hill, and a woman was run over, shattering one of her legs. She did eventually get assistance, in the form of an amputation, but according to B.K., this was around five hours later. To see what an amputation of the day might have looked like, one only has to go to Newcastle's Discovery Museum, where is displayed a case of early eighteenth-century surgical tools used for many years by the Company of Barber Surgeons. It is hard to see why a barber surgeon could not have been found more quickly, but the case certainly helped encourage the money to come in. Not that all donations were in cash – offers of linen and crockery, bricks and labour all poured in, as well as offers to put on fund-raising performances. (Boyes, J., 'Medicine and Dentistry in Newcastle upon Tyne in the Eighteenth Century', *Proceedings of the Royal Society of Medicine*, 1957)

DECEMBER 29TH

1941: On this day, ten bombs were dropped on the Matthew Bank area of Gosforth, and several others across the rest of Newcastle. One caused a 30-foot wide crater in the grounds of St Gabriel's Church, Heaton, and another seriously damaged eighteen Byker houses. But the worst affected area was Keyes Gardens and Matthew Bank, where over 100 houses were severely damaged and seven people were killed. Ten more were seriously injured, including a young lad who had to have his foot amputated to free him from the rubble of his house. A letter to the *Evening Chronicle* many years later recalls: 'A set of traffic lights at red, saved me and my parents from being victims of the Matthew Bank bombing in 1941. On the night of the bombing, my father, who was on leave from the Royal Air Force, had taken my mother and I to a variety show at the Empire Theatre, which was in Newgate Street, Newcastle. After the show we just caught the No.14 bus, because it had to stop at the Grainger Street traffic lights which were on red … After being in the house for a few moments there was a thunderous noise and the sound of breaking glass. The next morning we learned that Matthew Bank had been bombed, and that the next No.14 bus, which we would have been on, had the traffic lights not been on red, was arriving at Matthew Bank when the bombs fell.' (www.ne-diary.bpears.org.uk/)

DECEMBER 30TH

1775: On this day, the *Middlesex Journal* reported that a Newcastle woman attempted to enlist in the 71st Regiment of Foot, which was about to set off to fight in the American War of Independence. The paper reported that, 'a good-looking girl, about twenty-seven years old, dressed in mens cloaths, applied to Serjeant Miller, the recruiting officer here for Frazer's Highland regiment, and desired to be enlisted in that body, which the serjeant agreed to, and gave her a shilling. Her sex, however, was soon after discovered. She said the cause of this act was from a quarrel with her father, whose cloaths she had absconded in: and notwithstanding her sex, she would have no objection to the army, as she thought the exercise not superior to her abilities. She was, however, discharged.' [*sic*] We may never know if this really happened, or how the woman's secret was revealed, but it seems unlikely. New recruits often underwent physical examination, and additionally they were often put into bed naked the first night to reduce risk of desertion. The disguised female soldier or sailor was a common staple of songs at the time, but a lot less common in practice. (Hagist, D., 'The Women of the British Army in America', *Brigade Dispatch*, 1993)

DECEMBER 31ST

1993: On this day, notorious criminal Viv Graham was shot three times with a Magnum as he got into his car outside a Wallsend pub. He died a few hours later, and the getaway vehicle was found burned out in Heaton. Graham had presented himself as a Bigg Market bouncer, but his activities went far further than that into criminal 'fixing' and protection rackets (charging 'consultancy fees' to make problems go away), making him one of the biggest figures of the north-eastern criminal underworld. He was just thirty-four, and seen by some as a hero and protector. He had a charming side and, it is claimed, was keen to keep children away from drugs and crime. Still, when he died, he had only just finished a three-year jail term for beating up another doorman, from a rival club; this was followed by a suspended sentence for beating a man unconscious. People had also tried to kill him before. To date, no one has yet been charged with Viv Graham's murder, and it is one of the biggest unsolved cases in Tyneside's recent history. In the years since Graham's death various measures have been put in place to improve the reputation of the doorman, but many still have a grudging respect for Newcastle's 'Mr Big'. (*The Guardian*)